FROM D'BURG

—— TO ——

JERUSALEM

FROM D'BURG

— TO —

JERUSALEM

THE UNLIKELY RISE AND AWFUL FALL OF

A SMALL-TOWN NEWSMAN

CARL STROCK

Cover design by Andrea Costanzo
Book design by Emma Schlieder

Printed in the United States of America

The Troy Book Makers • Troy, New York • thetroybookmakers.com

To order additional copies of this title, contact your favorite local
bookstore or visit www.tbmbooks.com

ISBN: 978-1-61468-182-3

for Pearl

* * *

Contents

ACKNOWLEDGEMENTS

This book could hardly have been written without the patient support of my editor, Jeanne Finley, who encouraged me when I needed encouraging and made many valuable suggestions along the way—though she is not to blame for any deficiencies the reader might discover. Those are the result of my own obstinacy, and she must not be held to account. She has my enduring thanks.

I am also indebted to my former colleague at the Daily Gazette, Kathleen Moore, who reported some of the same stories that I have sketched in this book, read an early draft, and identified failings that no one else would have noticed.

I relied more than he can know on my Southern Humboldt friend, Steve Ladd, whom I shamelessly used as a sounding board, especially early on when I was lapsing into self-doubt. If not for his sympathetic ear, this modest tome might not have seen the light.

At the Jerusalem end of my journalistic adventures, I could not have seen what I saw, nor could I have extricated myself from the infamous Qalandia checkpoint and returned home to tell the tale, without the help of my new friend, Raed Sadeq. I would still be there in that accursed cage, wiser, perhaps, but forever trapped, so I am indebted to him uniquely.

In a perverse sort of way, I must acknowledge the contribution of Rabbi Matthew Cutler of Congregation Gates of Heaven in Schenectady, who more than anyone else impelled me to commit this tale to print, even if that was far from his intent.

And everyone else I pilloried over the years—cops, teachers, judges, bishops, prosecutors, school superintendents, psychotherapists, child protection caseworkers, SPCA animal-rescuers, ministers of the Gospel—who, if we had been in Mexico, would have hired a hit squad to eliminate me but who, in this country, restrained themselves. I couldn't have done it without them.

Foreword

I never expected to write this book, and I never would have written it if things hadn't gone wrong. I would have finished out a long and illustrious career at the *Schenectady Gazette* in upstate New York by collapsing at my desk, flecks of foam gathering at the corners of my mouth, and been wheeled out on a gurney by paramedics of the same fire department I had occasionally needled. At my memorial service public officials would have eulogized me as a fearless foe of injustice, hypocrisy and mixed metaphors, while those members of the reverend clergy who happened to be present would have inconspicuously made the sign of the cross and asked the Lord's forgiveness for attending.

I would have been happy—or at least as happy as a dead person can be. I would have said, well, the *Gazette* wasn't much of a newspaper, just a small-time broadsheet that lived off City Hall politics, and Schenectady wasn't much of a city, just a worn-out relic of earlier industrial glory, but I gave them both what I had, and I didn't make excuses. I didn't let myself off by saying this is a lousy newspaper and this is a lousy city, so it doesn't make any difference. I would have held my head high, if such a thing were possible and if I could have done it without startling the eulogizers.

But things did go wrong, and in the end I crept out the door without the drama of cardiac arrest or *grand mal* seizure and without the assistance of paramedics, cheating those whose speeches no doubt would have swelled the pride of my progeny.

So this book is a record of my rise and fall, if that doesn't sound too dramatic for so modest a history, told by medium of stories I worked on over the course of thirty-one years, terminating with the stories that turned out to be my doom. Those stories—to relieve the reader of the temptation to skip to the end and thus miss the preliminaries—dealt with a vacation that my wife, Pearl, and I innocently took to Jerusalem, hoping for nothing more than the pleasure of exotic cuisine and ancient architecture. The columns I wrote from there were not divinely delivered to me like the commandments unto Moses but emerged in the natural course of events from my own cerebrum, so I cannot plead helplessness. I was not a mere amanuensis but the active author of them, as I was the active author of some 3,500 other columns, so I cannot escape responsibility. Whatever I wrote, I wrote in full possession of my faculties, from beginning to end.

I reported fearlessly on the painting of the town garage roof in Duanesburg and also on the trial of two Muslim men in Albany accused of supporting terrorism, though there might have been just a twinge of fear in the latter case, just as there might have been in facing an auditorium full of home-schooled creationists at another time. I did battle with cops and teachers over their contracts, I valiantly stood my ground against psychotherapists who endeavored to diagnose me, I went toe-to-toe and eyeball-to-eyeball with the local Society for the Prevention of Cruelty to Animals, I did not shrink even from combat with child protection caseworkers. I look back with amazement at my own heroism and doubt if there has been anything like it in the annals of journalism. I grew so confident that I eventually took on God himself, or at least those who pretended to represent Him and speak for Him. In that regard I debated a chemist who claimed to "follow the data" to the conclusion that the universe is no more than 10,000 years old, in that auditorium full of homeschoolers, and I held up to ridicule the mighty Roman Catholic Church for suckering the people of the Mohawk Valley with a miracle that would have flushed the cheek of a medieval monk selling indulgences.

All these adventures and more I have set down in this book, hoping and praying for the approbation of the reader, but many more I have left out. In fact the great majority of subjects I explored in the *Gazette* I have left out. Most of them were necessarily trivial, there being a limited supply of thunderous events in Schenectady and environs. Few wars, revolutions, earthquakes, epidemics, though we did have a hill slide that buried a gas station and a flood that submerged several hundred houses, neither of which cataclysm, alas, made it into this volume.

Along with such events and along with such daily trivia as sewer breaks and gas station stickups, I also left out everything positive. You will find nothing about the City Mission, for example, which during my tenure in Schenectady morphed from a flophouse and soup kitchen into a fine institution that rescued down-and-outers from the streets, under the direction of a true believer in Jesus, Mike Saccocio, whom I was proud to count as a friend despite his true belief.

It used to be a common criticism of newspapers, when newspapers were still pillars of their communities, that they gave too much attention to bad news and too little to good, but I always suspected that the critics themselves would turn much faster to a story about a bus crash than to one about a bus that arrived safely. I followed that principle in my own writing, preferring the crashes to the safe arrivals, and the principle is reflected in this poor volume. I could write a book about the good work of the City Mission, but how many people would read it? So there is nothing here about Mike Saccocio, nor anything about the energetic Philip Morris, who turned the moribund old vaudeville house, Proctor's Theater, into an energetic showcase of the theatrical arts. Nothing about my dowdy friend Irene Prazak, who served in support of community causes with such irresistible spirit that she once even got me to a Salvation Army dinner, where I endured a heel-clicking flag presentation along with reports of good works. At the end of her years, when she was finally immobilized in the Kingsway Arms Nursing Center, she turned her concern to the immigrant aides who attended her and would boast of their community-college accomplishments as if those toiling young women were her own children. Nothing about her.

Nothing about Doris Aiken, who saved many a life with her anti-drunk-driving campaign even if the organization she founded, Remove Intoxicated Drivers (RID), did get out-public-relationed by Mothers Against Drunk Driving (MADD).

Nothing, either, about Frank Duci, populist politician, who served sixteen years as mayor and a whole lifetime as political showman. A man who, in his prime, which was a very long prime, couldn't walk a block anywhere in Schenectady without getting a toot of the horn, a wave from a porch, a cheer from across the street. Early in my *Gazette* career, when he was in his 60s and he came down with some minor ailment, the city editor commissioned me to write his obituary just in case he should die at an inconvenient hour and we should be left unprepared. I spent many days at the task, digging like a woodborer through drawers full of brittle clippings, and finally produced what I thought was a creditable mini-biography. Three decades later, when I had slunk out the door uneulogized, the same Duci, now ninety-one years old and shrunken to the size of a peanut, entertained me over a plate of ziti with reminiscences of our many feuds, and I entertained him with the tale of that obituary, the location of which I no longer knew. (Never careless of his own history, he wanted a copy.)

Nothing about him. It would take a book, but someone else will have to write it.

Nothing about Charlie Mills, the New York City assistant police chief who was recruited to come up to Schenectady and straighten out the crooked local police department, a man so gregarious, so street-wise, so foul-mouthed, so irresistible that Mayor Duci went into a dark jealous rage over him and drove him out of town. Charlie, alas, settled for a job as director of the state Bureau of Petroleum, Alcohol and Tobacco, on the 87th floor of Tower 2 of the World Trade Center, where he died on September 11, 2001, God rest his soul. Nothing about him.

Nothing about Bob Schulz, retired engineer and self-taught *pro se* lawyer who with great zeal sued the state of New York over its patently illegal practice of "back-door borrowing" and lost when the state's highest court decided that debt wasn't really debt if the state said it wasn't, this despite the fact that Schulz had single-handedly out-argued three of the biggest legal guns in New York before that same court. He was a hero of mine, insofar as I ever had heroes, until his zeal got the better of him and he spiraled into battle against the IRS, then spun into outer space as a "birther," challenging Barack Obama's standing as a natural-born citizen.

Nothing about the generous people who pitched in after the shameful conviction and imprisonment of two Albany Muslim men to help their wives and children survive without them. The finest demonstration of common humanity I witnessed in my years of journalism. Nor anything about the octogenarian Holocaust survivor who planted two peach trees on his farm in commemoration of the two men and several years later, on the anniversary of their arrest, presented the first peach to the youngest child of one of them. Too positive.

None of my ragging on dog owners, either, for their asinine projection of human qualities onto their obnoxious pets. Why alienate more readers than I need to?

Nothing about the influx of Guyanese immigrants into Schenectady under the mayoralty of my friend Al Jurczynski, nor anything about the hell there was to pay when one of them was observed slaughtering a goat in his backyard for dinner, an event that caused Jurczynski's prim successor, Mayor Brian Stratton, to rush to the address to investigate personally. Mayor Stratton took his meat shrink-wrapped only.

Not even a reprinting of my most incendiary columns so the reader might judge their merits for himself, or herself, since the individual chapters amount to distillations of the columns, often with generous quotes from them. I saw no need to burden the reader with duplication.

Schenectady was graced with a beautiful, bucolic Central Park, a gracious residential area originally built by General Electric Company executives, and a quaint brick-and-stoop neighborhood built on the site of the original Dutch Stockade, and so named—but it was mostly a dump. The downtown, later rebuilt by the redeployment of sales tax revenue, was half-empty when I arrived and pretty soon was completely empty, or close to it. Blank storefronts, doorways cluttered with empty bottles and windblown plastic bags, bums and winos demanding spare change. In the neighborhoods—Mont Pleasant, Goose Hill, Hamilton Hill— the old two-story, two-family houses that had once accommodated factory workers lately arrived from Italy and Poland were now dented and dilapidated, their chain-link fences bent and crooked, the new tenants often as not sitting on their porches nursing a cigarette and a can of beer, pit bulls roaming the weed-spiked street as the only, if pathetic, sign of vigor. And never mind the many houses that had simply been abandoned and boarded up.

General Electric, which employed as many as 45,000 people during World War II, had shrunk to just a few thousand. The American Locomotive Company, known locally as Alco, the other mighty employer, had closed shop altogether, leaving behind a vast block of rusting sheds and girders. A sign at the entrance to the city, with a nod to those two great corporations, had once declared, "SCHENECTADY: The City That Lights and Hauls the World. Population 100,000." It was hopeful even at the time, since the population never quite hit that mark, though there must have been Chamber-of-Commerce confidence that it soon would. When I arrived, the population had already dropped to 68,000, and by 2010 it had slipped further to 66,000, though the best demographers agree the out-flight would have occurred whether I wrote my three columns a week or not.

I started, by the way, as a lowly reporter in October 1981, advanced to the august position of columnist in December 1987, and finished in disgrace in October 2012. That is the period of time encompassed by this volume. I state it here for the record, since I choose in my narrative to ignore dates for the most part so as not to sound like a textbook, and also so the reader might relax in the poetry and drama of the story without being called away by matters so prosaic as years and months. This has also allowed me a certain liberty in arranging my material.

The newspaper for which I toiled, founded in 1894, was originally the *Schenectady Gazette* but in 1990 changed its name to the *Daily Gazette* for six days of the week and the *Sunday Gazette* for the seventh day. I refer to it as the *Gazoot* in a spirit of light-heartedness and without intending any disrespect.

As the reader will see who pursues this tale chapter by chapter, I eventually raised my journalistic sights from matters terrestrial, like sex abuse and police contracts, to matters celestial, like Biblical creationism, Catholic sainthood, and Jewish mythology, so it might be fair to confess myself, by way of full disclosure, a longtime non-believer. I was raised attending a Congregational Church presided over by the learned Rev. Dr. Carl Hermann Voss, whom I much admired for his professorial intellect, though I never felt any intimate connection to the God he talked about. By the time I was a teenager I had rationalized my Christianity down to the level of eighteenth-century Deism, telling myself there must be a higher power that presides over the world, and let's say this power is synonymous with "love" or "goodness" or some such anodyne quality, and I let it go at that for a long time before finally telling myself with a weary sigh, horsefeathers. The God-is-love business is just a dodge. There is no more reason to believe in that than there is to believe in Yahweh—or in Shiva or Huitzilopochtli, for that matter. There ain't no invisible man up in the sky looking down on us, and there ain't no gaseous spirit inhabiting the dandelions either. The whole thing is no more credible than Tinker Bell, and not essentially different from Tinker Bell. I do not make a big deal of this and do not hit other people over the head with it, but desiring to be open and aboveboard I here declare it so the reader may better appreciate my joustings with believers when the time comes.

My life did not begin with the *Schenectady Gazette*, and I did not come to the newspaper by design, but only by the kind of chance that steers us all. After venturing forth from my hometown of Saratoga Springs, I attended Tufts University, where I dived with enthusiasm into the novelties (for me) of Euripides and Socrates and felt little rapport with the aspiring dentists and engineers around me. I fell in with Quaker do-gooders in the poor black neighborhoods of Boston, I demonstrated in sympathy with civil rights activists in the South, I dropped out and ran away to join the American Friends Service Committee in rural Mexico, where I dwelled happily for two years. I eventually graduated with a degree in philosophy from what was then the New School for Social Research and is now the New School University, in New York City. I demonstrated against the Vietnam War and became so consumed with that holocaust that I rejoined the American Friends Service Committee for a two-year stint in Vietnam, a stint that ended with the Tet Offensive, after which I fell into journalism not from any sense of calling but just as a way to stay where I wanted to be. I stayed for six years—half in Vietnam, half in Laos—which was enough to convince me I did not want to be a journalist. I thought there must be more honorable ways to earn a living, though alas I never found any, not having any practical talents.

After taking refuge in the hippie, marijuana-growing hills of Humboldt County, California, for a spell, in a vain attempt to recover my equilibrium, I returned to Asia, to Hong Kong, to seek my fortune as an editor at the *South China Morning Post,* where my duties included editing *Asian Golf Digest,* the most absurd job I had ever had up to that point and which I allude to briefly in my narrative. There also I met my wife-to-be, the beautiful Pearl Bagalayos, whom I eventually dragged full circle back to upstate New York, where, needing employment to tide me over until we should move on again, I applied to the *Gazette* and was offered the demeaning job of reporting on the vanishingly significant affairs of the town Rotterdam, an appendage of the vanishingly significant city of Schenectady. It is there that our story begins. May Heaven keep us and preserve us.

1

THE RIGHT PAINT

"It's got to have fiber into it."

It was an unlikely way to hit upon a new direction in life, but there I was, sitting in a rinky-dink one-story town hall on rural Route 7 in Schenectady County, New York, taking notes as a bunch of fractious citizens earnestly disputed how to paint the town garage roof. I was a veteran of the murky arts of journalism in locations as exotic as Laos, Vietnam and Hong Kong, and this is what I had come to—reporter for the *Schenectady Gazoot*, responsible on this particular evening for covering the Duanesburg Town Board.

Duanesburg. Population 6,000, a population anti-social enough to be living by choice on seventy-two square miles of recently converted or abandoned farmland, as far from each other as possible. A population almost entirely white, almost entirely working, almost entirely truculent.

The chairman of the board's Buildings and Grounds Committee had brought to the meeting a can of what he insisted was the best paint available—pure aluminum. "It costs $20 a gallon," he declared, as if that settled the matter.

A town councilman, a technical type who worked at General Electric, didn't care if it cost $50 a gallon, and neither did the highway superintendent, whose cranium, shaped like an artillery shell, glittered under the fluorescent lights. "It's got to have fiber into it," each insisted, employing the rural vernacular.

The town supervisor, an earnest young Christian, agreed with fiber and added, "It's got to be an asphalt-based paint."

A curmudgeon from the back of the room hollered out that pure aluminum was good only on a roof with no leaks. The councilman agreed with that, and added that aluminum paint wouldn't bind around loose nails but would result in still more loose nails.

"It costs $20 a gallon," the chairman repeated. "I want to use the best. We painted the roof three years ago, and look at it now."

He also said the town could probably get the paint for $17 through a local dealer.

"It would be a lot cheaper in five-gallon buckets," the supervisor suggested.

"It would be a lot cheaper by the barrel," a smart aleck in the audience pitched in.

The town had budgeted $1,250 to paint the roof. The chairman figured that twenty gallons would do the job. The councilman calculated the area of the roof at

10,000 square feet and noted that a gallon of aluminum paint was advertised to cover 500 square feet, meaning that twenty gallons should be right. "But if it's got fiber into it, it won't go so far," he said. He proposed buying a little more than twenty gallons.

One of the cantankerous men who regularly sat in the back row and monitored the doings of the board, his arms folded, his lips pursed, volunteered to do the painting at no charge, to save taxpayer money, which was a large concern of the back-benchers. The problem was insurance. If he and the other back-benchers worked free, would workers' compensation insurance cover them? Probably not, the board thought.

"We'll pay you a dollar," the supervisor suggested by way of solution.

"We don't want a dollar," said the ever-obstinate back-bencher.

Wouldn't paying a dollar violate the minimum-wage law? the councilman wondered.

The town attorney said he would look into that one.

How much would it cost to buy extra insurance to cover volunteers? The attorney said he would look into that too. "I'll have the answer in two days," he pledged.

"We don't need insurance," the back-bencher said. "Anyone who can't get up on that roof without falling off, we don't want him." He suggested that the supervisor be "ground man," moving the ladder, so the volunteers wouldn't have to keep going up and down.

The supervisor said if the men were to be hired at a dollar a day, they would have to fill out applications like any other job seekers.

"If we're going to do the roof, at least you can do the paperwork," the back-bencher said.

I was close to slitting my wrists. How could I write a news story about this? It was getting late, and I had to drive a half-hour back to downtown Schenectady to the offices of the *Schenectady Gazoot* and write a story about these Lilliputian doings, and after a couple of hours of listening and taking notes I was at the outer limits of my sanity. I finally sat down at my computer in the crowded newsroom up on the second floor of 332 State Street, looked at myself, and said, screw it. I wasn't going to translate this miserable drivel into a formulaic news story—"The Duanesburg Town Board last night voted 4 to 1 to increase the town clerk's petty cash account to $75," starting with the seemingly most important item and working down through the other agenda items, winding up with "in other business," which is where the inconclusive discussion of the roof painting would have gone. I would focus on the matter most revealing of what the Duanesburg Town Board actually did at its monthly meetings, and I would write it as it happened, in all its banality.

Of course the banality was *my* problem, not the town board members'. They were tending to the town's affairs, and it wasn't their fault that the affairs were modest. But I was in despair at having arrived so low as a journalist, a trade that I did not even desire for myself, and that's how I handled it: I wrote up the discussion perfectly deadpan, as if it were a senatorial debate on an arms-control treaty. Who said what.

The next day the phone was ringing, and people were saying they didn't know whether to laugh or cry. "It's got to have fiber into it!" "Cheaper by the barrel!" "We don't want a dollar!"

I didn't necessarily think it was funny myself, at least not while I was writing it, but I wasn't going to complain. The exercise itself was a relief, and its reception a balm for my spirit, so then and there I resolved to do more of this species of reporting if I could get away with it, to relieve the boredom of the job if nothing else. I would just tell things as they were, even trivial things, even absurd things, even embarrassing things, and the devil take the hindmost.

The resolve didn't come out of the blue, nor was I so reckless as to chance writing a story in defiance of newspaper convention without a pretty good sense that I could get away with it. The *Gazoot* was a family-owned newspaper, but the family was so far removed from it, and from the world too, that you could get away with almost anything if you were cunning enough. The city editor, Dutch Boy Bob, who appeared to have been recruited from the loading dock, merely passed out press releases to the reporters and held to the philosophy "If they want it in the paper, they'll send it to us," as he told me once when I suggested a story that was not pre-packaged. Press releases and meetings like the Duanesburg Town Board meeting— that was the soil that we tilled. Except, as I discovered, if you went ahead and wrote a story without pitching it to Dutch Boy Bob or anyone else first, it went into the paper anyway, and what's more, it went in unedited, probably even unread, just as all stories did. Nobody fiddled with the copy to make it conform to company style and to avoid giving offense, as my copy had always been fiddled with before—at The Associated Press, at *Time* magazine, at *Newsweek*, anywhere I had worked, except at *Asian Golf Digest*, where I was fiddler-in-chief myself, which was the previous low for me, editing a golf magazine, of all absurd things.

I had adventured around Southeast Asia, I had sought refuge in northern California, I had toiled in Hong Kong, and now here I was in a decrepit old industrial city with a comical name in upstate New York, where the latest hope for revival was a concrete ditch downtown with paddle boats in it to suggest a long-gone stretch of the Erie Canal, and finally I said to myself, very well, I'll give it a go, right here.

I had already been through the Battle of the Shopping Mall and the Great Flats Aquifer, so it wasn't as if I was starting from zero. I had sat through days and even weeks of quasi-judicial hearings conducted by the state Department of Environmental Conservation on the question of whether a real-estate company from Rochester ought to be permitted to build a shopping mall above an underground natural reservoir, which was a question that burned fiercely in the breasts of both downtown Schenectady merchants, who feared further loss of business, and nature-loving suburbanites, who feared acres of asphalt where now grew grass. A freaking shopping-mall war. Day after day sitting on a metal folding chair in the Disabled American Veterans Hall down at Five Corners, listening to and taking notes on testimony from geologists, hydrologists, civil engineers, traffic experts, parking-lot-runoff experts, riprap specialists, ichthyologists, limnologists till my brain went numb, after which I would drive woozily back to the newsroom to distill the day's barrel of facts into a half-quart story for the next day's edition. So I was no stranger to laborious meetings by the time I confronted the Duanesburg roof debate. On the contrary, I counted myself battle-tested. The Duanesburg meeting was the turning point, that's all.

I had also lived through and reported on the high drama of the supervisor of the town of Rotterdam, John Kirvin, dropping dead on live television at the beginning of a campaign debate at the exact moment when the moderator introduced him, his eyes rolling up in his head and his body tipping over backward out of his chair. Fifty-seven years old. Which is not something you could expect in a national presidential race, so I didn't feel entirely shortchanged. I was privileged also to report on the ensuing election, which Kirvin actually won, there not being time to remove his name from the ballot and his fellow Democrats rallying behind him despite his alarming physical condition. "Dead Man Wins Election" was the headline in one of New York City's tabloids, while the *Gazoot* played my story on the bottom of page B1, under the more timid headline "Rotterdam Voters Pay Kirvin Tribute."

But mostly it was straining to make sense of things like planning board meetings, at which the chairman would say what sounded to me like "I don't know if this will meet seeker." I would write that in my notebook with a question mark after it, having no idea what he was talking about, even though the other members of the board seemed perfectly content, and not just content but well satisfied with the importance of their positions and the power they wielded over some citizen wishing to open a beauty parlor. They would ask solemn and pointed questions about "ingress" and "egress" and always that ever-loving "seeker," which I had to wait until the end of the meeting to find out was the State Environmental Quality Review Act, abbreviated SEQRA. How the hell was I supposed to know that?

Or Princetown board meetings at which the main topic of discussion was whether to have their annual lunch at Canali's restaurant in Rotterdam, as they did the previous year, and if so, which menu to choose, a discussion that could easily take half an hour. (As Rotterdam reporter, I was responsible not only for Rotterdam but also for the outlying rural towns of Duanesburg and Princetown.)

I will not claim I distinguished myself in reporting on these homely matters, but I will say I began to see a certain beauty in them, and I began to take a certain pleasure in writing them up, massaging the language to fit the majesty, or lack of majesty, of the events, even before I made the discovery that set me on a career path.

I sensed right from the beginning that the *Gazoot* was going to be different from anyplace else I had worked. When I first showed up for a job interview and was shown into the office of the family member who held the title of managing editor but who I later learned managed nothing at all, I was at pains to impress on him my worldly experience. I talked to him about the Vietnam War and the secret war in Laos, dropping the names of famous correspondents I had fraternized with and the names also of various national publications I had written for, even though I had been only a stringer and not a full-fledged correspondent, and I went on in this vein for some time, making myself out to be a journalist of some heft who would surely be an asset to so worthy a paper as the *Gazoot*, until finally Jack—that was his name—looked at me with one eye going this way and the other going that and said, in the dreamy remote way he had, "I'm a musician."

"I like music myself," I said, recovering with what I thought was admirable quickness, though I knew I was in new territory. Clearly this was not the AP or the *South China Morning Post*. This was the *Schenectady Gazoot* (later renamed the *Daily Gazoot*, in a futile search for a broader audience), and the guy who had inherited it spent his time picking bluegrass guitar with his friends. He didn't know Peter Arnett or Bernard Kalb from the man in the moon, and he didn't care. He did tell me that the *Gazoot's* Rotterdam reporter had just tendered his resignation, and if I wanted, I could have the position. I said I was confident I could do an able job of presenting the affairs of Rotterdam to the readers, and then I went home, got a map, and looked to see where Rotterdam was.

2

COPS ARE ROBBERS

*"Aiding and abetting a crack house—roll that over
on your tongue a few times."*

Even when immersed in the petty affairs of
Rotterdam and neighboring Duanesburg, I knew the
Schenectady police would be a rich source of material
if I ever rose so high in the *Gazoot's* ranks as to be able
to write about them—which I didn't necessarily expect
to do, they being property of the lofty City Hall beat.
What caught my attention, and everyone else's attention
in Schenectady at the time, was the matter of Patrolman
Ambrose Mountain, on trial for rape and sodomy,
accused of forcing a woman prisoner in a holding cell
to give him his pleasure. The woman had been arrested
in a bar fracas and brought to the police station in a
torn blouse with a tattoo showing on the upper part
of her breast, and Patrolman Mountain visited her in
her cell. The woman, with a laudable sensitivity to
forensics, spat the result of the encounter into a paper

cup thoughtfully provided by a jail matron, and as a result Patrolman Mountain was ultimately convicted and sentenced to four to twelve years in prison. Which was fine, and about which one could say, well, there's a bad apple in every barrel, except that Mountain's fellow cops belligerently supported him, paying for his defense, showing up every day at his trial, even endeavoring to trip the prosecutor when he walked down the aisle of the courtroom.

Now, *there* would be something to write about that would be a little more engaging than the hydrology of an aquifer or the painting of a garage roof.

Soon enough I learned there were cops in Rotterdam who also had a flair, like Sergeant Mike, a detective who was one of the first people I met when I went to the police station to introduce myself as their new designated reporter. He endeavored to befriend me by inviting me into his office to listen to a tape recording he had made of a little interrogation of his. A convenience store had been robbed, and Sergeant Mike had discovered that the young clerk on duty at the time had once been arrested on some minor charge and had not disclosed the fact on his employment application. Sergeant Mike put the screws to this clerk, letting on that he was the leading suspect in the robbery and threatening to tell his employer about the past arrest, which probably would have gotten the clerk fired.

"Here comes the good part," he kept saying to me as he fast-forwarded the tape recording—the good part being the part where the clerk whimpered and whined, insisting on his innocence, and begged Sergeant Mike not to get him fired.

"Did you really think he did it?" I asked.

"Oh, no," Sergeant Mike said. "He didn't do it. I was just having some fun. Listen, here it comes."

It was his way of being friendly with me, to let me in on this little joke, which he insisted was off the record. If it had happened later, when I had begun to find my way, I might have tried to shine a light on Sergeant Mike's way of amusing himself. I might have interviewed the poor clerk myself, for example, but at the time I just filed it away in my store of unpleasant memories of law enforcement, a store that had been building since my days of protesting the Vietnam War, when cops used to rip placards out of the hands of us demonstrators and then lie in court about what we had done to merit arrest. But on this day, as a newly minted small-town reporter, I was still at a loss, and I accepted Sergeant Mike's stricture of "off the record" without demur, allowing myself to be his confidant. It felt strange enough to be on the same side of the desk with him, in the inner sanctum of a police station, where I had never been before without handcuffs, but there I was, straight man to a small-town sadist with hair bristling out his ears, like my childhood barber.

The day would come when I would write a column under the headline "Are Cops and Criminals of a Kind?" and would use this incident as an example of the mentality I had in mind—without, however, naming Sergeant Mike—but that was after I had paid my dues not only as Rotterdam reporter but also as Schenectady

City Hall reporter—the big time!—and even as an assistant city editor for a brief unhappy spell, and had been elevated to the very empyrean of newspaperdom with a column of my own. (A new managing editor soon tired of my begging to be relieved of city desk duties and asked, "You want to write a column?" as a way of getting me out of his office.)

The Schenectady police were indeed a rich source of material for me once I attained the rank of columnist, all the more so when you consider that the *Gazoot*, like almost every newspaper in the land, traditionally treated the police with deference. It may not have employed the lickspittle language of big-city tabloids—"thin blue line," "New York's finest," that sort of thing—but the attitude was much the same. The police reporter for a daily newspaper in the United States didn't report on the police; he reported on criminals. He took the police at their word.

Simply to get hold of the police union's contract, read it, and then write about it in the newspaper was something unheard of, and it did not go over well at all when I undertook it— pointing out that the cops were allowed unlimited sick time and availed themselves of it lavishly, averaging twenty-six sick days a year per officer, not counting time off for on-the-job injuries. "It's frightening when you think about it," I wrote with concern, "the public depending for protection on such an unhealthy group of people." Spelling out how they amassed overtime so as to double their salaries by piggy-backing on each other's leave; reporting on how the 450 man-days off allowed for the conduct of union business, which did not need to be documented; checking to see how many officers showed up for work on the night of the union's annual dinner dance (five out of nineteen on the 4 p.m.-to-midnight shift, four out of seventeen on the midnight to 8 a.m. shift); explaining how they could earn overtime even while averaging only 179 days of work a year—these were novelties.

The contracts of public employees, along with the pay and benefits they receive, have since become mainstream news, but at the time I was doing this, beginning in the late 1980s, they were little noticed, and I pride myself on having been a pioneer in the field, even if a pioneer unnoticed by the rest of the republic. As far as reception in Schenectady went, it was mixed. For some, I might as well have been feeding nuclear secrets to an enemy state. Many a cop's wife or mother wrote to protest that police officers "put their lives on the line" to protect the rest of us, which was and still is the standard line, the implication being, one should not inquire how much they get paid or how many sick days they take, their work being dangerous. For some ordinary citizens, I am pleased to state, I was a hero, which was decidedly a new experience for me.

When Schenectady at one point hired a new chief to straighten things out, and on his watch a member of the department's vice squad, entrusted with catching drug dealers, was arrested for stealing cocaine from the department's evidence locker to feed his own habit, the new chief took to the microphone not to denounce the crook nor to heap scorn on the fellow vice officers, who must have been covering for him, but to praise all other officers, who "in these weather conditions"—it was snowing at the time—"are out serving the public, putting their lives on the line." I had a fine time with this, and even more of a fine time with the chief's sympathetic lament about "the obvious power that an addiction has" and his request for "courtesy and thoughtfulness" for the family of the coke-snorting officer, a lament and a request that no one ever heard on behalf of a civilian arrested for stealing or dealing drugs.

So I not only reported previously obscure facts; I also managed to inject a note of mockery, in good taste, of course. Once in a while I even got on my high horse and delivered a moralistic lecture as if I were a big-name syndicated columnist, though I'm not proud of that part and if I could do it over would exercise more restraint.

There was much to relish in the Schenectady Police Department as I felt my way along:

There was Patrolman Mike Guthinger, whose duties included guarding the parking lot behind Proctor's Theater on the nights when there were shows and who took advantage of his assignment to break into cars and rifle them for valuables, employing a tool that was actually provided by the police department. He was eventually set up by the State Police and caught in the act, the most notable thing about his case being that the police union left him to his own legal devices, declining to hire a lawyer for him, which was a rarity.

There was the $10,000 that disappeared from the department's evidence locker, which turned out to be not a locker but just a filing cabinet in the vice squad office to which all six vice squad officers had access, along with janitors and computer technicians who came and went. The mayor asked the chief for a written list of procedures to prevent such a disappearance from happening again, but never got it.

There was the case of the boys entertaining themselves on the occasion of a bachelor party by renting a bus to tour strip joints in the Albany-Schenectady area and afterwards, well-fueled, throwing eggs out the bus windows at passing cars in the very city they were employed to protect. I got tipped off to that a few days after it happened. A woman who didn't give her name called me about it, but I brushed her off. "Lady," I said, "I'm prepared to believe a lot of things about Schenectady cops, but I'm not prepared to believe they would throw eggs at cars."

Then I got another call to much the same effect, and with the same detail given by the first caller, that the cops had gotten into a dustup with a passing driver who had objected to their attentions. The driver supposedly got out and broke a window in their bus, and the cops roughed him up. Sure enough, the first bus company I called confirmed that a bunch of cops had indeed rented a bus and the bus had come back with a broken window. The police chief, who later went to prison on a drug conviction of his own, confirmed the story when I confronted him with it, and it was a lovely story indeed, even if he did screw me out of a scoop by releasing it to all the media right away. The *Gazoot*, bless its normally timid heart, sued to get the names of the cops involved, and when the case eventually landed in the state's highest court I sat with the chief in the courtroom and bet him an omelet we would win. Alas, we did not, so the names of the egg-throwers were forever denied to history.

There was the case of poor David Sampson, a low-level suspected drug dealer from the streets of Hamilton Hill, the poorest and most lawless neighborhood of Schenectady, who was sitting on a stoop one night about 9 o'clock minding his business when a patrol car stopped in front of him and the two cops inside, Mike Siler and Rick Barnett, decided to give him the business. They stood him up and searched him, and finding nothing, instead of letting him go put him into their car and drove away with him, west on I-890, to rural West Glenville. And there, partway up steep Rector Road, they relieved him of his shoes, threw the shoes off into the darkness and told him to start walking. Eight miles from Hamilton Hill. It was "so Schenectady," as people had a way of saying.

There he was, a young black street dude in an unlighted area only thinly populated by middle-class white folks, to give the story a racial angle, in his bare feet. A woman called the Glenville police and reported a black male in the road frantically waving as she drove by. The Glenville cop who responded wrote in his report that the guy was "irrational." Obviously. He claimed that cops had taken his shoes.

The city finally settled him with for $240,000, though by that time he was in state prison for unrelated felonious selling of cocaine. His lawyer was disappointed in not being able to take the case to trial, since he had had a great success with another Schenectady case, in which the cops had dragged a guy out of his house naked and beaten him both in the street and at the police station, in a case of mistaken identity. (If it had been the right guy, maybe it would have been OK.)

There was Mike Siler again, in uniform, skulking through a cemetery at night to throw rocks at cars driven by drug informants who worked for other cops. Part of an intramural feud. When I got a call about that one, from a tenant at a welfare motel, I knew better than to dismiss it. He didn't know what it was all about, he just saw it from the motel balcony—a uniformed cop crouching behind the fence of Vale Cemetery, pelting passing cars with rocks at about 9 o'clock on a Friday night, then creeping back to his patrol car and driving away. I actually staked out the scene the next Friday night to see if it would happen again, but of course it didn't, so that was the end of the matter as far as I was concerned—until a year later, when Siler took the stand in the trial of a couple of his comrades accused of drug dealing (he had already pleaded guilty in that one) and told about it. I almost fell out of my seat. It was the patrol division vs. the vice squad, as simple as that. Siler was a patrol cop, and he was busting on the vice cops by harassing their informants.

There was Lieutenant Mike Hamilton, one of the officers on trial in the drug case, accused and ultimately convicted of tipping off an informant of his, a low-level dealer, that her house in the Mont Pleasant neighborhood was being watched by the vice squad. "Aiding and abetting a crack house—roll that over on your tongue a few times," mused Judge David Hurd in federal court. Mike, who got four and a half years, was from a police family. Brother Jim was chief of the Rotterdam Police Department, brother Bobby was president of the Schenectady police union.

There was Ron Pedersen, a real beauty. Off duty late one night he tried to pick up a young woman in a bar—a striking-looking customer by the name of Becky DiSorbo, with long blonde hair. When she rebuffed him, he arrested her, wrenching her arm up behind her back and frog-marching her outside to a patrol car. When her sister protested, she was arrested by another cop, and both of them were taken to the police station, where the sister was shoved into a doorjamb and Becky was choked and had her head banged into a wall before being thrown face-first to the concrete floor and punched in the head. "I tried to stand up...they pushed me back down...I just stayed there. I thought if I got up they'd kill me," she testified through tears when the matter came to civil trial. The city of Schenectady was found liable and ordered to pay $1,675,000 (later reduced to $325,000).

Pedersen stayed on the police force another year, until he so frightened a prostitute he had picked up that she jumped from his truck at 3 o'clock in the morning and ran to a nearby house for help, and the latest police commissioner pressured him into resigning.

There was the Ninja raid on an unsuspecting family headed by a man who lived on disability payments and a woman who was a health aide at a nursing home— Ninjas being the colloquial name in Schenectady for the police department's SWAT team, whose members dressed all in black, including masks, for assaults on dangerous criminals. At 6 o'clock one morning, when it was still dark, the Ninjas broke down the door of the family's apartment—in a poor neighborhood, of course—swarmed in with guns drawn, and by the light of their flashlights dragged not just mother and father but also a twelve-year-old girl and an eleven-year-old boy out of their beds, threw them to the floor, handcuffed them, held guns on them, all the while shouting and cursing at everyone and not incidentally blowing their dog to Kingdom Come with a shotgun blast, as their two-year-old toddler stood by. This was to effect the arrest of their eighteen-year-old son for possession of about two joints' worth of marijuana. They said they had information he was dealing. I got eyewitness accounts from each member of the family, including the children. The police department's officially designated spokesman—whose bachelor party culminated in the famous egg-throwing—said their account was "a despicable attempt to disparage the Schenectady Police Department."

They were so sublimely sure of themselves, these officers of the law, they actually protested an order not to belittle people on account of race and the like. This was when Mayor Karen Johnson, in desperation, hired a police commissioner from outside to straighten things out. The commissioner issued what he called a human rights order, strictly boilerplate, like a Labor Department advisory in an employees' lounge that nobody reads, or a choking poster in a restaurant: "No employee shall either explicitly or implicitly ridicule, mock, taunt, incite, deride or belittle any person or group...employees shall not make offensive comments or derogatory comments based on race, color, sex, religion or national origin." Doing so would be considered misconduct, and anyone who committed it would be "subject to disciplinary action by this department."

The police union, humorously named the Police Benevolent Association, or PBA for short, filed what's known in the labor game as an "improper practice" charge with the state's Public Employment Relations Board, claiming any such rule had to be negotiated, meaning the city would have to give them something in exchange. I had a special place in my affections for the PBA president who took this action, since on his first day in office he had hand-delivered to the general manager of the *Gazoot* a letter demanding I be fired. It was a rare distinction for me.

As for their morale, don't even mention it. They would regularly show up at city council meetings to tell everyone how low it was. "I've never seen it so bad," I heard the PBA president say more than once, and never mind the study done by the state's Bureau for Municipal Police, which found that the PBA's very power had "inadvertently created an obstacle to high morale and effective discipline in the department." Having the run of the shop depressed them!

Well, I was happy, if they weren't. My morale was fine, what with all these treasures to write about, and it was getting finer all the time.

3

SCHOOL DAYS

*"We don't apologize for using clout to
get what students need."*

Part of my duties as Rotterdam reporter had been to cover the town's three school districts, and if you want a job guaranteed to shrivel your brain cells, ossify your synapses and benumb your whole *systema nervosum*, that's it, attending school board meetings and writing them up for a daily newspaper. It's only half a step above covering the Duanesburg Town Board, maybe not even that. School boards in New York have almost no power, educational policy being set by the state Education Department and terms of employment being set in labor contracts that are negotiated in secret. School boards debate the educational equivalent of how to paint the garage roof, and their members are earnest parents, serving without pay or perquisites, who simply manage to get elected. When I graduated from Rotterdam to Schenectady City Hall, and then eventually to column-writing, I did not weep at leaving school boards behind.

But I had learned a little in spite of myself, so when the *Gazoot* eventually ran a story about the teachers' union in the Schenectady City School District taking a righteous stand against what was known as "age promotion," that is, the passing of kids from one grade to the next regardless of whether they deserved it just so they could keep up with their age group, I was ready.

The union president was quoted as saying, "In the real world you don't get a promotion for not doing the work."

"Are you kidding me?" I wrote. "Automatic promotion is what teachers absolutely live by. It's not just something they tolerate, it's something they fight for. How can they be against it?"

I enthusiastically spelled out the "steps" in their contract, with the corresponding salaries, year by year, to which they were automatically promoted, and asked, "Do you know how they get from one step to the next? Just by hanging around for another year, that's all. Not by achieving anything, not by being more effective teachers."

It was a pedestrian-enough observation for anyone who knew anything about how schools work, and I thought little enough of it that I didn't even make it into a full column but just used it as an item, along with other items. But how the teachers reacted! How they wrote letters! How they berated me! They worked hard, they wanted me to know. They didn't just "hang around." Furthermore, children are our future. Education is extremely important. Teaching is difficult. My "diatribe" was full of hatred. My "rant" showed that I "do not have much value for life anymore"—even that.

So I knew I was onto something again, and I silently gave thanks for all those Draper, Schalmont and Mohonasen school board meetings I had doodled, daydreamed and muttered my way through. I would never have known about the workings of teachers' unions and school boards otherwise, and wouldn't have cared. What interest did I have in "step increases" or "age promotion"?

It also meant that I was prepared when the phone rang the next time and the caller said I had to keep her name out of it, but she had some unseemly business from the little town of Stillwater to tell me about. Stillwater, a down-at-the-heels old mill town on the banks of the Hudson River, upstream from Albany. She said the school board, meeting in secret, had put together a generous package of raises and guarantees for the teachers' union without even waiting for negotiations that were scheduled for the following year, and they were preparing to adopt that package at their next public meeting without divulging its contents. Very nice, I thought. Even better, five of the school board's nine members were teachers themselves, four of them in neighboring districts but resident in Stillwater and one retired from Stillwater.

It all turned out to be true. I managed to get hold of the secret package and wrote it up in my column:

Would you like an example of a school board being taken over by teachers?

Would you like an example of a school board engaging in a giveaway to its teachers, unrequested even by the teachers themselves but simply at the board's own magnanimous initiative?

Would you like an example of a board doing all that in secret, without telling the residents and taxpayers of its district what it's up to?

It was entertaining enough. I gave the particulars of the secret deal—the raises and the guarantees—and I identified the members of the school board who were themselves teachers, along with the districts where they taught. Not surprisingly there was a big turnout when the meeting finally came, at which the secret deal was to be ratified, keeping in mind that school board meetings anywhere rarely attract more than a few school employees and one or two unhappy reporters.

Here is how the meeting went, per my eventual report:

The people of Stillwater got a hosing from their school board the other night, no doubt about that.

They tried to speak up, they tried to protest, they tried to ask what the devil the board was handing over to the teachers' union, but the board ruled them out of order and told them to sit down and keep quiet or they, the board, would have them kicked out.

Indeed, two uniformed police officers stood by in case that was necessary.

No questions were allowed from the citizenry and no comments until after the board voted on its deal with the teachers' union and thus made questions and comments moot.

What deal?

You're not allowed to know until after it's ratified. That was the board's adamant position.

Can you imagine a democracy functioning like that? I thought, this must be how it's done in Sierra Leone or Uzbekistan.

In my years of attending public meetings, I don't believe I had ever seen anything like it—elected representatives flat-out refusing to tell their own constituents what they were voting on.

..."You're a disgrace to the community!" Stillwater Mayor Ernest Martin shouted at them from the floor at one point.

"This is taxation without representation!" hollered another man. But to no avail.

"You're out of order; we'll close the meeting," was all that the board vice president, Priscilla Mueller, would say as she repeatedly talked people down.

Former board member Valerie Masterson tried to speak and also got nowhere, but she trooped up front anyway to present a petition of protest.

And what were the terms of the deal that they were so reluctant to reveal? As I reported earlier, guaranteed three percent annual raises for teachers in the event a new contract is not agreed to (except for those at the top level of pay), which pretty much removes any incentive to negotiate, and a nice upward shift in the whole pay scale, getting rid of the lowest levels and adding new higher levels.

...Naturally, the board members were not happy that I blew the whistle on them, and as a result, I took my share of contumely and vituperation from them, along with accusations of disseminating misinformation when they voiced their own views at their microphones, but I didn't mind.

...My favorite defense of the giveaway, when the vote was finished and it came time for the public to speak, emanated from one Shawn McClements, a chemistry teacher at the high school, who took the microphone to shrilly declare that "there is a market value to teachers, like plumbers," and who then went on to read a list of average salaries in various school districts in this region, showing that Stillwater was near the bottom, 67th out of 69.

I have not checked to see if his numbers are correct, but it doesn't really matter. The argument harks back to President Eisenhower, who reportedly expressed dismay when he learned that half of all Americans have below-average intelligence.

Not only teachers but also police and firefighters argue from the same dismay. Nobody should get paid below average, is their position.

Do you want a below-average education for your children? they ask. Below-average police or fire protection? Of course not.

So up goes their pay, whereupon someone else falls below average, and on it goes.

As for there being a market value for teachers, that's really a hoot, since the very purpose of public employees' unions is to create a monopoly and make sure there is no free market.

Their salaries are locked into contracts negotiated by pliant school boards, of which Stillwater's is only the most egregious example, and that's the end of it. After that, there is no competition to see who can do the job cheaper, as there is among plumbers.

And if the taxpayers can't afford the salaries, too bad for them. They can move to Arizona.

The astute reader will perceive that by now I had strayed from the strictly deadpan reporting of garage-roof days and had stepped into the land of indignant polemic, which even now I'm not sure was a good move. There is much to be said for slyly laying out facts and allowing readers to make of them what they will, and it was my pride as a lowly reporter that readers sometimes reached very different conclusions, some laughing, others crying. An assault like the one above, characterizing the school board's action as a straight-out hosing, well, there wasn't much art in it. But it had its gratifications, or at least its seductions, and when I had the material to work with, increasingly that's how I handled it. I gave miscreants a hosing of their own.

In Southeast Asia I had seen humbuggery obviously on a grander scale and with grimmer consequences than anything Stillwater or Schenectady could offer, but I couldn't do anything about it. I had felt that telling the truth was impossible, or if not impossible then dangerous. Looking back, I realized I was just making excuses, but at the time a few pipes of opium at Hoang's or a joint at the morning market in Vientiane provided consolation adequate for the day. That another day would come when I would exercise my wits to get the goods on a school board in a little burg in upstate New York and would take satisfaction in it—well, who could have guessed?

I had felt I was onto something with cops, but I felt it even more with teachers. It wasn't just telling the plain truth that was satisfying while so much of the newspaper contented itself with press releases. It was violating a taboo: mocking those who *put their lives on the line to protect us all*, or exposing the secret dealings of those who *educate our children*. Telling forbidden truths about sacred persons, that was the ticket—a ticket that would carry me farther than I thought.

I hadn't had any illusions about cops since my experiences with them in anti-Vietnam War demonstrations. I remembered, for example, being arrested in Philadelphia by the celebrated police chief (later mayor) Frank Rizzo, then showing up in court along with other demonstrators and being briefed by our civil liberties lawyer on what to expect, which was that our arresting officers would testify first, and so forth, and my saying I was therefore off the hook, since my arresting officer wasn't present, an assertion that my lawyer shrugged off. "Doesn't matter," he said. "They'll just have some other cop testify that he arrested you." And sure enough, that's what happened, the casual perjury being taken for granted by old court hands.

But I still clung to my understanding of teachers as the low-paid, lightly regarded old maids I had known in No. 4 school in Saratoga Springs, not far from Stillwater, having missed the years when they became a major political force, which happened in New York with the passage of the Taylor Law in 1968, allowing public employees to unionize.

Now, a few decades later, teachers in depressed industrial-era towns like Stillwater and Mechanicville were making double the average income of their neighbors and they were still pressuring for more. They were a privileged class. They worked just half the days of the year, and if you wanted them to work more, to come in for a few days in the summer to look at new lesson plans, for example, you had to pay them extra. They were required to be on the job just six and a half hours a day. They insisted they worked more than that, at home, correcting papers and so forth, and no doubt some of them did, but they had plenty of free time during the school day for those chores too, contracts typically limiting actual teaching time to no more than three and a half hours a day.

And they were a political force—a political force and a half, you might say. At the time I was laboring on these matters, New York State United Teachers was the fattest cat at the state Capitol, No. 1 on the annual "Fat Cat" list compiled by New York Public Interest Research Group. They were spending a million dollars a year on lobbying and campaign contributions combined, and that soon grew to $2 million, ahead of every business lobby you can think of.

"We don't apologize for using clout to get what students need," the president of the union, Tom Hobart, wrote to the *Gazoot* in protest of my polemical reporting, and that was the line—the pay raises, the job protections, the early retirements, the outsized pensions were all for the kids.

In just a couple of decades the teachers' unions had extracted from the state legislature and from local school boards such sweet deals, and had amassed for themselves such power, that when some good-government types, known affectionately as goo-goos, attempted to call a convention to revise the state Constitution, teachers, fearful of losing their privileges, were in the vanguard of the resistance. Tom Hobart scoffed at the idea of ordinary citizens putting together "anything so complicated as a constitution," and he was joined by Robin Rappaport, vice president of the National Education Association, who argued that such a spectacle would make for "added cynicism among our children." In the end, thanks to a massive advertising campaign, they prevailed, and no convention was held.

We were supposed to believe, among other public relations pitches, that there was a critical shortage of teachers, owing to the hardships they endured, and the only way to rectify it was to pay them more and more. New York State United Teachers commissioned a survey, the artfully tailored results of which it distributed to the news media, and the news media, including the *Gazoot*, made the alleged teacher shortage into a major story for a time.

The survey showed that seventy-four percent of teachers aged fifty and older planned to retire in the next five years—alarming!—without noting that the union itself had fought for and won the right to retire at age fifty-five with a half-pay pension.

It showed that thirty-two percent of teachers aged thirty and younger planned to leave their jobs within the next five years—more alarming!—without also reporting that most of them simply planned to switch to other schools, not leave teaching.

It concluded that the best way to encourage older and more experienced teachers to stay on the job and stem the alleged crisis was to give them "financial incentives"—brilliant! and actually my favorite—because the way school districts had found to *get rid* of older and more experienced teachers, who are naturally the highest-paid, was likewise to give them "financial incentives" in the form of lump-sum payments. So if the union had its way, school districts would pay them extra to retire and also pay them extra not to retire.

When the state Board of Regents proposed that retired teachers be allowed to return to work at full pay without giving up their pensions, *The New York Times* called it a "stark concession to the seriousness of New York State's shortage of qualified teachers."

Years later these unseemly matters would come to a head in Wisconsin, where the Republican governor, Scott Walker, attempted to dismantle public employee unions altogether—or so it was reported—but at this time very little was heard about it, and even to talk about the power of the unions was considered indelicate. And even Governor Walker, for all his zeal, was not so impolitic as to include police and fire unions in his attempted dismantling.

The teachers' union, more gentle than the PBA, tried to divert me from my explorations into this forbidden territory by inviting me to teach for a day, so I could see for myself how arduous it was. I gave the flippant response that I would do it if I could get the summer off and retire at age fifty-five, but in fact I already had my eye on other matters.

4

DISORDERS DU JOUR

*"You are more creative, you are more energetic, you are more
intuitive, you are more original than most people.
That's really cool."*

It was a jolly time, and one of the things that made
it jolly was Ritalin. Not that I was taking it, but I was
becoming aware of it. A colleague at work mentioned
to me that it was becoming common for kids to be
prescribed this drug to help them pay attention in
class, and at certain times of the day these kids would
get up and troop to the nurse's office to get their daily
dose, or fix. Since this was at the same time they were
being told to "Say No to Drugs" and police officers
were giving anti-drug instruction in classrooms under
the DARE program (Drug Abuse Resistance Education),
I figured I could easily fill my allotted sixteen column
inches toying with the irony of it.

I learned that between three and five percent
of all schoolchildren in the United States were being

given Ritalin. I learned that the effects of the drug were similar to those of cocaine or amphetamines, that is, it concentrated the mind, and indeed Ritalin was a chemical cousin to amphetamines. In federal drug-control terms, it was a Schedule II controlled substance, right up there with heroin and morphine. "Pediatric cocaine," one critic called it—and there was a vocal if small body of critics who were writing books like *Talking Back to Ritalin* (Peter R. Breggin) and *No More Ritalin* (Mary Ann Block). There was even a national organization, Parents Against Ritalin, though it was no match for CHADD (Children and Adults with Attention Deficit/Hyperactivity Disorder). The chief defense of the drug was that "it works," as I heard from both parents and teachers when I looked into the matter. You get a kid in first grade, let's say, who is bouncing off the walls and can't focus on his ABCs for the life of him, you dose him up with Ritalin, and there he is, sitting quietly, focusing like Galileo almost.

Well, sure, I said, drugs work:

> *You feel sluggish, you have a cup of coffee. You feel wound up, you have a bottle of beer. You're tense, you smoke a cigarette. Maybe a little marijuana? A snort of coke? An injection of heroin? People don't do those things because they're ineffective...They do them because they work...But how dumb do we think our kids are?*

So I wrote, though I soon discovered that Ritalin worked mainly in getting kids to sit still. "The short-term effects on academic performance are minimal compared to the effects on behavior," a study at the time concluded. Basically, it made life easier for teachers and parents.

But the world of medicine being what it is— and the world of health insurance being what it is— doctors couldn't prescribe a medicine just to make kids sit still. That wouldn't be right. There had to be some underlying medical condition, some illness, that needed to be treated, and the American Psychiatric Association was there with a solution to that little problem: Kids who couldn't pay attention had Attention Deficit Disorder, or ADD, later expanded to Attention Deficit/Hyperactivity Disorder, ADHD. As far as diagnostic insight goes, it was like saying if your knee itches you have itchy-knee-itis— but never mind, the kids were sick! You could look it up in the psychiatrists' *Diagnostic and Statistical Manual of Mental Disorders*, fourth edition, which was the edition in use at the time. DSM-4, as it was known in the trade. ADHD was disorder No. 314.00 or 314.01, depending on type, which was the number a doctor would have to provide to an insurance company for billing purposes.

And what were the clinical, scientific criteria for this supposed illness, per the DSM-4? They were such utterly subjective and tautological manifestations as "often fidgets with hands or feet or squirms in seat," "often does not seem to listen when spoken to directly," "is often 'on the go' or often acts as if 'driven by a motor.'"

Did they mean to say only three to five percent of American schoolchildren were fidgety? Not hardly. CHADD, which was underwritten by the pharmaceutical industry, asserted that most children with this dread condition went lamentably untreated. In fact, only twelve percent of children who "met the diagnostic criteria" for ADHD in a particular study were being treated for it, meaning, if my arithmetic serves me, twenty-five to forty-two percent of all children were afflicted, so there was quite a market to be tapped. We were just getting started.

Things reached such a pass that a young couple in the rural reaches of Albany County were actually hauled into court for resisting giving Ritalin to their seven-year-old son. The kid was one of those who "bounced off the walls," by the parents' rueful admission, and at the end of his kindergarten year his teacher had told them they should get him evaluated by a doctor—the usual. The doctor diagnosed ADHD, of course, and prescribed Ritalin. He also suggested they take the boy to a psychologist, which they did, going to one who was recommended by the school. The psychologist told them she herself took Ritalin, and she advocated it. All of which was no more than expected, given the times. But then came the problems. On Ritalin the boy suffered some of the side effects that the Drug Enforcement Administration warned against, insomnia and loss of appetite. Plus, the parents said, he went from being overactive to underactive; he just sat around sluggishly. He began losing weight, and his grades in school actually went down.

So what did the parents do? They went to the school nurse and told her they were going to take him off the drug for two weeks to see how he fared, and you will never guess what happened next. The school nurse, with the approval of the principal, reported the parents to Child Protective Services of Albany County, and Child Protective Services filed a legal complaint with Family Court charging that the father, specifically, "fails to ensure that seven-year-old [name of child] takes medication prescribed for Attention Deficit Hyperactivity Disorder, thereby placing the child at risk of educational failure."

I met the parents when they were hauled into court. They were humble people, little equipped to deal with the labyrinth of caseworkers, lawyers, psychologists and judges that awaited them. Jill, the mother, was in the process of trying to get a General Equivalency Diploma, a substitute for a high school diploma, and Mike, the father, was a part-time gardener. They couldn't afford lawyers of their own so were assigned public defenders, one for each of them, and their son was assigned his own "law guardian," as a child's lawyer was then known. I caught up with one of the public defenders in the chaotic courthouse corridor just before their appearance and tried to find out if he was versed in the ambiguities of ADHD and knew about the side effects of Ritalin so that he might effectively plead their case, but he impatiently told me, "I've got fifteen cases today," so that was that.

In the end, the couple was ordered—safely enough, from a judge's point of view—to administer whatever medicine was prescribed by a doctor, which meant they had to give the kid his Ritalin, regardless of side effects, unless they could convince a doctor otherwise, on pain of having the kid taken away from them and put into foster care.

You might not have suspected such an outcome if you merely attended a conference of the local chapter of CHADD, as I did, at the Albany Marriot on Wolf Road, starring Dr. Edward Hallowell, Harvard Medical School psychiatrist, co-author of the best-selling *Driven to Distraction* and founder of the Hallowell Center for Cognitive and Emotional Health, who himself "had it," as the ADHD crowd always said, "it" being ADHD. You would have concluded that "having it" was "really cool," as the good doctor told a nine-year-old boy who had been brought along by his mother, a boy who hadn't actually been diagnosed but who undoubtedly had it, per his mother's account of his behavior. "Your brain is more powerful than most people's," Dr. Hallowell told him in the most dulcet tones as he beamed at him lovingly. "You are more creative, you are more energetic, you are more intuitive, you are more original than most people. That's really cool."

Didn't even know the kid. Never met him before. But it didn't matter. His mother said the kid "had it," so all that stuff must have been true. And the doctor must have known, because as he dramatically announced at the beginning of both his book and the conference, he himself had it.

All sorts of wonderful people had it. "It's in the American gene pool, big time," the doctor said, referring to the presumed restlessness of early immigrants. "You look at those colonists, it's like an ADD hall of fame," at which the audience of parents, special-ed teachers and pediatricians chuckled appreciatively.

How does one know if a child has this affliction, or this blessing, whatever it is? Easy. "Teacher reports, that's where you hang your hat," he said. There are tests, but not especially reliable tests, even just of the Q&A variety. "If the tests say no ADD and the history says yes, you believe the history"— meaning the account of a teacher or a parent of what the kid is like. If a teacher says a kid is restless or fidgety, then the kid has ADD, or ADHD, or whatever you want to call it. So it's a circular process. You take your kid to the doctor and you say, my kid is fidgety and can't pay attention, and the doctor, if he's doing his job right, takes that as conclusive, disregards any tests that might indicate otherwise, and serves up a diagnosis of Attention Deficit Disorder, with or without the Hyperactivity.

What if the doctor demurs? What if he has a different understanding? "You have to stand up to the doctor," a mother in the audience volunteered. "You have to be able to say, 'I know my kid.'"

"Very true," agreed Dr. Hallowell, beaming reassurance and comfort. "Until you get to where what you know in your heart and your gut has been recognized, you should not stop." In other words, keep shopping.

As for adults, there was another list of symptoms, or criteria, listed on page 201 of Dr. Hallowell's book, that as far as I could tell he created himself. These included "difficulty getting organized," "intolerance of boredom," "a sense of insecurity," "tendency to say what comes to mind," "mood swings," "easy distractibility," "chronic problems with self-esteem," and so forth— twenty such arbitrary and subjective characteristics. If you had twelve of them, you had ADHD. No explanation for that particular number.

It was odd enough. Dr. Hallowell, a smooth talker with the comforting manner of a successful insurance salesman, exhibited none of the telltale signs of his famous mental disorder himself during the day-long conference, despite his assurance that he had it. He was well organized, he never seemed bored, he acted entirely secure, he did not blurt out whatever came to mind, he exhibited no mood swings, he was not easily distracted, he seemed not to lack self-esteem or anything else. He was Dr. Feel-Good from beginning to end. But never mind. Another characteristic of people who had it was that they learned to "overcompensate," so other people couldn't tell. It was a near-perfect picture.

You couldn't imagine that just down the road, no more than ten miles away, a poor rural family was being hauled into court for nurturing misgivings about this Attention Deficit Hyperactivity Disorder business of his and was being ordered to give their kid an amphetamine-like drug for it, or else.

Nor was ADHD the only mental disorder ripping through this great land of ours. It may have been the most popular, but there were plenty of others listed in the profuse DSM-4, ready to be applied by the ranks of psychotherapists, psychologists and psychiatrists and for which the pharmaceutical industry just happened to have available the appropriate philters and prophylactics.

There was Mood Disorder Due To a General Medical Condition, No. 293.83, for someone who might be down in the dumps because of a toothache or a sprained ankle or lung cancer.

There was Antisocial Personality Disorder, No. 301.7, for someone who exhibits "disregard for and violation of the rights of others"—like maybe a cop who takes the shoes off a drug suspect and leaves him by the side of the road at night?

There was Oppositional Defiant Disorder, No. 313.81, for a child who "loses temper," "argues with adults," and "deliberately annoys people"—a brat.

There was Histrionic Personality Disorder, No. 301.50, for someone who indulges in "self-dramatization, theatricality and exaggerated expression of emotion"—like, I suppose, many a television celebrity.

There was Avoidant Personality Disorder. No. 301.82, the main feature of which was "a pervasive pattern of social inhibition, feelings of inadequacy," and so forth.

There was Generalized Anxiety Disorder, No. 300.02, which I was not aware of until someone called my attention to a four-page ad in *Reader's Digest* for a medication to treat it. "You may have Generalized Anxiety Disorder," the ad, from Bristol-Myers Squibb Co., warned. The symptoms were "restlessness, difficulty concentrating, irritability," and other similarly vague and ill-defined characteristics of what the uninitiated might call life. Remedy: BuSpar.

My favorite was not strictly speaking a disorder but rather an "Additional Condition That May Be a Focus of Clinical Attention," in the words of DSM-4. It was "Noncompliance with Treatment," No. V15.81.

Noncompliance with Treatment: If you don't go along with what your friendly psychotherapist suggests to you and you decline to take the pharmaceutical product he prescribes, you've got a condition. What might be the cause of such a condition? The manual suggests a few: "personal value judgments" (you think the therapist is full of it), "medication side effects" (the BuSpar hits you wrong), "denial of illness" (you think you're OK), and my favorite, "expense of treatment." Right there in the manual: if you think $75 an hour is too expensive for clinical attention, you need clinical attention.

I was vigorously denounced by any number of psychiatrists, psychologists and psychotherapists who accused me of making fun of mental illness and promoting "myths and stigmas" about those so afflicted. For defense I summoned up Paul R. McHugh, psychiatrist-in-chief at Johns Hopkins Hospital, one of the more distinguished practitioners in the land, who inveighed against his own profession more vehemently, and obviously more knowledgeably, than I could and who declared that "psychiatry has lost its way not only intellectually but spiritually and morally." Writing in *Commentary* magazine, he scoffed at "the fraudulent and dangerous fantasy that life's every passing 'symptom' can be clinically diagnosed," as psychiatry pretended. Of the DSM-4, he pointed out that many of the disorders are merely "normal responses of sensitive people" and that others are "purely the inventions of their proponents."

Proponents, those being psychiatrists who "receive extravagant retainers from pharmaceutical companies that profit from the promotion of disorders treatable by the company's medications." And of course Ritalin and ADHD, BuSpar and Generalized Anxiety Disorder came immediately to mind.

That wasn't the whole of it by a long shot. The voodoo sciences were exploring weirder recesses of the psyche than fidgetiness and the reluctance to pay one's bills. America was on a psychic ride, you might say, and I was pleased to be a spectator. A spectator and, in a small way, a chronicler.

5

SEX AND THE DEVIL

"What do you suppose is going on out there?"

Talk about a psychic ride. I was seated in the capacious Convention Center of the Empire State Plaza, that great monument to government built in Albany by Governor Nelson Rockefeller, listening to possibly the world's leading authority on Post-Traumatic Stress Disorder explain the origins of this novel condition, and naturally I expected a discussion of war and its many stresses. I expected case studies of Vietnam veterans, showing how some men cracked not during combat but many years later, when memories came back to torment them. I expected something that would illuminate the matter of the Schenectady cop who managed to sit home and collect full pay for fifteen years after being certified as a sufferer of PTSD, as it got tagged. To my way of thinking, he was just a hothead, a cop who beat up one driver and smashed the windshield of another after they had offended him in traffic stops, but in this season of rampant and fashionable disorders he had been able, as a Vietnam veteran, to get himself classified as a victim and turn his police career into an extended vacation. I was skeptical, but maybe there was something to it.

I had more than a passing interest in the subject, having spent a few years in Vietnam myself at the height of festivities there, not as a soldier but first as a doer of good with the American Friends Service Committee and later as a journalist, but still experiencing enough unpleasantness to wobble my kilter. Maybe I could learn something about my own ragged life after that adventure—though that's not why I was in attendance. I was in attendance because I had been urged to attend by the gentle psychotherapists of the Samaritan Counseling Center in Glenville, across the Mohawk River from Schenectady. I'd been making light in my column of all those fanciful disorders, beginning with Attention Deficit Hyperactivity Disorder, and they had taken exception. But rather than just denounce me in letters to the editor as a cad who insults the mentally ill, as some of their colleagues did, they invited me to their softly lit lair to speak reason to me, to listen patiently to my doubts, to urge me to read certain books and to attend this conference, featuring the eminent Dr. Bessel A. van der Kolk, director of the HRI Trauma Center at the Boston University School of Medicine and recognized authority on PTSD, that I might be enlightened. The conference was not for the general public but rather for the brotherhood and sisterhood of mental health professionals, though with a little effort I could get in.

That's why I was there, notebook in hand—to receive the light of truth. So the reader can imagine my surprise when, in the course of a full-day conference, the stress of war was scarcely mentioned at all. What the conference was about was the sexual molestation of children, especially of little girls and especially at the hands of their fathers and uncles. That's what was at the root of Post-Traumatic Stress Disorder, and many other disorders as well.

· "Psychologists almost always ignore the cause of why a kid is acting in strange ways," the doctor instructed us. "They diagnose something totally meaningless, like bipolar disorder, just as an excuse to medicate the kid—with Lithium or something."

Child rape is the real cause. One in four women were raped as children, he informed us—though I later learned that the definition of rape can be quite broad, so broad as to include dirty talk and leering. And I also learned that other enthusiasts put the number as high as one in three, so this was not an exact science. And as for overheated therapists encouraging memories of events that never actually occurred, so that some of these recovered memories were bogus—not in the opinion of Dr. van der Kolk. "In fact," he said, "the incidence of false memory is extraordinarily low." And the millions of cases of childhood rape reported annually are "just the tip of the iceberg."

A whole day of this, with many a lurid story of women recalling ghastly childhood experiences of fathers or uncles or grandfathers creeping into their rooms at night and violating them. A fourth or a third of all women—and that was just the tip of the iceberg! Holy leaping St. Dymphna! (patron saint of the mentally ill, who was murdered, according to legend, by her incest-minded father, and also, according to some sources, patron saint of those with memory problems). Could this possibly be? I couldn't help but doubt, and I wrote accordingly. No surprise: therapists responded according to their lights.

> [Carl Strock] *may indeed not believe that "the fathers and uncles of America, in great numbers, routinely rape their infant daughters and nieces," but they do. If he continues this quest against psychology, Carl will also likely reveal even more information about himself that may lead some therapists to label him with one of those diagnoses that he so despises.* (Jeannine M. Smith, Samaritan Counseling Center)

Well, it was definitely something that was going around, as I was learning, and there was abundant literature on the subject, including a book that was recommended to me by one of the therapists at the counseling center: *Trauma and Recovery* by Judith Herman, which made much the same claims as Dr. van der Kolk, principally that incest was "the common and central female experience."

Common and central, notwithstanding the universal taboo. Wow!

Another was *The Courage to Heal: A Guide for Women Survivors of Child Sexual Abuse* by Ellen Bass and Laura Davis, which was probably the main one, as hugely popular as it was, selling some half-million copies by then despite the lack of scientific credentials of its authors. Its thesis was the same, that great numbers, maybe even the majority, of girls in this fair land of ours were sexually molested in their most tender years, usually by male relatives. They buried the memories of these traumatic events—"the ordinary response to atrocities is to banish them from consciousness," wrote Herman—and then later they experienced all kinds of psychological problems from shyness to bulimia that they couldn't explain. With the help of a sympathetic therapist they were able to stir up the demons and thus exorcise them.

The mind might have forgotten, but "the body remembers," in the words of Dr. van der Kolk. This, I was learning, had become orthodoxy in the world of clinical psychology. Got a problem? Chances are you were sexually molested as a child. Now get to work remembering it. I'll help you.

Actually, Dr. van der Kolk had a method of helping that was different from Bass and Davis's denunciation of family members. He had "Eye Movement Desensitization and Reprocessing," or EMDR, which consisted of waggling one's fingers in front of a patient's eyes as the patient recalled events from her early life, which supposedly would lead her to remember the horrible truth, after which she would be OK. "I'm an EMDR fanatic," the doctor told us enthusiastically—just to show you how far out some of this stuff got.

The checklist of symptoms of childhood sexual abuse offered by Bass and Davis was as nebulous as that for Attention Deficit Hyperactivity Disorder, to no great surprise:

> *Do you feel different from other people?*
> *Do you find it hard to trust your intuition?*
> *Do you feel you have to be perfect?*
> *Do you tend to get involved with people who are inappropriate or unavailable?*
> *Can you say no?*
> *Are you overprotective?*
> *Do you have sex because you want to, or only because your partner wants it?*
> *Do you find that your relationships just don't work out?*

The orthodoxy of repressed memories of sexual abuse did not arise in a political vacuum, of course. "This book owes its existence to the women's liberation movement," acknowledged Judith Herman, who was a member of the Women's Mental Health Collective in Somerville, Massachusetts, besides being an associate professor of psychiatry at Harvard Medical School. It appeared, she said, "at a time when public discussion of the common atrocities of sexual and domestic life have been made possible by the women's movement." Bessel A. van der Kolk (a male) might have worn a cloak of scientific objectivity and spent a lot of time taking snapshots of the brain to see how the hippocampus contracted here and the amygdala lit up there when a patient experienced flashbacks, but Judith Herman welcomed the fact that women investigators "repudiated emotional detachment as a measure of the value of scientific investigation." The hell with emotional detachment. "There is war between the sexes," she said. "Rape victims, battered women, and sexually abused children are its victims." It was time to suit up.

Ellen Bass and Laura Davis likewise were feminist activists whose work was marked by the same sort of anti-male militancy. Dr. Paul McHugh, debunker of the *Diagnostic and Statistical Manual of Mental Disorders*, called their book "the Bible of incompetent therapists."

Whatever it was, it inspired a popular movement, and for a while celebrities seemed to compete with each other to get in on it, Roseanne Barr, the comedian, and Marilyn van Derbur, the 1958 Miss America, being just two examples, both of whom declared themselves "survivors" in 1991.

It eventually led to the creation of the self-defensive False Memory Syndrome Foundation and the publication of other books like *Victims of Memory: Sex Abuse Accusations and Shattered Lives* by Mark Pendergrast, but not before it had, indeed, shattered many lives. Families were breaking up and people were going to jail like nobody's business on account of "recovered memories," and never mind that in due time the whole business was scientifically refuted— first by Elizabeth Loftus, a cognitive psychologist at the University of Washington, in *The Myth of Repressed Memory*, co-authored with Katherine Ketcham, and later by Richard McNally, professor of psychology at Harvard University, in his *Remembering Trauma*.

No, we learned, if we indeed needed to learn, memories of traumatic events are not hidden in the body like fatty acids in fat cells. They remain all too vivid, as anyone who has undergone anything truly traumatic can attest. Survivors of the Holocaust did not bury the memories of it—far from it—just as I never buried the memory of hunkering under a staircase while Pleiku was being bombed around me during the Tet Offensive. Are you kidding?

"The notion that the mind protects itself by repressing or dissociating memories of trauma, rendering them inaccessible to awareness, is a piece of psychiatric folklore devoid of convincing empirical support," McNally wrote, and he noted that for military veterans there was financial benefit in psychic wounds, seeing as how ninety-four percent of those diagnosed with Post-Traumatic Stress Disorder applied for compensation.

"What do you suppose is going on out there?" Loftus remembers another cognitive psychologist, Ed Frischolz, asking her during a conversation about celebrity "survivor" claims and the attendant media frenzy. Indeed it was a question to ponder: what the devil was going on?

I had had my own experience with the social phenomenon of rampant accusations, and I'm sure it predisposed me in cases that came to my attention later. My twelve-year-old daughter came home from school one day in tears, running up the stairs, sobbing, "Tell them, Carl, tell them." (She always called me by my first name.) Right behind her were two stern-faced women who identified themselves as child protective caseworkers with the county Department of Social Services. They announced to my wife and me that I was the subject of a complaint of child sexual abuse, and I had never been so flabbergasted in my life.

"Who?" I asked. "Who has accused me of that?"

"That's confidential," they said, and they explained my various rights to me, explanations that just swirled around in my head and left no impression. Someone had accused me of following my daughter into the bathroom and pulling down her pants. That person had called the state hotline, set up for just such a purpose, and the complaint had been referred to these two caseworkers who were following up on it. I could see the report, if I made a formal request for it, but I could not know the name of my accuser. My mind ran through all the possibilities of people who might have a grudge against me, and came up empty.

I eventually got hold of the report, and it was truly incredible. It turned out the complaint had emanated from the mental health unit of the local hospital and had been referred to the state hotline by a nurse there. It showed that a certain Barry Lyndon (title of both a movie and a novel) had claimed to have followed his ten-year-old daughter (not my twelve-year-old daughter) into a bathroom and pulled *her* pants down. When I reached this nurse on the telephone, she informed me that the customer who gave his name as Barry Lyndon was a known nutcase and frequent visitor to the mental health unit. She was obligated by law to take down the particulars of his tale, no matter who he was, and, since it involved sex and a child, to file a report, regardless of the tale's credibility. She took his name as he gave it, she recorded other particulars as he gave them, without questioning anything, and passed the whole thing along.

It had nothing to do with me, nothing to do with my daughter. "Barry Lyndon" was denouncing *himself*, with regard to *his* daughter. But there was one connection, alas. He had given as his telephone number a number that turned out to be that of my mother, who lived near us. Almost all telephone numbers in town at that time began with 584, so if you said 584 followed by any four digits you would probably hit on somebody's actual telephone number, which is probably what happened. He made up a number, and that was it.

The caseworkers tracked the number to my mother, made the connection to me, and on that basis and no other took my daughter out of class for an interrogation that she later, as an adult, said was the most traumatic experience of her life. She insisted to them their story was not true, and they insisted to her she could trust them and should tell them the real truth, to no avail. Then they came to our house and with the most impressive gravitas this side of the Court of Oyer and Terminer, circa 1692, informed me that I stood accused of sexual abuse.

It was the most amazing thing I had ever experienced. They and their supervisor wouldn't apologize and wouldn't even call the school to admit they had made a mistake, after I put the pieces together and confronted them. All they would do was expunge the record. So when I began hearing about hair-raising charges regarding other people, I was primed to be skeptical.

But anyway, the repressed-memory movement was not an isolated phenomenon. By the time it came along we had already been through the Great Daycare Panic, when we were told that some of the people we had entrusted with our children as we went off to work weren't just playing Ring Around the Rosie with them. They were raping them, sodomizing them, forcing butcher knives into their anuses, dragging them through hidden tunnels, demonstrating animal sacrifice to them as a lesson in what would happen to them if they told. So this was all part of a continuum.

We might chuckle now about it, if we think about it at all, but it wasn't funny at the time. It was taken every bit as seriously as the witch investigations were taken in Salem, Massachusetts, 300 years earlier. This time it was a regular national phenomenon—even international, spreading to other countries.

The first really big case was the McMartin Preschool case in Manhattan Beach, California, which began when a mother, later determined to be both alcoholic and schizophrenic, claimed her two-and-a-half-year-old son had been sexually molested by a male teacher at the school. She also claimed people at the school were having sex with animals and the administrator of the school had "drilled a child under the arms."

Police couldn't find any evidence of such carryings-on, so they sent a letter to about 200 parents of current and former students, saying, "Please question your child to see if he or she has been a witness to any crime or if he or she has been a victim. Our investigation indicates that possible criminal acts include: oral sex, fondling of genitals, buttock or chest area, and sodomy, possibly committed under the pretense of 'taking the child's temperature.'"

California was ready, and the nation was ready. A nation that, let us note, had lately gone from Mom staying home with the kids while Dad worked, to Mom also being out in the workforce, liberated, and the kids being turned over to strangers for day care. You can bet parents questioned their kids, and you can bet they questioned them pretty aggressively, and you can bet that pretty soon professionals got involved too, from the Children's Institute International, a Los Angeles clinic that specialized in the burgeoning field of child abuse, and by the time they all got done with their questioning no fewer than 360 children were claiming to have been raped, tortured and molested in the most fantastic ways, involving underground tunnels, hot-air balloon travel, naked movie stars, and whatnot. It was absolutely riveting.

Seven administrators and teachers were finally arrested and charged with a total of 321 counts of child abuse involving forty-eight children. Some of them were released on bail to await trial, but the original accused teacher, Ray Buckey, was denied bail, and the administrator, his grandmother, had bail set at a prohibitive $1 million and so remained in jail. Amazing stuff. The trial was the longest in American history— three years—and in the end all the charges were dropped. There was no evidence for any of it, though by then Ray Buckey had been in jail for five years.

Saner heads determined that the questioning of the children had been highly suggestive, that the interviewers elicited the answers they wanted. "Many of the kids' statements in the interviews were generated by the examiner," concluded a British psychologist, Michael Maloney.

Interesting, no? That adults would be looking for such fantastic answers as they got and would actually "generate" them for the kids? Yes, but not really unusual, as we would learn.

There was a practice in psychology known as "facilitated communication," which was employed with severely autistic people who were unable to speak or write to help them communicate with the outside world. The autistic person would sit at a keyboard, and a "facilitator" would sit next to him and hold his hand, just to sort of steady him, and lo and behold, with just that little bit of help the autistic person would type words and whole sentences and sometimes even poetry. It was a very popular thing in the world of developmental disabilities, seeming to open a door for these unfortunate souls, or at least it was until the O.D. Heck Developmental Center in Niskayuna, next to Schenectady, ran a test that proved the so-called facilitators were actually doing the typing themselves even though they were not aware of it.

The interesting thing was, what exactly were these unfortunate autistic patients typing when their helpful facilitators were guiding their hands? And the answer was, on many occasions they, meaning in fact the facilitators, were typing accusations of sexual abuse. And another interesting thing is that when the deception was exposed, the facilitators were as surprised as anyone. They genuinely thought they were just steadying a few hands, just as devotees of the Ouija board believe their own hands are guided by some paranormal force.

It just seemed like the country was absolutely slavering for tales of sexual atrocities, there were so many examples.

There was the case of the Amirault family and their Fells Acre Day School in Malden, Massachusetts, where children were supposedly raped with knives and sharp sticks (leaving no visible wounds) in a "magic room" overseen by a clown.

There was the Wee Care Day Nursery in Maplewood, New Jersey, and poor Kelly Michaels— same thing sort of thing, with a key witness at her trial being one Eileen Treacy, peripatetic expert on "sexual abuse accommodation syndrome," who would soon enough show up in Troy, New York, for a trial that would occupy my own attention.

Most luridly, there was the case in Wenatchee, Washington, where, under the guidance of Detective Robert Perez, half the town went nuts, like some village in sixteenth-century Europe, with every family accusing every other family of witchcraft.

It got crazier and crazier. Not just "satanic ritual abuse," as these imaginary carryings-on were called, but abduction and sexual abuse by space aliens, as investigated and promoted by a Harvard psychiatrist by the name of John E. Mack—and please don't anyone ask me why so much of this stuff was coming out of Harvard. I have no idea.

Dr. Mack operated the Program for Extraordinary Experience Research under the sponsorship of the Center for Psychology and Social Change, and when he said "extraordinary" he meant extraordinary. He meant human beings getting picked up by space aliens and sexually messed around with, though not necessarily raped in the earthly sense.

He had patients, or subjects, or whatever they were, telling him how they had been taken into spaceships and probed by these alien creatures who extracted from them eggs or sperm cells, as the case might have been, or sometimes forced to engage in sexual intercourse with each other as another way of yielding up their life-giving material. "The abduction phenomenon is in some central way involved in a breeding program that results in the creation of alien/human hybrid offspring," he wrote in his book *Abduction: Human Encounters With Aliens*. This was "amply corroborated" in his clinical experience, he assured us. It almost made ritual abuse with knives and magic wands seem mundane.

More down to earth, there was simply the missing children phenomenon. You would have a carton of milk on your breakfast table to pour on your Cheerios, and there would be a picture of a wide-eyed child looking back at you. Missing. Date last seen, and so forth. For a short time you would pick up a Thruway toll ticket in New York and there would be a picture of a missing child on the ticket. That was the inspiration of a newly elected state legislator from Schenectady, Jim Tedisco, and so compelling was it that Governor Mario Cuomo himself got drawn into handing out the first such ticket, thereby boosting the career of a junior assemblyman from the opposite party. It was terrific publicity for the junior assemblyman, even if the program was soon dropped for the simple reason that drivers didn't retain those tickets but handed them back when they paid their toll and thus had no opportunity to study them. It was just for show, really.

You would go into some big store like the Walmart in Wilton, a little north of Schenectady, and right in the entryway, before a greeter could even say "Welcome to Walmart's," you would see a bulletin board full of wanted-style posters bearing pictures of children and the legend MISSING. It could take your breath away—all those children presumably kidnapped by rapacious predators, right there in suburban-rural Wilton, with its subdivisions, its commuters, its mammoth shopping centers.

If you looked into the matter, you found that many of these children were simply with one parent rather than another in a custody dispute, and so were not missing in any meaningful sense; many others were teenage runaways; they were from all over the country, not just from Wilton; and the cases went back years. But it didn't matter. Panic was in the air. You couldn't go anywhere without breathing it. Dr. Bessel A. van der Kolk could have waggled his fingers in front of almost anyone's eyes and gotten the same result. At the end of a day with him I staggered out of the Empire State Convention Center feeling like I had been abducted by space aliens myself, and counting myself lucky to have survived.

6

ADMISSION BY DENIAL

"We tried to get him every way we could,
and he wouldn't go for it."

In Troy, the kind of town the press always calls "struggling," across the Hudson River from Albany, there was no Dr. John Mack or Detective Robert Perez, but there was a fiery assistant district attorney by the name of Patricia DeAngelis, there was an earnest local police detective by the name of Steve Weber, there was a weird State Police investigator by the name of Ed Girtler, and there was a nurse-practitioner by the name of Jane Szary, all of them infused with the same fervor as their counterparts elsewhere in the country, all of them obsessed, you might say, with visions of diabolical sex and ready to find evidence of it in any crack or fissure of the social bedrock. On the prowl for it, poised to pounce on it, eager to punish it.

And there was also—too bad for him—a fortyish boat mechanic by the name of Jack Carroll, who a few years earlier had ditched his hard-boiled wife, Paula, in favor of a milder-mannered woman, Mary, and in the process had also more or less ditched his wife's eight-year-old daughter to whom he had been stepfather and really the only father she had known. More or less, because the girl—I'll call her Stacy—continued to visit him after he moved out, by arrangement with the mother, who needed a babysitter for her after school. Stacy would ride the school bus to Jack's marina and stay there a few hours until Paula would come and pick her up, and later he would visit her at their new apartment. The arrangement continued until Stacy was in junior high, thirteen years old, when Jack was arrested on charges of sexually molesting her over those years.

I knew nothing about it. Troy was on the periphery of the *Gazoot*'s territory and we paid little attention to it, besides which sex abuse stories were becoming as common as pit bull attacks by then, so the interest in them was diminishing. I probably wouldn't have paid attention even if I *had* known about it.

But one day I got a call from our state Capitol reporter, Bill Hammond, who had picked up an appeals court decision he thought I might be interested in, given what I had written about sex hysteria. The appellant, Jack Carroll, had been convicted of raping an underage girl, not further identified, and a tape recording of a telephone call in which he had protested his innocence had been kept from the jury. He appealed his conviction on that basis, saying the jury should have been allowed to hear it, and the first appeals court turned him down, leaving him in prison with a sentence of eight-and-a-third to twenty-five years. Well, that *is* interesting, I thought, and having nothing more urgent on my desk at the time I said, sure, send it over. I have since forgiven Bill for becoming a columnist at the tabloid New York *Daily News*, since this turned out to be the most intriguing and most wrenching story I had yet worked on.

I listened to the tape at the office of Jack Carroll's lawyer in downtown Albany, and it was an absolute stunner for me. There was Stacy's voice, hesitant and timid, saying she was going to tell people about the sexual things Jack had done to her, and Jack's voice, flabbergasted, saying, "Oh, my God, honey. I never did anything to you! Me? Jesus!" Having been through my own "Barry Lyndon" experience, I listened rapt, and naturally I identified with Jack, though his situation was far worse. This wasn't some bungling caseworker accusing him, based on a misread report; it was the girl herself. The phone call had been set up by the State Police as a way to trap Jack, and it was being made from a police telephone with Senior Investigator Girtler sitting by Stacy's side, coaching her by scribbling notes to her, notes that said things like, "You did sex to me," "You on top of me on couch," "Yes, you did," "I know you did and so do you," and holding them up to her as the conversation progressed. Of course Jack didn't know that. He just heard Stacy's voice, and he reacted with bewilderment: "Oh, my God! I don't know what the hell you're thinking of...I would never touch you in a sexual fashion...What do you think, I'm sick? Oh, my God, I can't believe you're doing this...Oh, sweetheart, I would never, honest to God, I swear to God to you I never would do that to you."

Well, this is a fine story, I thought. Man is accused by stepdaughter who is being encouraged by cop; man denies accusation; exculpatory tape recording is kept from jury; man is convicted; appeal is denied. I was fired up to write it, and it wasn't until I actually got back to my desk in Schenectady, assembled my notes and put fingers to keyboard that it occurred to me I had a problem: I couldn't identify the girl. It was the policy of the *Gazoot* and every other newspaper not to identify the victims or alleged victims of sex crimes so as not to add to their humiliation, and without being able to say that the girl in this case was the defendant's stepdaughter, alienated in a marriage breakup, the story wouldn't make sense.

Unwilling to walk away from it, I wrote it anyway, as best I could. I identified Stacy simply as a young girl, without signaling to the reader that she was a family member, and laid out the story as clearly as I was able, leaving a hole that I tried not to call attention to. "Taped Call in Sex Case Raises Doubts" was the headline.

I noted that the trial judge had barred the tape recording from evidence as "self-serving hearsay" but had allowed testimony of Investigator Girtler and Sergeant Weber regarding an interrogation in which Jack supposedly incriminated himself, which Girtler and Weber could have recorded but didn't. I wrote:

> *Imagine a judge not letting a jury hear an actual recording but permitting them to hear a cop's*

unsupported testimony about a later conversation, a conversation that the police could have recorded but chose not to!

The next day Paula was at the *Gazoot* with her latest boyfriend, a hulking jail guard who sat silently and looked grim while Paula ripped into me: "You son of a bitch! Who the fuck do you think you are?" and so on. I could barely get in a complete sentence. She was a babe and a half, I had to grant that, built like a brick but with a mouth like a sewer pipe. I could see why a man might first be attracted and then finally repelled. I could also see how she might have had something to do with Stacy making the accusations that she did. She was boiling mad at Jack for having thrown her over and, according to Jack, fiercely domineering of Stacy. She herself admitted that she "never really had a good relationship" with her daughter.

The sorry saga began, I learned, when a friend of Stacy's told Paula that Stacy had recounted to her a dream in which a young man, identified as a cousin, had "touched" her, and Paula had a fit, the use of "touch" as a euphemism being taken for granted. She sat her thirteen-year-old daughter down and demanded to know who exactly had done this "touching." Stacy wouldn't talk. Paula asked, was it this one? Was it that one? And eventually, was it Jack? At which point, according to Paula, Stacy nodded in the affirmative, apparently making the transition along with her from dream to reality, which was something that was never made clear in court, how the report of a dream got transmuted into a report of an actual event, and further how a cousin known by his initials got transmuted into Jack Carroll, stepfather. But however it happened, Paula took Stacy to a social services caseworker specializing in sex abuse, the caseworker and Paula together marched her to the Troy police, and you could almost imagine the rest of the story from there if you knew how these things played out elsewhere: the encouragement to make lurid accusations and the refusal to accept anything else as the truth. If this investigative technique was employed on a girl of thirteen who had been hurt by her stepfather's moving out, who had been rejected by her stepfather's new mate (Mary had banned her from her home on account of her "acting out"), and who was being prodded by a vengeful, jilted mother to boot, the result was foreseeable.

Sergeant Weber, the department's lead man in child sex abuse cases, interviewed her, then sent her to nurse-practitioner Jane Szary for a physical exam, the same Jane Szary who was his girlfriend and later became his wife. Szary, also a specialist in sex abuse, reported that Stacy's physical particulars were "consistent with disclosure," which was standard sex abuse jargon. From there she was sent to State Police Senior Investigator Girtler, another specialist in these matters, and Girtler had two sessions with her, five days apart, before crafting a written statement for her to sign, in the stilted language that would hold up in court—"And then I felt pressure between my legs and inside my vagina"—and which also met the requirements of a rape charge. Girtler had actually developed a specialty of drawing sexual "disclosures" from the teenage girls he interviewed, and he prided himself on his ability to get them to talk frankly, though he allowed to the jury, "The big V, that was a tough one," referring to the vagina.

After they had convinced themselves that Jack was guilty, just by talking to each other and without doing any outside investigation, Weber and Girtler arranged, first, the tape-recorded phone call, and when that didn't work, an "interview," as they called it, at the State Police barracks in East Greenbush, outside Albany, where they tried to trick him again. The gimmick this time was a printout of a lie detector test they claimed to have given Stacy to find out if she was telling the truth, though in fact they had given no such test and the printout was fake. It's a trick that police often employ to break a suspect, tell him they already know he's guilty so he'll give up and admit it. They showed Jack the printout and told him it confirmed that Stacy was on the level, and what did he have to say to that? Both Weber and Girtler later testified at trial that although Jack did not flat-out confess, he did not deny his guilt either, and when asked if Stacy was lying, said, "No, she's not lying," which of course amounted to the same thing as confessing. This is the interview that the detectives did not tape-record, even though obviously they could have. And this is the prejudicial testimony that the trial judge admitted into evidence even while barring the tape recording of the phone call.

I met Weber in his office, up on the second floor of the old brick police station at the corner of State Street and Sixth Avenue in downtown Troy. He was a big broad-shouldered man with a brush mustache and the confiding manner that cops sometimes adopt when they want to please a reporter, like the Rotterdam detective who played for me the tape of himself tormenting the convenience store clerk. He had nothing to hide, he conveyed with his welcome: "Come in and sit down." He was pleased at having nailed another pedophile, which was a word he used often to refer to Jack and other men he had put in jail, and he made no bones about having misrepresented what Jack had said in that interview. He freely admitted that Jack had never confessed to anything and even imitated him to me, for my enjoyment. "I didn't do it, I didn't do it, I didn't do it," he repeated in a mocking tone, and added, "We tried to get him every way we could, and he wouldn't go for it."

Very interesting. I suggested that Jack's remark about Stacy not lying, if he ever said it at all, must have been taken out of some such context as, "She's not a liar. I don't know why she would say this," and Weber responded, "I don't disagree with you."

"The law allows me to use trickery and deceit," he instructed me, and so I would not forget, he wrote the words on a scrap of paper for me, "trickery and deceit."

I delicately inquired why he would bend the facts in this manner, and he gave me the answer that I had learned was commonplace in the world of sex abuse investigations: "My job is to believe the victim first and then try to prove it beyond a reasonable doubt."

His effort to prove it did not include interviewing any of Jack's or Paula's family members, and did not include talking to the girl who had reported Stacy's dream to Paula. In fact, it included no legwork at all. It was all in-house, all within the small closed network of believers. It would not be an exaggeration to say I was taken aback, even though I tried not to show it but just scribbled my notes and kept my counsel—until I got back to Schenectady and wrote it up. "Cop Pulls Rug from Under His Own Testimony," was the headline. It was a nice job, if I say so myself. A man was in prison doing eight-and-a-third to twenty-five years, and one of the cops who put him there basically admitted that he and a colleague had lied on the stand to achieve the result. And I got it without using trickery and deceit but just by asking straightforward questions in a trusting and gullible manner, humbly writing down whatever the good detective said, which must have put him at his ease.

I interviewed Jack Carroll in a dreary room at Clinton Correctional Facility, the same room where parole interviews are held, which was an accommodation the prison made for me so we wouldn't have to talk into my tape recorder in the noisy visiting area. Jack was a small but determinedly fit guy—he said it helped him maintain his equilibrium to count calories and lift weights—and he was eager to talk. He was by now forty-five years old and had been locked up for three years. I knew that before his trial he was offered a plea bargain with a sentence of two to six years, which meant he could possibly have been free by now if he had pleaded guilty, and I asked him if he regretted not taking it.

"Not whatsoever," he said. "If I took that two-to-six I'd have to stand before the judge and I'd have to lie. I'd have to tell him I did commit these acts. If I had done these things I'd have certainly taken the blame for it, but it didn't happen, so they can keep me here for my full bid if they want"—bid is prison slang for a sentence—"but when I leave here I'm still going to be an innocent man."

He allowed that being locked up in one of New York's oldest prisons, a dungeon-like fortress, was not like a walk in Troy's Riverfront Park. "As time goes on," he said, "it's increasingly difficult for me, because when I first came in I kept looking forward to tomorrow, saying tomorrow will be the day that I'll be exonerated. Now I'm looking at my past."

I played excerpts of the interview on a radio show I had at the time, shortly before New York's highest court, the Court of Appeals, was to hear arguments in the case, and soon afterward an employee of the court called and asked me to please send copies of all the columns I had written on the case. I was happy to cooperate. The judges presumably would read my columns along with the trial record. I couldn't ask for more recognition than that. Of course they would also read the decision they were being asked to overrule, and I hoped they would enjoy it as much as I did. That decision, by the mid-level Appellate Division, held that Jack's original tape-recorded conversation with Stacy was "hearsay" and not an "excited utterance" in which the defendant was caught off-guard, which would have made it admissible. The judges who made that decision decided Jack's "normal reflective processes" couldn't have been rendered inoperative, as required for an "excited utterance," because—and the reader should hold on for this one—he was "alleged to have engaged in the sexual abuse of this victim for no less than seven years." Meaning, he couldn't have been caught off-guard by the accusations when Stacy called him, because he was guilty. There was no way out of an argument like that.

It was the emotional high point of my journalistic career when I eventually got a call from the court telling me that they had unanimously overturned Jack's conviction, and not just overturned it but actually dismissed the most serious charges, those of rape, finding that there was insufficient evidence for him even to have been indicted on those, so they could not be brought again. If the district attorney wanted to retry him on the lesser charges of sex abuse, he could do so. I looked out from my cluttered cubicle at the editorial writer across the room, and for a minute I couldn't find my voice. It was as if I was in a state of suspension. By God, I had won. Jack had won.

A judge scrambled to expedite Jack's release in time for Thanksgiving, and the very next day, which was the day before Thanksgiving, having been transported down from Dannemora, Jack walked out of the Rensselaer County Jail into a parking lot to be joyously greeted by family members who had gathered from as far as South Carolina and California, by reporters, by cameramen, and by me. It was a day to remember, a day to savor.

You might think that would be the end of the story, but no. The Rensselaer County district attorney and his aggressive assistant, Patricia DeAngelis, who was the one really fired up about sex abuse, obtained a new indictment on the lesser charges and moved quickly to a new trial. It was hard for me to adjust to.

I had worked on the story for more than a year, and it seemed to have a perfect trajectory: man convicted of heinous crime, evidence suppressed at trial, police witnesses exposed as liars, conviction overturned, man freed to the welcoming arms of his family. I was even named runner-up for the Heywood Broun Award of the Newspaper Guild for my efforts and trucked down to the National Press Club in Washington to collect a certificate. I couldn't have imagined a sweeter ending.

But now here we were in the ornate Rensselaer County Courthouse in downtown Troy to try Jack Carroll on six surviving felony counts of sexual abuse of a minor, and it had an air of unreality about it, at least for me.

For all her public bluster, Patricia DeAngelis behind the scenes actually had little enough confidence in her case that on the eve of the trial she offered to let Jack plead guilty to a mere misdemeanor of "endangering the welfare of a child" in exchange for a sentence of time already served, meaning he could have gone home then and there, albeit as a registered sex offender. Jack said no. He later told me DeAngelis had demanded what's known in the courtroom as an allocution, meaning he would have had to make a statement in his own words telling what acts endangering to the welfare of a child he had committed, and he wouldn't do it. He said if he could have just pleaded to the generic misdemeanor without any specifics, he might have been tempted, but he wasn't going to make a false statement.

In court nothing felt good, right from the beginning, when DeAngelis, now prosecuting for the second time, ripped and snorted in front of the jury for more than an hour without notes by way of an opening statement. She stormed, she sneered, she declaimed against this "pedophile" who had abused the trust of an innocent young girl and imposed his vile intentions on her, and when she was done I was almost ready to convict Jack myself. Jack's lawyer, Mike Koenig, by contrast was low-key and methodical and stuck to the facts. He folded his arms over his rail-thin runner's body, furrowed his prematurely creased forehead, and told the jury to wait till they heard the evidence. The score at that point was 1-0, and it never got better, not even when Koenig later demolished the testimony of nurse-practitioner Jane Szary and showed that she had concealed from both the police and the jury that Stacy simply had a yeast infection when she examined her, which fully accounted for the redness of her private parts, redness which Szary was forced to admit could not have lasted for the five weeks that had elapsed since Jack had supposedly last molested her anyway. It didn't make any difference, you could tell. Szary was defiant, DeAngelis was defiant, the jury was stone-faced, Jack squirmed in his seat, glancing nervously over his shoulder at his family.

DeAngelis's great inspiration was to play the previously suppressed tape recording for the jury herself, as if it were *her* evidence and she wanted nothing more in the world than for the jury to hear it. How to explain Jack's persistent denials on that recording? Easy. The same way that Weber and Girtler explained his persistent denials to them when they interrogated him in person. It was the theory of "admission by denial." If you denied something in a particular way, a way understood by police officers who had studied these matters in specialized training programs, then your denial was actually an admission. An experienced officer like Girtler, for example, who told the jury he had 1,500 hours of training in these arcana, had a "trained ear," as he testified, and could detect all sorts of "red flags" in Jack's protestations of innocence. For example, by insisting to Stacy on the telephone that he had never touched her sexually, Jack "tried to put doubt in her mind," Girtler explained. "That was important to me." And not just doubt, but by saying over and over in shocked tones that he had never done anything wrong, "He was injecting guilt, he was injecting reward, he was injecting fear, he was injecting love."

"There's red flags jumping all over the place," he told the jury. "More red flags than Tiananmen Square."

Any number of times, Jack made "religious references," exclaiming, for example, "Oh, my God!" or "Jesus!"

"That's a great one for admission by denial, seeking a higher source," Weber said.

"Those are red flags for me," Girtler said.

"Bingo!" DeAngelis would exclaim when one of these red flags popped up during the playing of the tape. Admission by denial!

Didn't Jack deny the allegation against him?

"He was in denial. He did not deny it," Girtler said, making a distinction of scholastic subtlety.

Well, admission by denial, what does that mean?

"When someone's trying to tell himself that he didn't sexually abuse the child," Weber answered.

Could it be someone simply saying no?

"In some cases that is true," he consented.

Did Carroll supposedly say at one point, referring to Stacy's allegations, "I can't believe she's saying that"?

"I interpret that to be an admission by denial," he said.

The detectives also testified that they had been trained in body language and so were able to discern, during the interrogation, that when Jack crossed his legs he was "locking down," as Girtler put it, and "that tells me we're starting to get to some of the issues that he doesn't want to talk about." When Jack handed a piece of paper back to Girtler, "He opened his legs," Girtler said, "which was significant to me... because that means he was starting to open up." They admitted they had not performed any similar analysis on the postures of Stacy or her mother during their interviews with them.

Of course the detectives did not record this interrogation, in which Jack supposedly said, "She's not lying," which was the single most incriminating thing about it that the cops testified to. No video, no audio, not even notes. The jury had nothing to go by but the cops' own word, which for reasons never clear to me was not considered hearsay and which was never challenged in court except for one time when Koenig asked Weber, "Why didn't you take notes?" and Weber answered defiantly, "Because it makes my job easier... and your job as defense attorney more difficult."

As for his having imitated Jack Carroll to me, saying, "I didn't do it, I didn't do it," Weber denied it: "No, I never told Carl Strock that." Alas, I had not surreptitiously tape-recorded our conversation but had only taken notes, and Koenig chose not to call me as a witness and present my notes to the jury. I never did ask why, though if I had been on the witness list I wouldn't have been able to attend the rest of the trial.

When Stacy was called as a witness, DeAngelis escorted her into the courtroom, and passing the defense table where Jack sat she theatrically placed herself between Stacy and that table, like a football player running interference, glancing fiercely over her shoulder as they passed, as if daring Jack, the depraved pedophile, to try to pounce. She would block him for sure. The whole courtroom could feel it.

Stacy took the stand, and she was no longer a child. She was now seventeen, a big, heavy-jawed girl but still quite pretty. She kept her head down and spoke in barely a whisper, making statements that were obviously memorized. What had Jack done on such-and-such a date as charged in the indictment?

"He would roll me on my back and get on top of me. Then he'd move my bathing suit to the side and kiss my breasts...I told him to stop and get off me...I would try and push him away...He told me we had a special relationship and not to tell anybody, because they wouldn't understand, and they'd blame me." On another date, same thing, practically verbatim.

Or a variant, at a different location: "He put his hands up my shirt and touched my breasts, and down my pants...He would touch my vagina...I would tell him to stop and push away from him...he would push me up against the couch," the pushing being necessary to establish force, for a higher-level crime. "He told me we had a special relationship," etc.

Over and over, for each specified date.

But gone were the rote repetitions of, "And then I felt pressure between my legs and inside of my vagina" from the first trial, which had been used to support the charge of rape. The charge was gone, so now in the second trial the testimony was gone also.

A colleague whispered to me, "It sounds like she's remembering what she's supposed to say, not what happened." And indeed, she admitted under cross-examination that she had spent most of the past month practicing the questions and answers with DeAngelis. Anything outside of what she had practiced, any details that Koenig inquired about, she answered, "I don't know," or "I don't remember."

As for why she sought Jack out every day, calling him on the telephone asking him to bring her things at the new apartment where she lived with her mother, the very apartment where he was supposedly groping her over her protests, she had no answer. It had to strain the credulity of even the most eager of crusaders, I thought.

Jack, on the witness stand, looked nervous, his eyes darting this way and that. He had the aspect of a trapped cat. And he kept his answers short. On such-and-such a date had he touched Stacy's breasts? "No." Had he pushed her against a couch? "Absolutely not." Had he done this, that or the other, as charged? "No." It wasn't much for the jury to work with. Stacy had said one thing, in a highly rehearsed manner, barely audible. Jack said no. An elderly woman juror I interviewed later, who had never before seen a real trial, said she was sure Jack was guilty because when testimony was given against him he did not jump out of his seat and protest his innocence, like they do in the movies, but just sat quietly.

Eileen Treacy, a then-unlicensed psychologist, veteran of the Kelly Michaels case in New Jersey, was there to testify that the nurturing and caring behavior of Jack toward Stacy, including bringing lunch money to school for her, was typical of how sex abusers "groom" their victims. And Stacy's failing for several years to complain to anyone about behavior of Jack's that she supposedly hated, and her continuing to go voluntarily to his workplace after school, when she could easily have refused, and her frequently calling him on the telephone and asking him to visit—that was all part of the "sexual abuse accommodation syndrome," which was a cornerstone in the mental architecture of sex abuse experts.

When the jury went out I had a dark foreboding, and it turned out to be justified. The verdict was guilty again. The sentence this time, even with the top charge of rape not part of the picture: ten to twenty years, compared with the eight-and-a-third to twenty-five he had gotten previously. I walked out of the courthouse onto Second Street feeling empty, as if disemboweled, passing the district attorney who was talking swell-chested to the television cameras, passing Mike Koenig, who was trying to explain why the minimum sentence was longer this time, passing even Jack's brothers, mother, new wife, and new in-laws, who were hugging each other.

Jack's appeals were rejected this time, the jury having been allowed to hear the crucial tape recording, and he wound up serving a total of eleven years, including the three he had already served. He was finally released on parole after one of the parole commissioners who had previously turned him down pleaded guilty to soliciting sex with underage girls on the Internet.

Patricia DeAngelis was elected district attorney and won the Young Alumni Award from the Alumni Association of Albany Law School, as well as the Woman in the News Award from the Women's Press Club of Albany, before being formally rebuked for her conduct in several other cases, falling out of political favor, and disappearing from public life.

Jack later told me the worst for him was getting sent back not just to the same prison but to the same six-by-eight-foot cell from which he had so recently been sprung. "That was tough," he allowed, "real tough." I will not compare my own despondency to his.

7

NOWHERE TO LIVE

*"We shouldn't be managing them, we should
be stopping them!"*

Up on the sixth floor of the Schenectady County
Office Building, a cheaply built aluminum box from the
1960s, the atmosphere was pretty highly charged. The
spectator seats were full of clergymen, psychologists,
civil libertarians, town officials and above all anxious
parents, though "anxious" is hardly adequate to
describe the state they were in. Hysterical would be
more like it. Ed Kosiur, county legislator and soon-to-
be-candidate for the state Assembly, was perfectly in
synch with them, like Lang Lang playing Tchaikovsky's
Piano Concerto No. 1 with the Philadelphia Orchestra
up Route 50 at the Saratoga Performing Arts Center. Beat
for beat, measure for measure.

He had brought a tape measure, and supposedly for
the benefit of his fellow legislators, twelve of them, but
really for the benefit of the spectators, he stretched it out,

right under the noses of the chairwoman, the clerk of the board and the country attorney, to demonstrate precisely twenty-one feet, which he said with fiery indignation was the distance from the curb in front of the house where a registered sex offender was living and the curb in front of an elementary school. "Four hundred children are there!" he exclaimed. "These are our children!"

It was enough to send shivers down the spines of the assembled parents: twenty-one feet, just a leap and a bound, you might say, and a predator could grab hold of one of their own children. When it came the turn of the public to speak, several of these parents choked up with tears as they pleaded with their elected legislators to do the right thing. One man said, chokingly, that the law they were considering still wouldn't be enough to protect his little daughter. A woman moaned about "these monsters," referring to sex offenders, and pleaded, "Children are so precious, they do not deserve to have these things happen to them."

The law on the table would have banned anyone on the state's registry of sex offenders, meaning almost anyone who had ever committed a sex offense, whether against a child or an adult, from living within 2,000 feet of any "school, playground, public park, public swimming pool, youth center or licensed daycare center," meaning not only that registered sex offenders couldn't move into such areas but that one-time sex offenders who already lived there would have to move out, which was a step beyond what other towns and counties had already done, and quite a big step at that. It wouldn't matter what kind of record a person had maintained since his offense, or even the gravity of the offense. The state put sex offenders into three classes, based on the estimated likelihood of their committing new crimes, but the Schenectady law would have treated them all the same. Some guy had diddled around with his younger brother or sister once upon a time and was considered a low risk to repeat the transgression, now owned his own home, had a family and was gainfully employed—no matter, he would have to pack up and leave. Where he would go was unclear, since almost any spot in the county except in the westernmost rural reaches would be within 2,000 feet of some school, playground, public park, public swimming pool, youth center or licensed daycare center.

To say the Schenectady County legislators were considering this law is to stretch somewhat the meaning of "consider." Bob Farley, known snickeringly as Baby Huey because of his pear-shaped resemblance to the cartoon character of that name, took the oratorical lead, standing when his turn came and positively shouting, "Two thousand feet is not enough! I'd like to see it 3,000 feet, maybe 4,000! I don't want them in our county! I don't trust them!"

Had a psychologist in the audience said that sex offenders needed to be properly managed? "I don't want to manage sex offenders!" Farley hollered. "We shouldn't be managing them, we should be stopping them!"

I was sitting right behind him, in a row of seats reserved for county officials but often invaded by reporters, and I wanted to whisper to him, "Bob, sit the hell down and stop embarrassing yourself," but I stuck to my note-taking.

One member you could fairly say did consider the proposed law was the former judge Michael Eidens, who declared the law would do "nothing in my judgment to protect our community" and further that there was "no correlation between residency restrictions and sex offenses," as I had already discovered and reported, but he was not only voted down, he was so ostracized and browbeaten as a result that he soon left the legislature.

Schenectady was on the same roll the rest of the country was on, and this was its latest manifestation: sex offender residency restrictions. It had reached such a pass in Miami-Dade, Florida, that registered sex offenders had nowhere legitimate to live at all and had taken to pitching camp under a bridge, where probation officers actually sent them, there being nowhere else. The delicious irony was that the bridge was actually within the proscribed 2,500 feet of eight schools, two daycare centers and a treatment center for victims of child sex abuse. It was wonderful.

No, there was no evidence that any of this did any good. The Iowa County Attorneys Association put out a statement saying, "Research shows there is no correlation between residency restrictions and reducing sex offenses against children." Research in Colorado showed registered sex offenders who committed new crimes lived no closer to schools and playgrounds than those who didn't commit new crimes. Research in Minnesota showed the same. Jill Levenson, assistant professor of human services at Lynn University in Florida, concluded, "Housing restrictions are not a feasible strategy for preventing sexual violence"—just as, presumably, keeping bank robbers from living near banks and car thieves from living near parking lots would have little effect on deterring those types of crimes.

With sex crimes there was the further notion, widespread in the land, that sex criminals, even just one-time sex criminals, could not control themselves and were bound to repeat their offenses. They had a recidivism rate that was "off the charts," as Farley put it in his impassioned speech. Indeed, the official "intent and purpose" of the Schenectady law began with the statement that "the high recidivism rate among convicted sex offenders after their release from confinement necessitates a heightened awareness by local government officials."

On examination this turned out not to be so. In fact, the recidivism rate of sex criminals was lower than that of other types of criminals, according to any number of studies, as I prided myself on discovering.

One study from 1994 by the Bureau of Justice Statistics, U.S. Department of Justice, which tracked 272,111 people who were released from prison in fifteen states, found that sixty-eight of those ex-prisoners were re-arrested for new crimes within three years, but only five percent of male sex offenders were re-arrested for new sex crimes, and only three percent of child molesters were re-arrested for new sex crimes against children, thus making the recidivism rate of sex offenders vastly lower than average and the recidivism rate of child molesters even lower.

A study by the New York State Division of Probation and Correctional Alternatives in 2006, a "meta-analysis" of eighty-five other studies, found that while former sex offenders had a recidivism rate comparable to those of other criminals for all kinds of offenses (thirty-six percent), they had a "significantly lower" rate (thirteen percent) for new sex offenses.

An analysis by the New York State Division of Criminal Justice Services found that of 19,458 males on the state's Sex Offender Registry, only two percent were arrested for a new sex offense within one year. That number went up year by year, to a maximum of eight percent after eight years.

Another, older study cited by the New York State Division of Probation and Correctional Alternatives found that of 917 sex offenders on probation in seventeen different states, only 4.5 percent were arrested for new sex crimes within three years. The agency concluded: "Thus, sex offenders are arrested and/or convicted of committing a new sex crime at a lower rate than other offenders who commit other new non-sexual crimes."

All of this I dug up in my self-assigned role as monitor of lunacy, hysteria and *delirium tremens*, and all of it I duly reported in the *Gazoot*. None of it mattered. Whenever the subject of sex offenders came up, their astronomical recidivism rate was always taken for granted. I worked my fingers to the bone digging up all those facts, and the county legislators, in their discussions and speeches, never mentioned any of them. I never felt so unappreciated, and at every turn I gave them the business better than before.

The idea of regulating the post-prison lives of one-time sex criminals originated with the rape and murder of a seven-year-old girl, Megan Kanka, in New Jersey in 1994. The man who committed that enormity was living across the street from Megan's family after having served a prison term for a previous sexual assault against a child, and when that became known, state after state rushed to see that such a thing could not happen again, requiring first of all that those released from prison for sex offenses register with the state, providing their addresses, places of employment, type of vehicle they drove, and other identifying information. The registers were to be open to the public so everyone could check to see if any former sex criminal was living across the street. Other restrictions were adopted too, including residence restrictions. Eventually these laws were passed in one form or another by all fifty states. Individually they were known as Megan's Law.

How effective were they? A team of researchers at the New Jersey Department of Corrections studied a random sample of 550 sex offenders over a twenty-one-year period, from both before and after the passage of Megan's Law, and concluded that the law had "no effect on reducing the number of victims," "no demonstrable effect in reducing sexual re-offenses," "no effect on the type of sexual re-offense," if there was one, and "no effect on community tenure," meaning the time during which a former offender stays out of trouble after being released from prison. It was just something that made people feel good.

Nevertheless, as time went by and as panic over the sexual abuse of children flourished, a lot of local governments felt they had to go their state governments one better and adopt even tighter restrictions, giving rise to a weird sort of competition between towns. We'll see your thousand-foot limit and raise you a thousand, was the idea. We'll see your playground restriction and raise you a swimming pool. In New York, Schenectady was the most daring, seeing everyone else's can't-move-in rule and raising them a gotta-move-out, harking back to the banishment that in the ancient world was an alternative to the death penalty.

One customer caught up in this movement was twenty-one-year-old Rich Matthews from Scotia, across the river from Schenectady, who had pleaded guilty to committing a sex act with a younger boy, a family member, when he himself was eighteen. He had served nine months in the county jail, and when he got out he was classified as a Level 3 offender, which was the most dangerous, and he so appeared on the state registry. When his landlord found out he evicted him from his downtown Schenectady apartment, and Rich Matthews had nowhere to go.

He was taken in by a former mayor of Scotia, Will Seyse, and his wife, who had known him when he was a classmate of their daughter's. Will Seyse had visited him regularly in jail, and now he invited him to live in his and his wife's tidy middle-class home on tidy middle-class Washington Road in tidy middle-class Scotia. I never saw anything like it. Neighbors up and down the street encircled their shrubbery with yellow CAUTION tape and planted signs in their lawns saying, "This neighborhood and this house is [sic] unprotected from those who would prey upon the most innocent among us, our children."

The Seyses tried to talk to them and even invited them to meet their houseguest, but to no avail.

"There's no need to meet the guy," one neighbor told me when I canvassed the block.

Another said, "The reason they can do what they do is they're charming and nice on the outside." That man's son, a lawyer, actually wrote a letter to the Seyses denouncing young Matthews as "a vicious, deceptive, horrible human being," able to "charm people with his smile and words," without having met him. Another neighbor told me a mother no longer would bring her baby to his house for babysitting because of the proximity to this registered sex offender.

The Seyses woke up one morning to find a dead fish wrapped in newspaper on their doorstep and a three-by-five-foot sign fastened to a tree in front of their house, consisting of a collage of clipped-out tabloid headlines: "RICHARD the Savage," "EVIL FELLA," "Neighbors Pay Their Respects," "Anything can happen," "REVENGE," along with a photo of hearses at a funeral. It was wild.

It turned out the county legislature, in adopting the most draconian residency law in the state in order to protect children from out-of-control "predators," hadn't even checked with the district attorney to see if there was an actual problem with registered sex offenders committing new sex offenses. Nor did they check with the county sheriff or with any of the five local police chiefs. Nor with the Probation Department or the criminal courts. The whole thing was purely in their heads—and in the heads of their constituents, like those on Washington Road in Scotia.

When I checked, I found there had not been a single case in Schenectady County during the past two years (the longest period I get could information for) of what the legislators were in a lather to stop, that is, registered sex offenders preying on unknown children at schools, playgrounds, swimming pools and the like. The district attorney's office had processed 113 sex defendants during the previous two years, and of those a mere six were on the state registry. Of those six, only two were charged with offenses against children, and of those two, neither was a stranger to the child but rather a friend or family member. Which only confirmed what was well known anyway— that most sex offenses against children are committed by friends and relatives. The dirty-minded stranger lurking behind a bush at the neighborhood playground who haunted the dreams of absent parents was an extreme rarity in waking life.

It was also revealing how Rich Matthews lived even without the new residency law but just under the terms of the state's existing Megan's Law. He wore both an anklet and a GPS device on his belt that sounded an alarm if he dallied for more than a few minutes near any place "where persons under the age of eighteen are likely to be present, including but not limited to: parks, playgrounds, arcades, and public pools." Since those places were not mapped out for him, and since he wasn't told exactly how far away from them he had to stay in any case, he had no way of knowing in advance when he might be treading on forbidden ground. The buzzer on his belt would sound, and he had to call his probation officer to explain and then get moving. He remembered being in a video store with Seyse to rent some movies when that happened. Seyse said it was probably because the store, on a main road, backed onto school property, and never mind that the two properties were separated by a hurricane fence and the school was closed anyway, it being nine o'clock at night. He had been enrolled in a culinary program in Rhode Island, and he couldn't return to that because he was forbidden to leave New York.

No sooner had Schenectady County adopted its groundbreaking residency restrictions than trouble began. The New York Civil Liberties Union announced its intention to sue, and worse, leaders of the various towns that were subdivisions of the county groused that since they were less densely populated than Schenectady, with their schools and playgrounds more widely spread out, the effect of the law was likely to be that "predators" like Rich Matthews would move into their territory— into Niskayuna and Rotterdam and Scotia-Glenville and Duanesburg and Princetown—which left the legislators who represented those places looking pretty foolish. First they had conjured these mostly imaginary predators, then they had recklessly dumped them on their own constituents!

So pretty soon the legislators backpedaled, partially. They kept the basic residency law, but they repealed that part of it that required people to move out of their homes and leave town, which was blatantly an added-on punishment imposed retroactively for crimes that had already been paid for.

It wasn't enough. First one county, then another saw its residency law challenged in court, and one law after another was overturned—not because it was fundamentally ridiculous but because it encroached on the authority of the state. The state Megan's Law "pre-empted" any local laws. When Schenectady's turn came, it was the same, and after all the hysteria the law went in the wastebasket.

Ed Kosiur with his tape measure suddenly looked silly, and he lost his race for the Assembly. The various counties, cities and towns that had their laws upended could have appealed to the state's highest court, but they wisely chose not to. Wisely, because once the top court spoke, then all local residency laws in the state—there were about eighty of them by then—would have been automatically voided. Better to let the matter drop. In the end it was just one more wave in the sex abuse panic that began with diabolical doings at the McMartin Preschool and continued with missing children and the recovered memory movement. People like Gerald Amirault, Jack Carroll and Rich Matthews were just unlucky enough to be caught up in it.

For me it was one of the few moments of practical satisfaction I experienced (setting aside the short-lived satisfaction of the Jack Carroll appeal). I always said I wrote solely for entertainment, without expectation of changing the world, and it was largely true. Certainly I had no effect on police or teachers' contracts and didn't expect to have any. Likewise with the plague of novel mental disorders. But when this one was over, the county attorney asked me, "How does it feel to have won?" and I thought, well, yes, you could look at it like that. But I had to be careful not to let such a notion distract me. I wasn't in this to change the world; by now I was living my life, that's all, and was having a merry time of it.

8

CHILD SNATCHERS

"You've got to dance to their music a little bit."

Yes, "you've got to dance to their music a little bit," a lawyer explained to Angel confidentially outside Family Court, and he was certainly right about that. A young mother like Angel—high school dropout, unskilled, living on public assistance—had to dance to the music of Family Court more than a little bit, actually. She had to dance till her feet went numb and her brain came close to exploding, like in one of those dance marathons of the Roaring Twenties, if she wanted to get her children back.

Angel—big, fat welfare mother who dropped out of school at age fifteen to deliver her first child—had two children by now, a ten-year-old boy and a six-year-old girl, by two different fathers, and child protective caseworkers from the Schenectady County Department of Social Services had been part of their lives since they were born. In fact, when I tried to piece together the history of her predicament and asked her when these caseworkers had first come into her life, she didn't seem to understand the question. They had always been in her life, even before her children were born. Her mother had been a drug addict, and as a child Angel had bounced from one foster home to another, always monitored by one social services agency or another. This latest jam she was in, in which her own children had been taken from her, was just one chapter in a long and dismal story. She had been cared for by strangers, and now her children were in the care of strangers—strangers who had volunteered for that role and who got compensated enough to cover their expenses. Surrogate parents, paid by the county.

At this moment she was in the corridor that led from the courtroom to the chaotic waiting room of Family Court, having just pleaded guilty to one count of child neglect as a way, ironically enough, to get her children back, and her lawyer was explaining to her about the need to dance. The judge and the caseworkers called the tune, and she couldn't just flip them off.

So she had taken the plea. The deal was that she would get her son back in two weeks and her daughter in about two months. Both had been gone for five months, and during that time she had had only very limited visits with them, under supervision, so she was anxious to have them home, so anxious that she had called me, as a newspaper writer, to plead for help, since I had already written about another such case. I wondered if she might have mistreated her kids to have them taken away from her, but that turned out not to be the case. In fact, a report prepared for Family Court by the non-profit Northeast Parent and Child Society found that Angel "usually recognizes and attends to the needs of [both] the children," that she was "fairly accepting of and affectionate to [both] children," that there was no domestic violence, no alcohol, no drugs in the family's life, that "nutrition, clothing and personal hygiene" were "adequate," that she "appears to have average cognitive skills," that she "uses adequate coping skills in most situations to manage stress," and as for "safety factors that place the children in immediate danger of serious harm," the report said "none."

So what was the problem? It was our old friend sex in the case of the girl, and ADHD in the case of the boy. The boy, aggressive at school, had been diagnosed with Attention Deficit Hyperactivity Disorder, and a doctor had prescribed Adderall, an amphetamine alternative to Ritalin. Angel had given it to him for a while but then had stopped, because she said it made him worse. The girl had kissed another child, had followed a child into the bathroom at school, and—the clincher—had engaged in some kind of sexual contact, unspecified, with a four-year-old, which Angel had not seen but had been told about by her son. Endeavoring to be cooperative, she told an "in-home respite worker" about it. That person in turn told a county caseworker, and the next thing she knew the caseworker was knocking on her door. Angel, angry at being reported, wouldn't let her in, and the next thing she knew after that, in a matter of just a few hours, she was hauled into Family Court and both children were taken away from her. During the months that they were gone, Angel proved a poor dancer. She kept some of the appointments that were required of her with various social services agencies but did not keep others, and this caused the children to be kept ever longer. "Breaking the rules," the caseworkers called it, and the court agreed.

This was how things worked in Family Court: An unemployed, uneducated, single mother would be neglectful in some small way, and child protective caseworkers who were already part of her life would flex their muscles. They would file a "petition of neglect," as it was called, and a judge would basically rubberstamp it. The mother would not have a chance, and neither would the children. They would all be represented by court-appointed lawyers, but for the most part these lawyers were just functionaries who came to work at 9 o'clock in the morning and sat in court with one assigned client after another for $75 an hour, often without spending any time at all with that client. It was not unusual for a lawyer to meet his or her assigned client for the first time in the waiting room just a few minutes before being called into court. It was not unusual for a child's assigned lawyer not to meet the child at all, even though the state recommended at least one meeting. The legal standard for making a decision on a case like this was the child's best interest, but it was rare for that standard even to be discussed. The real standard was how to punish the parent, and the conventional answer was, take the children away and put them into foster care, in the homes of strangers, without and discussion of what the emotional or psychological effects on the child might be, as if the children were no more than repossessed cars.

I didn't know any of this as I pursued cop and teacher stories. Family Court in New York State had always been closed to the public, and if I thought about that at all, I thought it was just as well. What went on there was no doubt private and personal and of no legitimate public interest—divorces and custody squabbles. The last thing a newspaper needed was more trivial government functions to cover, to add to the zoning boards and budget committees.

My eyes first got opened when a colleague at the *Gazoot* discovered that a woman visiting Schenectady from New Jersey had her three kids taken away from her because she had left them alone for a few hours while she was at the Department of Social Services headquarters applying for food stamps for them. Now there is a nice twist, I thought. There is a neat column waiting to be written. And indeed it was, especially since in the meantime the state had decided that family courts in New York should be open to the public the same as any other courts.

It turned out that Family Court judges were slow to adapt to this change, and the first time the aforementioned colleague and I tried to sit in on a hearing in this case, we were kicked out on the curious grounds that the matters to be discussed were "sensitive and involved children." It took a letter from a *Gazoot* lawyer, explaining the law to the judge, to get us in the next time, but in the end it was indeed a fine story.

A young woman by the name of Debra, fitting the usual profile of poor and uneducated and having three children by three different men, had come to Schenectady to try to reconcile with the father of the second of those children, who was lodged in the county jail, and had taken a temporary apartment on Van Vranken Avenue, a couple of blocks from the Department of Social Services. When she left them there she expected to be gone an hour or so, but the hour turned into four just because the process was slow.

When she got back she found taped to her door a NOTIFICATION OF TEMPORARY REMOVAL AND RIGHT TO A PROMPT HEARING, and the kids were gone—a ten-year-old boy, a three-year-old boy, and a one-year-old baby girl. Another tenant in the same building, with whom Debra had managed to get on bad terms, had noticed the children were alone and called the cops. The cops came and called Child Protective Services, and the usual and predictable followed from there, with one branch of the social services operation snatching her children while another branch, a few blocks away, was entertaining her with applications for food stamps.

She had a right to a prompt hearing, but what with one holdup and another it was nine days before she actually got the hearing, and of course during that time her children were living with another family, a family they didn't know, in another town, another county, without any contact with their mother and with no way of understanding what had happened to them. I don't know what went on in the hearing, since that's the one my colleague and I got kicked out of, but the upshot was that the judge ordered Debra to undergo a psychological evaluation and establish a stable home before she could get her kids back.

Amazing, I thought. She hadn't mistreated the kids in any way other than leaving the two little ones in the care of the ten-year-old, who probably was not mature enough to handle an emergency, which was arguably a poor thing to do. But the only harm the kids had come to was being snatched away by the authorities. And now she had to prove what other parents in Schenectady did not have to prove: that she was sound of psyche and had a stable home.

How about a psychological evaluation of the judge and the caseworkers? I wondered. How about determining that the kids would be safer in the home of strangers, in the face of studies showing that actually kids are more likely to come to harm in foster homes than in their own deficient homes?

It was a fine story. Debra did get cleared by a psychologist—no disorders, oddly enough, given the rich assortment available—but there was still the matter of a stable home. She was by now back in New Jersey with her newest boyfriend, the father of her youngest child, and how to determine that their apartment provided stability? Send a Schenectady caseworker down there to have a look? No, the law didn't provide for that. A better answer was to recruit the lawyer who represented the children to go have a look, which is what happened. In time the lawyer reported back that the apartment was satisfactory and he didn't have "any reservations about the children living in that," but incredibly the caseworkers still objected to the children being returned on what I thought were the revealing grounds that they and their mother would then be beyond their "supervision," as they called it. They wanted the return delayed until arrangements could be made with their New Jersey counterparts for a year of supervision in that state—"They deserve some protection and stability," a caseworker argued in court—which was probably the most hilarious twist of all, since the New Jersey Division of Youth and Family Services, which would have been responsible, was at the time being sued by the federal government after four young boys were found starved by their adoptive parents and the body of a foster child was found hidden in a basement. An investigation had concluded that the state's child welfare policy was "almost meaningless," and in the words of *The New York Times* the system was "broken almost beyond comprehension." The Schenectady people didn't want to let Debra and her children go unless they could be watched over by *that* agency!

In the end, the judge overruled the caseworkers, which was remarkable enough, and Debra got her kids back two months after they had been taken from her, but it was an eye-opener for me. I had no idea this was how the protection of children worked. So I was not altogether shocked when Angel later came to me with her story. I had already been initiated.

Angel's adventures did not end nearly so neatly. She got her son back on schedule, but social services kept her daughter in foster care for another two and a half months as punishment of Angel—without even a claim, I noted, that it would be beneficial to the daughter. The punishment was for "breaking the rules," as stated over and over in court. For example, she had had a childhood friend present during one of her scheduled visits with her daughter—a "contract" cobbled together by her caseworker required her "not to allow any inappropriate people in her home," without defining "inappropriate"—so she was deemed to have violated the contract. She was even punished for having briefly taken a job as a cleaner at the Saratoga horseracing track, which had prevented her from keeping one of her scheduled dates with her daughter. A welfare mother punished for taking a job, or maybe I should say her *child* punished, which was more like it, though no one in the system ever looked at it that way.

Finally, after eleven months of basically being held hostage, the little girl was allowed to come home; the family, including Angel's wasted mother, grateful for my reporting on this matter, presented me with a teddy bear bearing the legend "Best Friends," which I had no immediate need for but which remains a memento on my bookshelf; and I figured that was the end of that. But three years later we were back. This time Angel had been babysitting for nine kids, including her own, who now numbered three—yet another kid by yet another man—and in the chaos and disorder two of them had gotten into a bottle of pills, swallowed a bunch and fallen into unconsciousness. One of the kids was Angel's latest, two years old. The medicine was Clonidine, designed to counter the side effects of stimulants like Ritalin and Adderall and help kids sleep—thus does the pharmaceutical industry provide. Half a pill had been prescribed at bedtime for one of the kids Angel was babysitting, and she had also given half a pill to her own kid. A short time later they both discovered the bottle and started gobbling. Angel called an ambulance and they were both rushed to Albany Medical Center, where a nurse later said it "could have gone tragic." They survived, but caseworkers from Schenectady County were soon on the scene, and the upshot was, not only did they take the two-year-old away from Angel and pack him off to foster care, they also took the older girl and boy, who were by now nine and fourteen.

The standard for such rapid snatching is supposed to be "imminent danger to the child's life or health," and it was hard to see how that might apply to the two older kids. Even with the little one you could argue that the danger to his life and health was in the past, not imminent. Angel had carelessly allowed the kids to get at the Clonidine, but she had responsibly gotten them to a hospital as fast as possible. So what was the imminent danger even to her two-year-old? In court a few days later for a hearing to review the snatching, the question did not even come up, not in regard to the two-year-old, not in regard to the nine-year-old girl, not in regard to the fourteen-year-old boy, who had grown enough that it took three police officers to subdue him and get him away from his mother. The caseworker in charge even admitted that she had not determined if Angel had any prescription medicines in her home that would present a new danger. The court-appointed lawyer representing the children did not mention the relevant legal standard, nor did Angel's own court-appointed lawyer, and when

I asked him about it before the hearing out in the corridor, he said, "Well, that's subjective." What he said to Angel was that the county had a strong case against her because she had admitted giving her kid that half-pill, unprescribed.

Indeed, that's what the judge hung her judicial hat on, seeming not to understand that the kid had swallowed half a bottle or so of pills on his own. Angel "gave the child a pill that was not prescribed, and he became so sick he lost consciousness," the judge said, reading from a decision that she pulled out as soon as testimony in the hearing was completed, meaning she had written it ahead of time and had not been influenced by what Angel or anyone else actually said. The decision, of course, ratified the snatching of all three kids.

It didn't matter that the caseworker had conceded that "Angel and her family are a very close family" and that "the family really does love each other."

It didn't matter that the lawyer appointed to represent the children had said, "My clients desperately want to go home with their mother."

"You want them to go home now?" the judge asked incredulously.

"I'm advocating for the children," the lawyer responded defensively, as if to say, I'm just passing along what they say, it's not what I think myself.

It took five months of being jerked around for Angel to finally get her kids back—five months during which nothing substantially changed in her family except for the disruption and upset imposed by the caseworkers and the court.

It was not easy to get an answer as to how this state of affairs came about, but it was pretty clearly an extension of the hysteria over child sex abuse. Don't take any chances, was the idea. If there is the slightest indication that a child might be in danger in his or her own home, take that child away and never mind the psychological trauma that such a "removal" is bound to cause in a kid. A former reporter from the Albany area, Richard Wexler, wrote a book about it, *Wounded Innocents: The Real Victims of the War Against Child Abuse*, and also founded an organization to try to rectify it, the National Coalition for Child Protection Reform, both of which I cannot commend highly enough.

"The war against child abuse has become a war against children," he wrote. "Every year we let hundreds of children die, force thousands more to live with strangers, and throw a million innocent families into chaos. We call this 'child protection.'"

Indeed it was a fine progression—from many years of ignoring the physical and sexual molestation of children to suddenly deciding it was everywhere. The targets, naturally, were poor people, not middle-class people who could afford lawyers and might know their way around government agencies. Poor people who lived in shabby neighborhoods, had poor habits of keeping appointments, acquired and dropped paramours frequently, drank booze or smoked pot. You could bust on them for any of those faults and charge them with neglecting their children. There was always at least a little truth in it. Poor people themselves got in on it, calling the state Child Abuse Hotline to anonymously report their neighbors, as a way of settling a score. "Hotlining," it was called, and you would hear it a lot in Hamilton Hill, something like: "I wouldn't let her park in my driveway, so she hotlined me." With the result that the person would be subjected to a torturous and humiliating investigation.

It got so people didn't actually have to *abuse* their kids in any proactive sense, like break their bones or scald them or starve them, though from time to time cases like that did come to light and of course served to justify the ongoing campaign. You didn't have to nail them on neglecting all their children, either. If you could nail them for neglecting one child, you could nail them for "derivative neglect" of the others, and I encountered several cases in which newborn babies were taken away from their mothers right in the hospital on those grounds.

It was a wild business, and the satisfaction for a reporter was that very few people knew about it outside the poor neighborhoods where it happened, and if you told them, they often sided with the governmental authorities, figuring they must be right. The authorities wouldn't do anything so cruel and stupid as I described.

Once I had acquired a reputation as a champion of these unfortunate parents others would call me, telling me their stories, and the stories were so much alike that I just couldn't write them all. The readers would get tired of it, and I confess I eventually got tired of it myself. "Nothing new here," I would think as some tearful mother told me over the phone how her child had been taken away because she had missed an appointment at a drug counseling program, which she couldn't get to because her car had broken down. I would sympathize and wish her luck. It was awful.

I remember the couple in rural Schoharie County who were driving down a road arguing, the woman at the wheel, the man next to her, their two little kids in the back seat. The man reached over and angrily tried to pull the keys out of the ignition, the car swerved, the woman kept control and drove to her father's house. Out in the driveway they all argued, the couple and the woman's father, yelling at each other but with no physical violence. The father called the police, the police came, and since kids were involved, they called the county Department of Social Services. Caseworkers raced to the scene and snatched the kids on the unstated grounds of "imminent danger." Months later, having long since reconciled, the couple were still in and out of court trying to get the kids back. The basis of the neglect charge against them was simply that the kids had been in danger in the back seat with the car swerving. The solution was to take them away and send them to live with strangers, requiring the parents to go to all kinds of counseling and undergo all kinds of drug tests, some of which they were likely to miss, as the courts and the caseworkers well knew from experience, so they could keep their hooks in them that much longer. "Set them up for failure," as one frustrated lawyer put it. How devastating and terrifying this must have been to the kids, I never once heard mentioned in court.

There was one lawyer I knew, in the Schenectady County Public Defender's office, who really felt it personally. He had been born with facial deformities and when he was nine years old his parents took him to a hospital in Boston for eye surgery and, unable to afford a hotel room for the anticipated ten weeks, left him there. He told me he never forgot the terror of abandonment as he used to sneak away from the other kids and cry privately behind a big globe in the corner, and that's what kept him going in Family Court, trying to protect other kids from that experience.

As for failure, there was Angel. She had difficulty walking any long distance on weak ankles. Of course she had no car. She would have an appointment for one kid on one side of town and an appointment for herself on the other side of town, and it would be raining, and she would skip one of the appointments, and then the caseworkers would "violate" her, as the jargon had it.

"I got violated," she would call and tell me. I thought she meant raped, but no. They had charged her with violating her court order, and now, for sure, she would have to wait that much longer to get her kids back.

I asked myself if I was doing better reporting on these homely matters than if I were pursuing an honest trade like locksmithing or lawnmower repair, and I didn't know the answer, but at least the desire to slit my wrists had left me. True, I wished no more intercourse with Duanesburg, but I was happy enough to see caseworkers set their jaws and look grim when I walked in the door of Family Court. There were worse ways to make a living, I figured, than being an irritant to these child-snatchers.

9

TOO MANY CATS

"There's humane, and there's inhumane."

You could argue that Family Court was a step above kittens and cats, at least on the evolutionary ladder, but I found that kittens and cats were not to be despised as a subject of journalism either. True, I found it somewhat belatedly, months after the *Gazoot* and every other newspaper and television station in upstate New York had reported on the arrest of an alleged kitten-killer at a trash-transfer station in a rural stretch of Saratoga County and had followed his court appearances with the sort of attention normally reserved for Hollywood stars, but find it I did. At first I thought, well, here is more small-town news, or, here is more sentimental fervor over animals, which was running second only to child abuse as a favorite of editors and news directors.

Then came the day when the story appeared to have run its course. The kitten-killer, Ron Bruzdzinski by name, pleaded guilty to a reduced charge of "attempted animal cruelty," was spared a jail sentence and was simply ordered not to keep more than one cat at the Clifton Park trash-transfer station, of which he was supervisor. It was a slow day for me, and I decided to pop over and say hello to Mr. Bruzdzinski and see if I could squeeze a column out of his misadventure. It would be a pleasant drive, and an animal torturer might make lively copy, I figured.

Ron Bruzdzinski was a weary-looking fifty-three-year-old man. I found him in his particle-board office stroking a cat that was curled up on top of his desk, the only cat he was permitted to keep. I asked him about what had happened, and he told me in the most woebegone way possible, "I don't understand these people," referring mainly to the people from the county SPCA but also, I gathered, to the law enforcement people who backed them.

Ron, it soon became clear, was not some perverted animal torturer as I had imagined, but on the contrary was the softest-hearted animal-lover, and especially cat-lover, that you could imagine. At home he and his wife had seven cats and a rabbit, and the first thing he did was show me photos of them, like a doting parent or grandparent—Precious, Pooh Bear, Max, Charlie, and so forth, here on a rocking chair, there asleep on a bed with his wife. At the trash station, where he had worked for fifteen years, he used to feed stray cats that happened by or that had been dumped by the side of the road by what he called "cruel people." The food bowls still stood behind his office, under a rough shelter that he had built to keep the weather off.

What happened was this: On a Sunday afternoon the previous summer, Ron drove to the transfer station to feed the stray cats as usual, and there, among the weeds at the base of a fence, found four tiny kittens, still wet, their eyes closed, one with the afterbirth attached, with no mother in sight. He picked them up individually with a towel so as not to frighten off a returning mother with his smell, and put them in a small unused doghouse with food next to them, though he knew they were too young to eat on their own. The next morning when he came to work he checked on them and found that "two were moving OK, and the two others were very slow." The morning after that he found one bleeding internally from the ear, one with maggots on it, and the other two dead. He called his wife and asked her to call a veterinarian, which she did, but the veterinarian would not euthanize the remaining kittens without payment and would not take them in without the mother.

"If they had their mother, they wouldn't be dying," Ron said with exasperation. "I couldn't understand that."

He sat in his office for half an hour, trying to work while listening to the dying squeaks from outside his window. Finally, he said, "I just couldn't stand to hear them cry no more," so he did what his father used to do when Ron was a boy growing up on a farm nearby. He got a bucket of water and held the two kittens under till they stopped moving, which he says was only a matter of seconds. Then he got a loader to dig a three-foot-deep hole next to the landfill, put all four dead kittens in the hole, and shoveled in dirt to fill it.

The next day was a day he would long remember. Two representatives of the Upstate Society for the Prevention of Cruelty to Animals, responding to an anonymous call they had received, showed up at the transfer station, produced their badges as state-sanctioned peace officers, and demanded to know what had happened to the kittens. Ron told them and at their insistence dug up the four corpses and turned them over. They thereupon issued him a ticket ordering him into town court on a charge of violating Article 26, Section 353 of the state Agriculture and Markets Law, which deals with the torture, maiming and unjustifiable killing of animals.

Thus began what Ron called his "nightmare." Local television went berserk, as local television invariably goes berserk over animal stories, and Ron began getting calls accusing him of animal torture. He was officially charged with four misdemeanors, one for each kitten, each punishable by up to a year in jail, a $1,000 fine, or both. When it emerged that he had ten cats hanging around the transfer station, living off his charity, he reluctantly agreed to get rid of all but one of them.

"I almost cried when we took them out of here," he recalled. The nine exiled cats were sent to the Saratoga County Animal Shelter, where they were kept for the legally required five days and then—please get ready for this—were *killed*. Injected with sodium phenobarbital. For a column-writer in search of material, it was too good to be true: The person charged with animal cruelty had been caring for the cats, and the rescuers killed them!

I later asked Cathy Coultier, head of the Upstate SPCA, if she saw any irony here, and she did not. "There's humane, and there's inhumane," she said. And she made clear that for her, feeding stray cats, not to mention drowning dying kittens, is inhumane, whereas a quick injection of phenobarbital sodium is humane. Furthermore, she said, "A transfer station is not supposed to be a pet farm." This is what moved unsophisticated old Ron Bruzdzinski to say, "I don't understand these people."

I was bound to note in my column, just as a fillip, that while New York punished anyone who "unjustifiably injures, maims, mutilates or kills any animal, whether wild or tame," it positively encouraged the shooting of deer, bear, turkeys and other wild animals—with television commercials promoting the state as a sportsman's destination, with hunter safety courses, and with the issuance of hunting licenses. Which meant you could drive a titanium arrow into the rump of an unsuspecting deer and leave the animal to suffer in the woods until it died of infection and gangrene if you couldn't catch up with it, but you could not drown a half-dead kitten in a bucket of water to put it out of its misery. This was material beyond my expectations.

Anyway, I now had an inkling of what the animal protection business was all about, or at least partially about, just as I had more than an inkling of what the child protection business was about, so I was not surprised sometime later when I heard from a woman a little farther north, in the farm country of Washington County, that she had been turned into a criminal by the same Cathy Coultier of the same Upstate SPCA for the same offense of caring for stray cats.

What the devil was going on here? I wondered. All these stories I kept reading in the local papers and seeing on local television about animals being "rescued" from horrible conditions and others being left to die in piles of their own excrement, with ghastly photos of dogs and cats with open sores and protruding ribs— were they all of the same sort?

The woman in the cow country to the north was Jane Meneely, who lived modestly with her husband, Bill, on four acres of farmland. Jane was food and beverage manager at a golf club—at least she was until she got branded as an animal abuser—and Bill was a groundskeeper at the local school district. They, especially Jane, had a weakness for cats. There were times when they would find cats or kittens by the side of the road near their house, and they figured that people who owned those animals and didn't want them had dumped them there, which was a reasonable guess. People often disposed of unwanted pets that way. Jane would call the SPCA about the cats, but the SPCA had a policy of not taking in "feral" cats, so her choices were limited. She could take them in herself, or she could leave them alone and let them fend for themselves as best they could, which in most cases would probably mean a slow death. So she took them in—and took them in and took them in. It got to the point where people knew of her generosity, so when they had a litter of kittens they didn't want, that's where they would dump them. Or when they had a sick or injured cat. Sometimes dead cats too. Bill and Jane had a burn barrel for those. They'd pick up cat carcasses by the side of the road in front of their house and burn them in the barrel.

It got to the point where they had so many live cats, sick and well, injured and sound, that they actually built a twenty-by-thirty-foot addition onto their house to accommodate them all. They were spending $125 a week on cat food, kitty litter and veterinarian bills and were falling behind.

"I know I needed help," Jane told me. So she called in someone to help clean the place up, and that's where the trouble began. The cleaning person took one look around—at the excrement and the open sores—and called the SPCA. Cathy Coultier, brigadier general of animal rescue, did not contact the Meneelys to ask what was going on and did not visit their home or make any other investigation, as far as I was able to learn. And she made no effort to relieve them of their self-imposed burden. She went to the district attorney and to the sheriff, she got a search warrant, and she attacked. Jane got a phone call at work from an SPCA staff member telling her to get home within ten minutes or they would break her door down. She did get home, she and Bill were charged with multiple counts of animal cruelty, and the cats were rounded up with nets. Pictures of the worst ones were provided to local newspapers and television stations, which passed them along to the reading and viewing public with the appropriate indignation, leaving the impression that the Meneelys had inflicted the injuries themselves. Why, who knew if the burn barrel, also pictured, might not have been used to incinerate live cats in some devilish ritual reminiscent of the McMartin Preschool story?

What was glorious to me was the SPCA's own shelter, run by Cathy Coultier herself. I visited it, to enrich my understanding of animal rescue, and Santa Maria! You want to talk about "animal hoarding," which was the phrase used to describe what the Meneelys and other people did. You want to talk about stink! I walked into that shelter on the outskirts of Glens Falls and damn near retched. I didn't see the Meneelys' house before it was raided so I don't know what that might have looked like or smelled like, but it couldn't have been much worse than the SPCA's own shelter. Cages full of dogs and cats were everywhere, not just in the designated kennels and holding areas. In the lobby I counted seventeen cats in cages; in the laundry room, six dogs; in the staff kitchen, nine cats; in the bathroom, five cats; in the pharmacy, more dogs and puppies that I neglected to count; in every corridor, in every nook and cranny, more cages of barking dogs and curled-up cats, often stacked one on top of another.

The place had an official capacity of seventy-six cats and sixty dogs, General Coultier advised me. The current occupancy was 303 cats and ninety-eight dogs, and the place smelled accordingly. Thirty cats from the Meneelys' place alone were in one large cage. "Court cases," Coultier said with a wave of the hand at the agglomeration of cages. It was a new world for me.

The Meneelys pleaded not guilty, their case went to trial, and a jury convicted them. At their sentencing Jane read a statement in which she recalled "the trips to the veterinarian's, on emergency calls or just for health checks, trips to the feed store, the sheltering, the sleepless nights nursing a cat or kitten under the guidance of my veterinarian, all because no one wanted a sick or injured or healthy cat."

"We are financially drained," she told the court. "All money saved for my husband's health and our future is gone...to be convicted of this is the worst nightmare, because you never wake up from it...there was never any cruelty by Bill or myself...as far as Bill and I are concerned, animal cruelty and human cruelty were both committed on June 3 [the date of the SPCA raid] and continues on by Ms. Cloutier and her army."

The judge agreed and effectively vacated the verdict by declining to punish the Meneelys beyond pro-forma probation. "This entire case could and should have been handled in an entirely different manner," he declared, and he rejected the SPCA's demand for payment of $27,784.50 from the Meneelys for room and board for the cats. That his name not be lost to history, it is John Holmes, Hartford Town Court, State of New York. Eventually the guilty verdict was overturned on appeal.

After this and half a dozen other similar cases, I thought I had reached an understanding of the animal rescue game, and I was ready to move on to bigger game. What I was not prepared for was a lawyer from Long Island launching his own SPCA right in Schenectady and recruiting me as a supporter—not that I understood what was going on in the beginning. I'm as susceptible to flattery and soft-soaping as anyone.

His name was Mathew (one "t") Tully, and he cut a figure— big, self-confident, with a presence, as they say. He was building a successful law practice in the Albany area suing the federal government on behalf of veterans and Social Security recipients. He was a lieutenant colonel in the National Guard. He was a onetime prison guard. He had worked for an SPCA in Long Island and as a result was a certified "peace officer," a distinction that he shared with Cathy Coultier. It was a category of citizen that might be unique to New York, I wasn't sure about that. A "peace officer" was somebody tangentially connected to law enforcement—a prison guard, a probation officer, a park ranger—and under New York law such a person had authority to "make warrantless arrests," "use physical force and deadly physical force," "carry out warrantless searches," and so forth, which I believe a lot of people didn't know about. These powers were especially sobering because the officers of an SPCA, unlike park rangers and prison guards, were not public employees, and if you thought they got out of line, there was no public official to complain to. You couldn't go to the mayor, or the county sheriff, or anyone else. An SPCA was a private organization, answerable to no one.

Mat (likewise with one "t") invited me to lunch to reassure me he was not going to be like the bad bullying SPCA I had written about to the north. "With animal hoarders it makes very little sense to make an arrest of a little old lady who got in over her head," he told me. "My goal is not to seize animals. We want to help people."

I was wary of the police and military trappings he had adopted—the mail-order police-type uniform and badge, the black-and-white police-looking car with PEACE OFFICER written on the side, the Glock .45 handgun, his self-appointment as "Chief of Department" and "Chief Humane Law Enforcement Officer"—but he sounded sincere enough, and thereafter I ignored the minor news stories we ran about multiple cats being "rescued" from some little old lady's apartment and about Tully's repeated complaints that the private animal shelter in Glenville wouldn't accept all his "rescued" animals.

It took a long time for me to realize that he was waging a frenetic war against the Glenville animal shelter, a perfectly harmless operation run by perfectly harmless and good-hearted people, that had been in operation since 1931. Without advertising it, he had demanded that they entirely finance his paramilitary operation, and when they declined, and also declined to lodge all the animals he "rescued" because they simply didn't have the space, he threatened them with a "hostile takeover" and told them they would be consigned "solely to the history books." All of this in e-mails that I eventually got hold of.

It came to a head when the director of the animal shelter, Rosalie Ault, left two pit bull puppies at the Schenectady police station, puppies that had been picked up from the streets of Schenectady and dropped at the shelter in Glenville. (The shelter had a contract with a few neighboring towns to accept stray animals but not with Schenectady.) The police had no place for the puppies, so the matter soon became public, and the SPCA responded by saying Rosalie should be arrested for abandoning those puppies. Tully added that such a crime should be elevated to a felony if committed by an animal welfare official, like the shelter director, and what's more, a new law making it a felony should be named for that official—Rosalie's Law!

Poor Rosalie, mild-mannered friend of cats and dogs, under assault by a paramilitary fantasist who must have thought he was in Afghanistan facing down the Taliban. He wrote to his supporters about the shelter's "blitzkrieg assault" on one occasion and about its "weak counterattack" on another. He promised that the media would "smell blood in the water" and that "counterattacking is helping us get attention for the next round." Weird stuff that I printed as soon as I got it. He responded on our website by calling the write-up "an APF smear with Carl as a puppet," APF standing for Animal Protective Foundation, the organization that ran the animal shelter.

Me, a puppet! I wanted to roll over and die. He further said I wrote what I did because "the APF has many full-time people to kiss Carl's ass." So down the tubes went our jolly relationship in which I ignored his animal raids, and I can't say how sorry I was that a short time later he got called up for a thirteen-month tour in Afghanistan to train Afghan police officers. I was pumped by then for a whole series of rip-snorting columns, so chagrined was I at having been played for a sucker at the outset, and I had to keep those columns bottled up inside me where they caused no end of heartburn. By the time he returned to Schenectady, possessor of a Purple Heart, I had already slunk from the field of battle, so I never could disgorge those columns. I make note of it here so that when a pathologist finally does an autopsy on me, he will be able to account for the blockage, which otherwise might puzzle him.

10

INVENTING TERROR

"The court appreciates your demeanor
in this courtroom."

It was quite a scene for Albany, which despite
being the capital of the Empire State is very much
a provincial city. Next to the federal courthouse
down on Broadway there was parked a bus-sized
black van with HOMELAND SECURITY emblazoned
on its sides and a satellite dish affixed on top, as if
scanning the atmosphere for bleeps of an attack. On
Broadway itself a phalanx of cops both on foot and
on horseback. Up on the roof of an office building
across the street from the courthouse a pair of
sharpshooters, like you might see at the U.S. Embassy
in Libya. Flak jackets all around. And of course,
television vans with their own dishes and towers
and cables, and photographers aplenty pressing for
shots, and poor print scribes like me, identifiable by
our narrow reporters' notebooks, hungrily looking

for quotes. You might have thought Khalid Sheikh Mohammed, the celebrated "Mastermind of 9/11," was on trial.

It wasn't him, but it was Mohammed Mosharref Hossain, proprietor of the Little Italy pizza shop on Central Avenue, Albany's third-world-like commercial drag, and Yassin Aref, imam of the storefront Masjid As-Salam mosque, also on Central Avenue, the two of them accused of "providing material support and resources to a foreign terrorist organization." Something to do with a surface-to-air missile. In Albany!

Hossain, or Mosharref, as his friends knew him, was an American citizen originally from Bangladesh who had been in this country for twenty years, had a wife and five (soon to be six) children, and lived humbly off his tiny pizza shop and two dumpy little buildings that he was trying to renovate for apartments. Yassin was a Kurdish refugee from northern Iraq who had come to this country only five years earlier, sent here by the United Nations Refugee Agency with his wife and three (eventually to be four) children. He had worked as a janitor at Albany Medical Center while learning English, was intense and bookish, and eventually was appointed imam, or prayer leader, of the mosque, where Muslim immigrants and some disaffected black Americans worshipped. Neither one had a criminal record. Mosharref was forty-nine at the time of indictment, Yassin thirty-four.

The evidence seemed to me thin, just looking at the public documents. The criminal complaint filed by the FBI claimed only that Mosharref had agreed to accept $50,000 in cash from a "confidential informant" and return $45,000 of it in checks, keeping $5,000 for himself, money that the confidential informant was supposedly making from the importation of weapons and ammunition. Though the complaint was intended to support the arrest of the men and thus could be expected to make the strongest case possible without giving the defendants' side, it still conceded that Mosharref, in conversations secretly recorded by the FBI, had said "now was not the time for violent jihad" and that the importation of weapons was illegal, and that he did not need as much money as the confidential informant was pressing on him in the form of a business loan. Further, he "expressed reluctance" about transporting a missile to Kingston, which in any event he didn't do.

As for Yassin, the basic charge against him was that he "agreed to witness the transactions," that is, the handing over of money to Mosharref, in his role as imam, acting more or less as a notary. That allegedly implicated him in a conspiracy of "threatening to use...a weapon of mass destruction against any person in the United States," the targeted person in the United States supposedly being the Pakistani ambassador to the United Nations. He also faced lesser charges of lying to an FBI agent when he was arrested and interrogated. The most damning thing against him was that he had been referred to as "commander" in a notebook found in an alleged terrorist camp (or village) in Iraq—"Kak Yassin," with an old Albany telephone number next to it, which we later learned was what triggered the FBI operation in the first place. They had set out to nail this commander, cleaning toilets at a hospital in Albany, New York, and Mosharref was the avenue to reach him.

But you couldn't read the charges, plowing through all the legalese, without thinking, is that *it*? Weren't these guys going to blow up the state Capitol? Weren't they point men for al-Qaeda, planning to pump cyanide into Albany's Alcove Reservoir? One of them accepted what was presented to him as a loan for his business, and the other acted as notary? And also without thinking, who the devil is this "confidential informant"? What's that all about? Was he a friend of Mosharref's and Yassin's who turned against them and began snitching on them? Or was he an FBI plant, or what?

Soon enough we found out he was a disreputable Pakistani character by the name of Shahed Hussain, code name Malik, who had been arrested for falsifying driver's license exams for pay on behalf of immigrants and was cooperating with the FBI as a way to avoid being deported. Cooperating not so much as an informant, as the FBI let on, but as an *agent provocateur*, that is, someone who doesn't simply report on crimes that are happening anyway but who makes crimes happen—though it took me a while to understand that, and I made the mistake in my early reporting of referring to him as a "snitch."

The FBI called the operation a "sting," the idea being to give someone the opportunity to commit a crime and see if he takes it. That's what the FBI did here, by its own account. They invented a crime and tried to get Mosharref and Yassin to participate in it. Nobody even alleged that the two men were involved in any support for terrorism before the FBI baited them.

The atmosphere surrounding the case from the beginning was, the two men must be guilty. Not only had Governor George Pataki declared when they were arrested, "There are terrorists among us who would do us harm...we are taking these threats to our freedom very seriously," and not only had Mayor Jerry Jennings promised, "We will continue to be proactive," but there was this massive display of security surrounding the trial—local police, federal marshals, immigration agents, FBI agents, horses, patrol cars, sharpshooters, flak jackets, metal detectors, and that big Homeland Security van with the satellite dish on top. The government surely had not taken all those precautions on account of a pizza shop owner and a janitor-turned-prayer-leader who were minding their own business, two family men struggling to make a living in a foreign country. Nor had the FBI run a year-long undercover operation and the U.S. Attorney agreed to prosecute and a grand jury agreed to indict if the two men were blameless. That would have been hard for any solid citizen to imagine.

What's more, we were in the aftermath of 9/11— the undercover operation began in 2003, the arrests came in 2004, the trial was held in 2006—when the whole country was alert to maniacal Muslims, and these two guys, did they ever fit the profile! Mosharref, brown-skinned, with a long and full gray beard and some kind of fez on his head, could have been cast as the Prophet Mohammed himself if a movie were being made. And if you caught a glimpse of his wife in the background, fully shrouded and veiled, like she just blew in off the desert, it was worse. Yassin, with his full black beard, his intense look and his title of imam, could have been on the nightly news as the latest terrorist to be picked up in the nick of time—and indeed he *was* on the nightly news that way.

For my part, I had misgivings about putting people to the test to see if you could get them to commit crimes, and wondered what would happen in Albany if an undercover operator tried to induce a couple of sons of Eire to provide material support to the Irish Republican Army—heavily Irish Albany, where anytime Gerry Adams of Sinn Fein, the IRA's front organization, came to town he was given a hearty welcome by the mayor and every other politician who could squeeze into the picture.

I had further doubts when the U.S. Attorney's office conceded it had mistranslated "kak," and it did not mean "commander" after all but rather "brother," and was in fact the standard male courtesy title in Kurdish, used much like "mister." Well, well, I thought. And well, well, thought Judge Thomas McAvoy also, who on the strength of that concession released Yassin on bail. (Both men had been jailed without bail after their arrest. After a few weeks Mosharref was released to await trial, but the "commander" continued to be held as seemingly the more dangerous of the two.) If he was not a commander but just a plain old mister, what was the significance of his name and telephone number appearing in someone's notebook in his native land? Not much, I figured.

Both of them now being out on bail, I took the opportunity to look them up, and that deepened my doubts. I found Mosharref in his hole-in-the-wall pizza shop being warmly welcomed home by neighbors coming in off the street—neighbors black, brown and white. His wife told me from behind her veil that he was not going to talk to the press, but when he saw me with my notebook he invited me to sit down anyway.

"I love this country, this is my country," he insisted. "If something happens here, my children die, I die."

I asked him about Malik, and he said Malik had ingratiated himself by visiting the shop and giving his children a toy helicopter. "Whoever loves children, what can be wrong with that person?" was his reaction. So he did not suspect anything when that same Malik, supposedly a rich businessman, began offering to lend him money to prop up his business. And no, he did not regret having come to the United States in the first place: "I know I'll be free. I haven't done anything to harm no one."

I found Yassin in front of the mosque, which from the street was nothing more than a derelict-looking old store window papered over. I had spotted him as I cruised slowly down the opposite side of the street, had immediately pulled into a parking space and hustled over to him. We talked for a while, he intense and searching for the English words, when he said, "Is that your car?" A parking officer was standing over it, writing out a ticket. In my hurry I had neglected to put a coin in the meter. I ran over, but too late. When I came back, ticket in hand, Yassin said, "Please give it to me. I will pay it."

"Thank you, that's very kind of you, but I can't do that," I said, and I gave him a little talk about journalistic ethics.

He looked serious and insisted. "I don't want you to be hurt because of me. It's my faith."

So here he was, an obviously poor man, in an awful jam, looking at the possibility of spending many years in prison, with three children and a pregnant wife to worry about at that point, and he was insisting that he pay my $40 parking ticket so I not be hurt on his account. It was his faith! I asked him, as I had asked Mosharref, if he had made a mistake in coming to the United States in the first place.

"I don't think so," he said, "especially after I saw the court"—meaning the massive Art Deco James T. Foley United States Courthouse on Broadway with its marble floors and gilt pilasters that wouldn't quit. "I believe justice is there."

He would find out soon enough, but by the time the trial started, with all its attendant theater, I was thinking there was more than one thing wrong with the picture. And by the time it was over I was as ashamed as I had ever been by anything I had seen in a court of law. It was bad right from the beginning, right from jury selection, when men and women who couldn't think of an excuse to get out of it, and who had in common that they would not be missed at their jobs, trooped forward one at a time to be questioned about their ability to look at these two bearded Muslims accused of terrorism and give them a fair shake, and one after another answered no, frankly, he (or she) didn't think so. The events of

9/11 were still too vivid, too wrenching. And that person was, of course, excused, but I had to believe those were simply the honest ones, and I wondered, what about the others? Did they really think any differently? I was also impressed with how little they knew about Islam or for that matter about the world, the most learned among them stating only that he could place Bangladesh on a map. Also with how little they knew about this case, which had been prominently in the news for two years by the time the trial convened. They sort of remembered seeing something about it on television, but it made no impression. Only one admitted to believing that if the government brought the case there must be something to it, though others must have believed the same. I half-believed it myself, just looking at the lineup of court officials, lawyers and FBI agents. It couldn't all be a misunderstanding, could it? Or a desperate attempt by the FBI to make its bones in the War on Terror?

Which I finally decided it really was. After 9/11, we learned, the FBI was given as its top priority the catching of terrorists before they could strike again, and organized crime and everything else was pushed to the back of the stove. The Albany case was just one of many that followed a similar pattern: invent a terrorist plot and cajole, trick, even bribe a few targeted Muslims into doing just enough in support of it that they could be arrested and charged with supporting terrorism, to the greater glory of the FBI. But I didn't know that when the trial was in progress. I thought the Albany case was unique, and I was fired up at the opportunity to report on it.

The principal witness was Malik, as we thought of the *agent provocateur*, and I can honestly say he was the worst witness I had ever observed in my years of observing witnesses. He squirmed, he evaded, he contradicted himself, he rambled unintelligibly. He wouldn't even admit that when he presented himself to Mosharref as a rich businessman, per instructions from his FBI handler, Tim Coll, it was a ruse.

"I don't know if it was true or not true. It was a one-way street, I'm telling you. Wasn't I had to make up story. What Agent Coll told me that morning of the assignment that I had to do, so I would go and do the assignment—to assign—it was a day assignment I had. He used to tell me, 'This is your assignment for today. Go in and talk.' If it's true, not true, I do not know." (I copied that down later from the transcript. It was impossible to take notes at the time. It wasn't just the syntax; his accent made it sound like he had a mouthful of uncooked chickpeas.)

For the benefit of Agent Tim Coll, whom he was trying to please, he interpreted every word and phrase of Mosharref's in the most toxic way possible, to the point where it was downright laughable. Mosharref had said in response to a bait-question from Malik about the attack on the World Trade Center, "This, of course, this was bad...We can't frighten others like this...We should have a good relationship with the unbelievers. Then, because of our goodness, Islam will spread and continue spreading," which hardly fit the profile of a terrorist. As for who carried out the attack, "I don't rightly know whether bin Laden did this or someone else did it, for whatever reason. God the master knows this." (The conversation was captured on tape.) In the trial, Malik testified that Mosharref had said, "If the other guy did it, it was bad, but if bin Laden did it, it was good because it was holy war."

Everything turned upside down and inside out.

He was so bad that at the end of an excruciating cross-examination by defense attorneys, in which he came across as nothing but a pathetic creep, when it was the turn of prosecutors to question him again and try to rehabilitate him, they declined the opportunity. "Nothing further," they said. I was downright embarrassed for them.

But it didn't matter. Nothing mattered except the missile launcher. The missile launcher, an Army-green tube about six feet long, was fatal. It didn't need any interpretation. You could see it. The prosecutors brought it into the courtroom and even had an expert on hand to demonstrate its use, pointing it this way and that, including at the jurors themselves for dramatic effect, and explaining the technology. And then you saw it in one of the surveillance videos, filmed in a bogus office the FBI had set up for Malik to transact his bogus business in. He was lending Mosharref cash to help him with his rental properties, and at one point he pulled out and hoisted onto his shoulder this dark green tube. "This, look this," he said on the video, *apropos* of nothing. "This came from China, right? Do you know what this is?"

"No," said Mosharref.

"This is for destroying airplanes. This is sensor heat, you know? This comes from our *mujahid* brothers."

Mosharref paid little attention. At one point he commented, "Good money can be made from this, but it's not legal." At another point he said, "I don't believe in your method. That's why I don't take that path."

He obviously had no interest in or sympathy for whatever Malik was up to, but neither did he drop everything and call the cops. And that was the ruin of him. Nobody in the courtroom, it's fair to say, could get that missile launcher out of his mind, or Mosharref's nonchalance about it, even if there was no reason to believe he made any connection between the "sensor heat" and the business loan that Malik was pressing on him.

As for Yassin the notary, whose English was still rudimentary, it was awful, him talking with Malik— Malik of the fractured syntax and mouthful of chickpeas. Following instructions from Agent Coll, Malik tried to lure Yassin into expressing support for an Islamic militant group fighting in Kashmir, Jaish-e-Mohammed, known as JEM, which the State Department classified as a terrorist organization. Yassin said he didn't know anything about the group except what he heard on television. Malik persisted, and Yassin persisted, each in his own bumbling English. At one point Malik told him the president of Pakistan was against JEM, and "That's why, the mizz-ILE, that we sent it to New York City to teach...President Musharraf the lesson not to fight with us," and he asked Yassin what he thought.

Yassin went into a long rambling disquisition of the kind that, if you knew him, you soon got used to: "I don't know that organization, but I believe any Muslim organization and people, if they are needy, special thousand of the women, special a lot of orphans, special a lot of people they lost their house and they send them out, they live in the mountains without house, without anything, maybe they are needy in the cold weather, there is mountainous, maybe like all here the cold weather. They are needy, maybe, for, for food, for anything, I believe you can help them, help them, why not? Even the people they don't like. Because you are not helping the terrorism, you are helping their children. You are helping their womans. You are helping those people. They have no food to eat." Without any mention of any "mizz-ILE," which was how Malik pronounced "missile," or any indication that he had understood it or it had registered with him in any way. (Malik often threw incriminating words and phrases into a conversation, out of the blue, just to get them on tape.)

In court, asked to summarize Yassin's response, Malik outdid himself, saying it was "Use the mizz-ILE but do not tell anyone."

In the end both Yassin and Mosharref were convicted of money laundering "to facilitate the covert importation of the SAM that, in turn, was to be used for an attack on the Ambassador of Pakistan in New York City," along with various counts of conspiracy.

One bit of evidence against Yassin was that at a meeting in his apartment, Malik had supposedly said something about a "chaudhry," which was his code word for missile, a code word possibly known only to him, and Yassin or someone had supposedly said something about "New York" and "1" and "44," which could mean 1st Avenue and 44th Street, which was the location of the United Nations. But, alas, there was no audio recording of that exchange. Malik's recording device had supposedly fallen off before he arrived at the apartment, and we had only the word of Agent Tim Coll, who said he was sitting outside in his car monitoring the meeting, able to hear the sound through a transmitter that Malik still wore.

Convenient as hell, I thought. Like the all-night interrogation of Yassin after he was arrested, also conducted by Agent Coll, when Yassin supposedly lied about a couple of fairly minor matters. The FBI managed to record conversations everywhere else to make its tenuous case but did not trouble to record an interrogation at its own headquarters down on McCarty Avenue. So the resulting charge of perjury against Yassin was supported only by the word of his very interrogator. It reminded me, of course, of the interrogation of Jack Carroll, and I remembered Detective Steve Weber at trial telling Jack Carroll's lawyer, "It makes my job easier... and your job as defense attorney more difficult." No one asked Agent Coll the question, but I guess there was no need. Of course Yassin was convicted of that relatively minor charge also, or at least one of the two such charges. Actually, he was acquitted of twenty of the thirty charges against him, but that didn't do him any good. Ten counts were plenty. Mosharref was convicted of all twenty-seven charges against him. Both faced up to thirty years in prison, which is what the prosecution asked for.

I wrote a column in the form of an open letter to Judge McAvoy, urging not a lenient sentence as many other citizens did but rather a complete overturning of the jury verdict. I did it in High Oratory fashion, I'm afraid, after the manner of a Christian preacher at an outdoor rally:

> *Can you possibly believe in the privacy of your heart that this is right?*
>
> *Can you possibly believe the government was justified in marshaling its resources to trick these two men?*
>
> *Can you possibly believe the jury was justified in finding them guilty?*

I reminded him of his astounding instruction to the jury, that the government had "good and valid reasons" for targeting the two men, but the jury was not allowed to know those reasons because they were classified, so highly classified that even the defense attorneys, who had received security clearances before the trial began, were not allowed to see the supporting evidence, just as they were not allowed to see evidence of illegal wiretapping. (Even the government's own prosecutors were not allowed to see evidence of wiretapping.)

I worked on this story as hard as I had ever worked on anything in my life, straining all day to hear and understand testimony, all evening to distill dozens of pages of notes into a succinct column that I hoped was not only accurate but also truthful, till I was dizzy with brain fatigue. A couple of things left deep impressions on me. One was the sentencing, at which Yassin stood and spoke boldly: "I swear by God I never had any intention to harm anyone in this country...They"—

indicating the FBI agents lined up in the front row—
"they knew I never did any violence. The government,
they knew. You knew. I didn't come to this country
to harm anyone," as Judge McAvoy's face grew redder
by the minute under his thatch of Irish white hair and
Yassin continued to give him what-for, thereby risking a
punitively longer sentence.

Then Mosharref, poor Mosharref, with his
veiled wife, Fatima, and their six kids huddled in the
back of the courtroom. Not trusting himself to speak
extemporaneously, he had prepared a statement, but
trying to read it he choked right away.

"When Malik first came into my life, he had
everything I did not. He was smart, he had export-
import business, he had cars, he had more money than
he could spend," and so forth. "I did not know about
terrorism and shooting and bombing, but I could tell
you how many pounds of flour you need for pizza." All
of this in near-tears, his voice trembling, as his wife and
children looked on miserably.

Judge McAvoy had replied sarcastically to Yassin,
the brave one: "It's nice for you to believe you're
innocent, but the jury found you guilty." What's more,
"The court," meaning him, "reviewed the verdict
and decided they were correct." To poor trembling
Mosharref he replied with what I thought were the most
revealing words of all the many thousands of words
that were uttered in the twelve days of trial: "The court
appreciates your demeanor in this courtroom."

Yes, the court—meaning he himself but most
likely also U.S. Attorney Glenn Suddaby and Assistant

U.S. Attorneys William Pericak and Elizabeth Coombe, as well as the buzz-cut FBI agents sitting erect in the front row of the spectator section—appreciated and downright relished Mosharref's pitiful quaking in front of his wife and children. It was the payoff for them. Then and there it occurred to me that in a funny, reverse sort of way, this had been a terror trial after all.

That wasn't the end of it. A couple of weeks later, these government worthies (minus the judge) trooped over to Schenectady for a meeting with the editors and me. Glenn Suddaby, U.S. Attorney for the Northern District of New York; William Pericak, assistant U.S. Attorney; John Pikus, agent in charge of the Albany office of the FBI; Timothy Coll, special agent—all gathered around the conference table up on the second floor of the *Gazoot* building on Maxon Road Extension for the sole purpose of denouncing me and my reporting. I had never in my ragged career felt more honored.

And another thing that left a deep impression: after the sentencing was done and Yassin and Mosharref were led away in their jail suits to begin their fifteen-year sentences (not the thirty they might have gotten), I encountered Mosharref's shrouded wife out in the parking lot, appearing as always like a remnant of another, sand-swept world. She looked at me over her veil, her eyes full of tears, and said, "Thank you, thank you"— thanking *me* for my reportage. I will not forget that as long as I live.

11

JANITOR RAMPANT

*"You have crossed a line with me. I am not
a tolerant person to begin with."*

Me, denounced as a liar. I could hardly believe it.
And right in the middle of a school board meeting, no less.
Good lord in heaven, I thought, I should have stuck to my
resolve never to attend another school board meeting in
my natural life. But there I was in the auditorium of Mont
Pleasant Middle School in Schenectady, up in the front
row so as to hear as well as possible, with the daughter of
the board president choking up with emotion, thanking
her father for "putting up with all this CRAP!" as she
shouted it, and turning to me and angrily declaring, "You
lie about my father!"

Lie, when all I had ever said was that her father,
Jeff Janiszewski by name, had protected and politically
schemed with a psycho who was now in jail without
bail charged with terrorism, and had done so in cahoots
with the school superintendent and a couple other

administrators. And had gotten her slenderly qualified mother a nice-paying job in the school district while managing to avoid a Civil Service exam for it. And a few other things, like creating fake organizations to campaign for passage of the school budget and the election of his own hand-picked candidates for the school board. As a result of which a crowd of angry taxpayers was now in the auditorium demanding to be heard as Dad attempted to gavel them into silence. Dad finally relented, he would let a few people speak, but the first person he recognized was his own adult daughter, who alternately praised him and ripped me a new one, as they say. And Dad didn't leave it at that but declared on his own account that "the superintendent has been the victim of character assassination in Carl Strock's column," while I sat there and endeavored to take notes in a professional manner the same as if they were talking about a budget amendment. It was worse than being back in Duanesburg and getting upbraided in plenary session for having omitted from a previous story some audience member's oratorical eruption.

But it was all true, what I had said, and a lot more that we didn't know about yet. The Schenectady school board and the Schenectady school administration had coddled and protected a bizarre grounds worker by the name of Steve Raucci, who bullied and terrorized his subordinates and anyone else who offended his dignity. They had promoted him to the management position of supervisor of buildings and grounds even as they abolished that title and labeled him merely "head utility worker," so that he might still earn overtime pay, might continue as union leader of the workers he managed, and might also avoid having to take a Civil Service test, just as Mrs. Janiszewski had avoided such a test. They did this because Steve Raucci helped them stay in power. Come election time every year, when voters would approve or not approve the coming year's budget and would elect new or the same school board members, old Steve would round up janitors and custodians to work the phone banks at the regional headquarters of the union they all belonged to, CSEA, calling residents to urge them to vote the right way. And he would also deliver them to various local taverns like Brandon's on Van Vranken Avenue, where they would sit at a table with Janiszewski or his alter ego, Warren Snyder, and would stuff envelopes with letters from "Friends of Schenectady Schools" urging the same. "Friends of Schenectady Schools," as I discovered, was just them. It was just Janiszewski and Snyder and these hapless janitors. School boards were not allowed by law to campaign for their own budgets, so this is how they did it, behind a false front. CSEA printed the letters, and the teachers' union paid the postage, all *sub rosa*.

Janiszewski himself admitted it to me when I first got curious and inquired about the nature of these mailings. "I was certainly engaged in these democratic endeavors," he told me on the telephone, full of confidence in his powers of persuasion.

But now they were furious, all of them, that I had written it up and was writing up more of it every day as new information kept dribbling to me from disgruntled employees, including the fact that Raucci also helped the administration by seeing to it in his capacity as union president that no labor grievances ever got filed.

"None of us deserves to be dragged through the mud by our local newspaper," the superintendent, Eric Ely, declared on the school's website. He quoted his father as having said, "Believe nothing of what you read and only half of what you see," and he added, "Reading the recent editorials and newspaper stories I have come to the conclusion that, as usual, he was right," which was quite a lesson for an educator to trumpet on a school website: Don't believe anything you read.

Superintendent Ely (pronounced EE-lee)—he was beautiful in his colored shirts, his wide ties, his Midwestern accent, looking and sounding for all the world like a 1970s Ohio car salesman. But a thoroughly nasty guy, who early on forbade the school's official spokeswoman to speak to me, and when I asked him about it told me it was because "I don't like your style," though I didn't know I even had a style.

Steve Raucci's trial was yet to be held, so we didn't have all the facts yet. We didn't know yet, for just one example, that Ely had actually tipped him off to the criminal investigation of him when he learned about it through a back channel—a "heads up," Ely called it in an e-mail that was eventually introduced into evidence. He suggested to old Steve that they take a "head-on approach pretty soon," but by then it was already too late. The State Police were putting together the bits and pieces of unsolved crimes from the various towns and counties where they had occurred, crimes that had previously been investigated only by local police, and everything pointed to Raucci, "head utility worker" and chief political operative of the Schenectady City School District—this wiry sixty-year-old leaf-raker-turned-manager with curly hair and a hunted, darting look who bragged on tape about his relationship with Superintendent Ely: "He listens to me. If I tell him this is what you should do, that's what he'll do," and of whom Ely said in return, "There aren't many I trust. You are one. Thank you."

What exactly did old Steve do to land in the can and be held without bail? A jury ultimately found that he had three times vandalized the house and vehicles of Hal Gray, a subordinate, and Hal's wife, Debbie, a minor CSEA officer, mainly because he believed it was Debbie who had written a letter to her CSEA superiors saying Raucci was running his department "like something out of a gangster movie."

The first time, striking late at night when all was dark and peaceful in suburban Burnt Hills, he sprayed red paint on their house, garage, pickup truck and car, working methodically so as to ruin not only the house's siding but also the doors, windows and deck, and not only the bodies of the vehicles but also the tires, bumpers, windows and even license plates. Plus RAT in big red letters on all sides of the house. The next day he rounded up a few employees and drove them up to Burnt Hills to see his handiwork, just as a lesson to them, for which he got a mild reprimand and nothing more from the assistant superintendent.

The second time, he poured red paint on their pickup and left a note on the porch: "#2 QUIT THE

UNION AND LEAVE JOANNE ALONE," Joanne being a union comrade of Steve's and the "#2" apparently being an indication that it was the second warning.

The third time, he slopped yellow paint on the porch. The Grays had by then installed surveillance cameras, but they showed only a wiry guy springing onto the porch, his face not visible.

He punctured the tires and planted an explosive on the vehicle of the school's athletic director, Gary DiNola, because he was angry at DiNola for asking for keys to a gymnasium so coaches could get in during athletic events. Raucci had refused, just as a way of exerting his bureaucratic power. DiNola asked again, and then again. Raucci e-mailed him: "You have crossed a line with me. I am not a tolerant person to begin with. I'm even less tolerant of people who show me disrespect." It rained that night, and the cigarette left as a fuse got extinguished, so the explosive didn't go off. When DiNola reported the planting of the explosive to Superintendent Ely, Ely told him it was a police matter, not a school matter.

He surreptitiously punctured the tires and splashed paint on the vehicle of an employee who had filed a worker's compensation complaint against the school over Raucci's repeatedly grabbing his crotch as a way of bullying him.

He did another paint job and planted another explosive at the house of a woman in nearby Rensselaer County whom he didn't even know, apparently as a favor to the aforementioned Joanne, who had just ended a romantic relationship with that woman.

Several years earlier he had planted an explosive that actually went off on the front door of a house in Rotterdam as a favor to someone he knew only second-hand—a woman dispatcher for the Rotterdam police who was having a hard time with a sergeant. He left a note along with that one: "Your [sic] good at harassing our friend because she's a girl, well let's see how tough you are dealing with men." That fit, because we learned along the way that Raucci had a singular obsession with manliness and regarded sneaking around under cover of darkness, vandalizing people's homes and cars, as a righteous manifestation of it. In various tapes and documents, he described himself as "a man's man" and his activities as "street justice." Alas, he hit the wrong house in Rotterdam—he had gotten the address mixed up—so it took the police a while to figure that one out.

When old Steve was arrested he actually had an explosive device hidden in a potted plant in his office, in the school building where we now sat, and we soon learned that he commonly kept a "quarter-stick" in the glove compartment of the school pickup truck that he used. In his opening statement at the trial, Raucci's lawyer, trying to soften the evidence that he knew was coming, admitted with lawyerly ruefulness that old Steve "likes to joke with firecrackers—that's one of his faults," which did not strike me as the strongest possible defense. And indeed District Attorney Bob Carney, who prosecuted the case himself, got a lot of mileage out of debunking the comparison with firecrackers. Raucci's quarter-sticks, FBI tests showed in dramatic videos, packed 300 times the explosive power of mere firecrackers.

But what was really fascinating in my view was not so much Steve Raucci's curious idea of manliness and his paranoid defensiveness against almost everyone he dealt with, but his cozy relationship with Superintendent Ely, as well as with the director of human resources and the assistant superintendent for business. You might find a rogue employee anywhere, but where else could you find a rogue employee who was so favored by the chief executive that the chief executive would give him a heads-up on a criminal investigation or would ignore a complaint that he was trying to bomb cars? And where else could you find a director of human resources who would present this rogue employee with a photo of Marlon Brando as the Godfather? (Which was interesting, because anyone who wanted to complain about old Steve had to go through that same director of human resources). And where else could you find an assistant superintendent who would administer no more than what a secretary called a "slap on the wrist" to someone who took employees on a guided tour of vandalism he had committed?

I had become accustomed to a certain amount of moral lassitude in police departments, but nothing had prepared me or anyone else in Schenectady for a bomb-planting wacko in a school district, coddled and cozied by top administrators and sheltered by the school board itself. "I do whatever I want," Raucci wrote in a journal that he kept on his computer. "I'm like the dog that can lick himself."

Indeed, Superintendent Ely and old Steve so admired each other that not only could Ely tell Steve he was one of the few people he trusted, but old Steve could write to Superintendent Ely:

> *I have often told you that you and I are alike in many ways, we just have different backgrounds. We both like to win and we do not care how we do it as long as we win. We both tell it like it is and if someone doesn't like what we say, that's too damn bad. If we do not like someone we let them know about it and usually do something about it. There we may differ a little. According to rumors, when I don't like someone, I force them to go away or make them disappear. When you don't like someone, you have to wait until they die of old age (unless you give me their name.)*

It was beautiful, right down to the sly insinuation that if Ely needed someone taken care of, old Steve was available.

Couldn't Ely and the others have been prosecuted as some kind of accessories or enablers of Raucci's? District Attorney Carney didn't think so: "It's non-feasance or misfeasance in office, and that's an administrative matter, not a criminal matter."

As for Ely's tipping off Raucci to the State Police investigation of him, "Our conclusion was you couldn't form a criminal charge on that, because he was not privy to police information"—since he had gotten the information second-hand, from a lawyer. "It was good evidence of his bias and his protection," that's all.

So old Steve got twenty-three years to life in prison—which might seem pretty steep for vandalism in which no one got physically hurt, but first-degree arson for setting off that explosive in Rotterdam was a killer—and old Eric Ely got nothing. But at least he got fired, right? At least he got blackballed from the world of public education, right? At least he got tied to a rail, slathered with tar, decorated with feathers, and given a ride to the Schenectady city limits, right? After all, the school board of Jeff Janiszewski and his woodchucks had been disgraced and the majority of its members ousted in the next election—Janiszewski himself wisely declined to run again—so new people were in charge who had promised to clean things up and restore "transparency," as the buzzword had it.

But that's not how things worked out. Ely's contract provided that he could be fired "for cause," which could be anything the school board said it was, like maybe tipping off a rogue employee to a criminal investigation, or allowing the same rogue employee to collect $50,000 in overtime pay without any documentation showing that he had earned it. The superintendent would have the right to a hearing, but the board itself would conduct the hearing, according to rules of its own devising. A record wouldn't even have to be kept. And the board would render the final verdict, with no provision for appeal.

Yet the new board chose to buy him out instead—give him more than $100,000 to go away—rather than get enmeshed in a quasi-legal process that a good lawyer could probably have complicated endlessly. We need to think about the kids, they said. We need to move on. Put all this unpleasantness behind us. So they negotiated a deal, and the deal not only called for the payout, it also called for the board members to hide the truth from any prospective employer who might inquire down the road.

"The members of the Board of Education," said the settlement document, "agree that individually and collectively they shall make no derogatory comments about the Superintendent..." What's more, Ely himself would get to "designate two current or former Board members from the District to offer employment information," and if any other board members were contacted they would have to refer the inquirer to Ely's chosen spokespersons. And even those chosen spokespersons "shall provide an agreed-upon letter of reference," meaning Ely would get to approve even that, taking no chance that any other school district in the country would ever learn the truth about him from Schenectady's board of education, transparency or no transparency.

In the event, Ely immediately landed a superintendent's job in the small town of Southbridge, Massachusetts, without missing a day of employment, though within two years he was suspended from that job by a local board that apparently had more gumption than Schenectady's, and soon after that he resigned. The *Gazoot's* website was for paid subscribers only, so poor Southbridge couldn't find us through Google and probably didn't know what they were getting in for.

As for me, well, I could boast of having brought to the readers of the *Gazoot* some novel and entertaining facts that I discovered, as well as the larger understanding that Steve Raucci was not a lone operator but rather a key player in the way the school district was run, was in fact the "muscle" of the school district, as a colleague described him, but taken all around, it was not a performance I was especially proud of. The sorry truth was that I got several tips about old Steve's tyrannical doings before anything became public and more or less blew them off. I was still riding the energy of the invented-terror case, and by comparison complaints about a bullying utility worker in the Schenectady school system seemed almost *infra dignitatum*. I didn't care if Steve Raucci could legitimately serve as both union head and manager, which a couple of callers complained about. I didn't care how much overtime he got paid, which a couple others alerted me to, so it took me too long to realize what a splendid story this was in its own right and to get on it.

Then too, I admit I was increasingly preoccupied with matters celestial. I was ready to leave petty local matters behind, leapfrog the national and the international, and go straight to the divine. Anyone watching could have seen I was heading for destruction.

12

THE GREAT DEBATE

"We know a great many people
whose lives have been ruined because they
put too much faith in science."

Eventually I found myself on the stage of the Carl B. Taylor Auditorium at Schenectady County Community College, sitting at one end of a table with a nuclear chemist by the name of Jay Wile at the other end, and Ernie Tetrault, retired television newsman, between us as moderator, the three of us looking out over a capacity crowd of mostly teenagers, waiting for the specified hour of 7:30 p.m. to arrive. Nothing to do but wait. Nobody else was coming—nobody else could come. The place had been packed for an hour, the teenagers being Christian home-school students who had arrived that early, many of them by bus, from all over creation, to make sure they got seats and not incidentally to make sure no one else did. But the official start time was 7:30, so we sat and waited. We looked at the audience, and they looked at us.

I kept telling myself not to be nervous, but my palms were sweating, and I couldn't help it. "You're prepared," I said to myself. "You've got the answer to the Second Law of Thermodynamics. You know the flaw in Michael Behe's argument of irreducible complexity. You understand genetic drift. You know the Omphalos hypothesis that God craftily created the world already looking old. You know how to rebut the Cambrian Explosion argument about the sudden appearance of new species. You're versed on supposed gaps in the fossil record, and you know archaeopteryx like an old friend. You're ready to pounce on the contradictions in the story of Noah's Ark. You've been coached on the science by outstanding people—Ricki Lewis, a geneticist who writes college textbooks; Donald Whisenhunt, a chemist at the General Electric research center; George Shaw, professor of geology at Union College. And most importantly, you're right. Darwin's theory of evolution is supported by overwhelming evidence and is accepted by every major scientific institution in the world; 'intelligent design' is just a thin and dishonest cover for old-fashioned, backwoods, Biblical creationism."

But it didn't matter. My head was so stuffed with facts, many of them strange and unfamiliar to my non-scientific brain, that they were ricocheting around like so many atoms in a particle collider. I thought I could give a rambling five-hour lecture, possibly, with all I had learned, but could I give a punchy two-minute response in a debate? And most intimidating of all, could I do it against a guy who had a Ph.D. in chemistry and who was going to insist that the world was no more than 10,000 years old?

Heaven help me, I thought. How the devil did I get into this? But I knew. On a slow day, working out my dismal fate, I had written a column about the state of Georgia requiring stickers in its biology textbooks declaring evolution to be "a theory, not a fact," and also about schools in a town in Pennsylvania requiring the teaching of intelligent design alongside evolution. I expressed mock amazement at how little intellectual progress we had made since the Scopes trial of 1925. I said if students were going to be taught intelligent design alongside evolution they ought also be taught astrology alongside astronomy, alchemy alongside chemistry, and so forth. I scolded myself for my innocence in supposing we had left backwoods religion behind us with William Jennings Bryan, noting that forty-five percent of Americans agreed with the Gallup Poll statement, "God created human beings pretty much in their present form at one time within the last 10,000 years or so." Almost half the country! A proposition that I thought hadn't been seriously entertained outside the Ozark Mountains during my lifetime.

It was a playful effort that in upstate New York I thought might provoke a smile or two, but I was wrong. The letters started arriving in no time:

> *It is important to remember that Darwinism is a theory, and throughout scientific history many theories have been proven wrong. For those of us who*

believe in a loving creator God, the evidence is all around us. All we need to do is keep our eyes, and our mind, open. (Jim Fischer, Ballston Spa)

All of the many experiments, theories and philosophies that have been devised, down through the ages, have yet to disprove the word of God. (David R. Lewis, Schenectady)

Real science concludes that the order we see in nature requires a designer, and evolution simply doesn't require one. (Edward Razz, Ballston Lake)

...there is no mechanism for evolution. It's no surprise that there are thousands of scientists in the U.S. alone who reject evolution. (Darrin Anton, Albany)

Why are so many left-wing evolutionists so afraid of creationism? (Stephen D. Griffis, Schenectady)

Thousands of scientists all over the world, many with Ph.D. and post-doctoral research experience, completely reject the theory of evolution— every single one of these people possess [sic] more scientific information than Mr. Strock. (Stephen Bartholomew, Burnt Hills)

The world is too orderly and too perfectly put together for me to believe it was an accident. (Jill Hogan, Niskayuna)

This did not deter me. On the contrary, I was greatly encouraged. I had hit upon a subject, unlikely as it might seem at a small-time newspaper, that was both cosmic in its reach and local in its impact, and I girded my loins appropriately and strode forth onto the field of battle. I wrote column after column poking fun at fundamentalist Christianity and rebutting the angry letters that arrived in response, until finally, reacting to a letter that insisted I was ignorant of the Bible, I indulged in a rhetorical flight of my own and declared of these Christian enthusiasts, "I will meet any of them in open forum, and we'll see who's ignorant of what."

Of course, I didn't mean it, at least not literally. I was just defending my honor, but—wouldn't you know?—someone took me up on it, someone by the name of Charlie Stoker, whom I did not know, who wrote to the editor, "A friend of mine and I would like to take up Mr. Strock's challenge to an open forum debate over the Bible, Creationism vs. Darwinism, and other aspects he's attacked on the Christian faith."

Oh, boy, I thought, now what do I do? I talked it over with a few colleagues and decided I couldn't very well refuse, but I wouldn't have to make a big deal of it either. If they wanted to hold a debate in some neutral location like a fire hall or library, OK, I would do it, and we could quote the Bible back and forth to each other for half an hour, and I would explain the theory of evolution to them, based on my reading of Charles Darwin's *On the Origin of Species by Means of Natural Selection*, which I had actually read and actually loved.

But then I talked to Charlie Stoker and discovered 1) he was just a kid, and 2) his "friend," who would do the actual debating, was not some hallelujah preacher from down the street in Schenectady but Jay Wile, co-author of Charlie's homeschool biology textbook,

Exploring Creation with Biology, a 582-page opus hefty enough to prop open a church door on a stuffy day. He was the head of Apologia Educational Ministries Inc. based in Indiana, publisher of many textbooks and other educational materials—lab equipment, videos, CDs—"built on a creationist foundation," in the words of its catalog. He had a Ph.D. in nuclear chemistry from the University of Rochester, of all things. Charlie had recruited him when he saw my smart-alecky challenge, and Wile had of course accepted. "Of course," because it's no secret that Biblical creationism, or its cover, intelligent design, is in bad odor everywhere in academia except in fundamentalist Christian institutions and its proponents cannot get a hearing anywhere else. They will jump at any chance at all to debate an "evolutionist," as I learned, even if it means flying at their own expense from Indiana to New York to meet an example of the species no more distinguished or qualified than a columnist at a local newspaper whose credentials end with Biology 101, taken to meet a science requirement.

Jay Wile was very gracious about all this. I called him to feel him out, and he right away offered to let me back out, since, with the mismatch in our *bona fides*, a debate would obviously be no contest. That piqued my pride just a little, and I said, "Well, you're certainly better qualified, but on the other hand I have the advantage of being right, so maybe it will balance out." And we were on. He offered to send me his textbook and various promotional materials from his Apologia Educational Ministries so I would know what I was up against, and I in turn offered to send him the few scraps of paper that were my anti-intelligent-design columns, and thus was the challenge consummated.

But I was rattled. To exchange barbs with a local Baptist preacher would have been one thing. To go up against a guy who was simultaneously a Biblical creationist and a genuine scientist—that would be something else. It was enough to give me a clammy premonition of making a fool of myself. All I could hope to do at that point was limit the damage.

I had three months to educate myself—we had agreed on a date that far off—and I began to scramble. I reread *On the Origin of Species*, and I read *The Blind Watchmaker* by Richard Dawkins, the best exposition for the layman I have read to this day on the workings of natural selection and one that I recommend to both the beginning and the intermediate student. I prowled the Internet for creationist websites and had a hallucinatory time studying the arguments at answersingenesis.com and reasons.org, two outfits that passionately support the proposition that God created the world, evolution be damned, but just as passionately scratch at each other like alley cats over little details, like whether he did it billions of years ago or just the other day. I read bits and pieces of Jay Wile's textbook, including his introductory warning that "we know a great many people whose lives have been ruined because they put too much faith in science," and his further warning that "science will always be flawed," but "because the Bible was inspired by One who is perfect, the Bible is perfect." I studied the argument, as best I could, of Michael Behe, a professor of biology at Lehigh University, that evolution can't be true because some organisms are so "irreducibly complex" they could not have developed by stages but could only have come into existence all at once, at the hand of an unknown but indubitably intelligent designer. (I also read the disavowal of his position by the rest of the Lehigh biology department.)

I submitted Wile's textbook to the aforementioned geneticist, Ricki Lewis, who lived in nearby Glenville, and also to the aforementioned geologist, George Shaw at Union College, both of whom liberally papered it with notes saying things like, "this guy knows a lot of facts and is good at twisting things," "this is so wrong I can't bear to read it," "this entire section is absurd," "pure rhetorical obfuscation" and "classic logical error (though probably intentional, either that or he's just plain stupid)," the last of which I would actually read aloud in the debate, to a reception of dead silence.

I learned, among many other things, that intelligent design dates as far back as Thomas Aquinas in the thirteenth century but that in its modern iteration it is traceable to English Archdeacon William Paley, who in his Natural Theology of 1802 laid out that if he is walking on a heath and comes upon a watch, he knows perfectly well that it didn't land there by itself but had to have been made by some craftsman or other, and if that is true of a watch, how much more must it be true of the vastly more complex living organisms of this world?

I learned all sorts of things that I didn't know before, but two things especially impressed me. One was the utter daffiness of much of the creationist world. They had me studying matters like how to fit representatives of all the animal species of the world into a wooden boat 300 cubits (450 feet) long, which they had worked out to the finest detail, right down to the watering of the beasts, the exercising of them, and the disposal of their excrement. Even the number of them: 16,000. They had me lying awake at night contemplating counter-arguments from talkorigins.org, like the one that said the excrement couldn't just be shoved overboard because many of the animals would be below the waterline, so it would have to be carried up a deck or two, and with only 600-year-old Noah and seven of his family members on board that would be an impossible task. I felt at times like I was going nuts. (Many of the creationist calculations had been worked out by a certain "John Woodmorappe," much cited on creationist websites but identified by Wikipedia as actually Jan Peczkis, a Chicago elementary school teacher who was cashiered in 2006.) They had me considering the possibility that Noah and his contemporaries really did live to immensely ripe old ages and that God had reduced those life spans to those of today in order to "limit the spread of wickedness," as posited by Hugh Ross, Ph.D., captain and commander of Reasons to Believe. Further, with shorter lives an enzyme complex called telomerase, which correlates with cancer, does not have much chance to develop, so "by limiting the growth of cancer, and minimizing human suffering, God again showed his mercy toward the human race." Wild, fantastic stuff, earnestly rebutted by persons of science, who must have had as many sleepless nights as I did.

The other thing that impressed me was the dishonesty, not only of the out-and-out creationists but more especially of the disguised creationists, the advocates of intelligent design. They misquote, they misrepresent, they distort, they dissimulate, and they mine sources that they know are bogus, I learned to my anguish. They will snatch a fragment of a quote from a distinguished source like British philosopher Karl Popper—"Darwinism is not a testable scientific theory"—knowing full well that Popper later changed his mind and explained his admiration for Darwin's theory, and they will circulate that quote around and around until the feathers are falling off it and still not put it on the compost heap.

Wile himself, in a book of his called *Reasonable Faith*, likewise made crafty use of a quote from *The Origin of Species*. Darwin was about to explain how the eye might have evolved, but to set up the explanation he first deployed a rhetorical gambit: "To suppose that the eye, with all its inimitable contrivances for adjusting the focus to different distances, for admitting different amounts of light, and for the correction of spherical and chromatic aberration, could have been formed by natural selection, seems, I freely confess, absurd in the highest degree." Then he proceeded to show why it's not absurd. I found that quote, isolated from the explanation that followed, over and over again as I plowed through intelligent design literature. Wile concluded from it: "So we see that Charles Darwin himself agrees that his theory is hopelessly inadequate for explaining the existence of complex organs and organisms in nature."

Finally it took a trial in federal court to smoke out the intellectual bogosity of intelligent design. This was the trial to determine the constitutionality of the Dover, Pennsylvania, school board's requiring the teaching of intelligent design alongside evolution, and the star witness for the school board was none other than Professor Michael Behe of "irreducible complexity" fame who, under cross-examination, was forced to agree that "there are no peer-reviewed articles by anyone advocating for intelligent design supported by pertinent experiments or calculations which provide rigorous accounts of how intelligent design of any biological system occurred."

As for the Dover school board members who voted to require the teaching of intelligent design, Judge John E. Jones III said, "It is ironic that several of these individuals, who so staunchly and proudly touted their religious convictions in public, would time and again lie to cover their tracks and disguise the real purpose behind the ID policy."

Lie like bankers.

I wish I could have done as forceful a job as the judge when 7:30 p.m. finally arrived at Schenectady County Community College and the debate began, but I felt like I had lockjaw. Jay Wile, boyishly handsome under a thatch of iron hair, was as smooth as a television weatherman, and I was as stiff as a Presbyterian deacon, notwithstanding the eye-dazzler bow tie I had chosen. I was not at all helped by the youthfully exuberant audience that either groaned or remained deathly silent at my best lines and cheered joyfully at every inanity uttered by their hero, my adversary. I knew I was in trouble right away, during my opening statement, when I said Jay was not a real scientist because he claimed to know the truth in advance, contained as it was in his "perfect book," and held up a Bible I had brought along as a prop, and the kids cheered, not at my perspicacity but at the sight and mention of the Holy Bible.

I had labored on my opening statement a long time, and it sounded like it. Wile opened with an exuberant and seemingly spontaneous tribute to the Ampullae of Lorenzini, a cluster of cells in the shark's nervous system, which I had no more idea of than I had of the Purex method of extracting plutonium from nitric acid: "These cells sample electromagnetic fields that are coursing through the water...the Ampullae of Lorenzini select all these electromagnetic fields, send the information to the brain, the shark's brain is able to filter them all out, and let's suppose the shark wants a flounder today, it looks at all those electromagnetic fields, gets rid of anything that doesn't mean flounder, then triangulates the position of the source of those electromagnetic fields, finds the precise location in three-dimensional space, and the shark goes and eats the flounder. Now, these Ampullae of Lorenzini are more compact, more precise, have a wider range of detection, and consume significantly less energy than the best electronic field sensor that human technology can make," and so forth, all of which he rattled off the top of his head with the vivacity of a hopped-up radio jock delivering the morning traffic report: "Fender-bender on the I-890 interchange—watch out for the curiosity factor there—it's backing up all the way to Exit 4..." It was merely William Paley's watchmaker argument restated, but all I could think as I waited my turn was, "Ampalini Lorenzelli? Lorenzini of Ampuzetti? What the devil is he throwing at me?" All the exotic dishes I had sampled in my preparations, and here was one I never encountered.

I knew by now that intelligent design advocates tried to minimize their religious commitment and pretend they were concerned only with science, so I tried to steer him to the Bible. I asked him in what order God created human beings and animals, figuring the Bible was his "paradigm," which was a word he liked, and he ought to be able to defend it. It was a trick question, since as any reader outside of a Pentecostal Sunday school knows, there are actually two versions of the creation story in Genesis. In the first one, God creates man and woman at the end, on the sixth day, after he's done with the plants and animals, while in the second version, he creates man first, then the plants and animals, and then finally woman, out of man's rib.

Jay Wile seemed unaware of this. His first hesitant answer was, "Uh, the animals first, then man," but when I pointed out to him the discrepancy he recovered like a champion. "It was written in Hebrew," he said, "and there's nothing in Hebrew to indicate sequence...You tell the story in chronological order and then go back and concentrate on the main character, it's a standard storytelling technique." The audience cheered and applauded.

I tried to trip him up on the Flood, with the same miserable results. Did it last forty days, as stated first, or 150 days, as stated next, or some garbled version of seven months and seventeen days as stated next, or fifty-four days as stated finally?

At first he said, "I'm not sure how long the Flood lasted," which I thought was amazing, though no one else did, but then again he recovered and began reading from Genesis itself, rattling it off and declaring with great verve, "This makes perfect sense, it doesn't give you different times, it just tells you how things are going on... this is clear chronology." The auditorium cheered again.

He steered me back to his preferred terrain: "In science you go by the data...for example, there's only one theory that correctly predicts the value of planetary magnetic fields in the solar system. Two of those planets were predicted seven years before they were measured. When the planetary magnetic fields were finally measured it was the young-earth prediction that was right on the money, it was the old-earth prediction that was off by a factor of 10,000."

I had no clue. I was up on hundreds of obscure and arcane matters, but I had missed planetary magnetic fields.

When we got to questions from the audience, most people wanted to make speeches and deliver sermons, and Ernie, the moderator, had to keep demanding, "What is your question?" They were really fired up. Questions ran along the lines of, "Why would science ignore the fact that there are *Tyrannosaurus rex* tracks and hominid tracks in the same rock?" Though one fellow did ask Wile, "If God is perfectly omnipotent and omniscient, how do you explain that a baby is born deficient? Did God make a mistake?" A classic tough one, you might think, worthy of any medieval scholastic, but Jay from Indiana handled it with aplomb: "No, God doesn't make mistakes. And I take exception if someone says a handicapped child is less than perfect," which elicited still more applause. All children are perfect, bless them. I came up with withering responses to all these statements of his—the next day, gnashing my teeth at home.

The high point from my wife's perspective was our being escorted out the back door by a security guard at the conclusion of the festivities and put into our car, which had been parked there by pre-arrangement for a quick getaway, before the Christians could lynch us. She thought that was very classy.

Then came the letters:

> *I was proud of our Schenectady young people and their unshaken faith.* (Wanda Knapp, Voorheesville)
>
> *Hitler would have been proud of Strock's continual "appeal-to-the-majority fallacy," saying "all" and "every" scientist and university disagreed with Wile, so he had to be wrong.* (Jeff Minniear, Schenectady)

It was a grim experience, and it did nothing to endear evangelical Christians to me. Of course, Christians were not alone in their preference for Scripture over science. About the same time as our debate, ultra-Orthodox Jews in the Jerusalem neighborhood of Mea Shearim, which I had never heard of, posted an open letter denouncing a certain rabbi-scientist, declaring,

"He believes the world is millions of years old—all nonsense!" and insisting the rabbi should "burn all his writings." Muslims likewise. "There are people who say that long ago man was a monkey and he evolved. Is this true? Is there any evidence?" was a question posted on the website islamonline.com. The answer was, "Praise be to Allah. This view is not correct, and the evidence for that is that Allah has described in the Qur'an the stages of the creation of Adam." But it was Christians who were leading the way in the land of the free, and it was Christians who were keeping me on my toes in Schenectady, so it was Christians I concentrated on. Praise the angels in heaven, I thought, and pass the Ampullae of Lorenzini.

13

GUNS, GOD AND GREED

*"God and guns were part of the foundation
of this country."*

"God wants you to be rich."

They were a bunch, these Christians. My favorite event indicative of their thinking happened not in Schenectady but in Colorado Springs, Colorado, at the New Life Church, a so-called megachurch that had been founded by my favorite televangelist, Ted Haggard, president of the National Association of Evangelicals, before he was discovered to have a fondness for crystal meth and male prostitutes. Some madman who had already killed two church members at a camp and two more people just outside the church burst into the church itself during a service, armed and shooting. A volunteer security guard inside, a woman, shot him and dropped him, which was well and good, except that she then thanked God for steadying her hand, and the pastor praised her for saving a great many lives, which she no doubt did.

I checked the church's website to confirm what I suspected, that the church regarded the Bible as "the authoritative Word of God, inspired, infallible and inerrant," just as every evangelical church regards it, so then I wondered in print, what about the much-quoted injunction from Jesus to "love your enemies" and to "turn the other cheek"? How does that play? How can you say the Bible is inspired, infallible and inerrant and then ignore one of its most famous teachings? How can you call yourself a Bible-believing Christian if you gun down your enemies? And how can you thank God for his assistance? I also quoted readers' responses to the original story in *The Denver Post*, like, "My problem is how in the heck God helped her kill this guy when He could have prevented it in the first place," which I thought was a fair question. And I also thought it fair to ask, if God steadied the hand of the security guard, who steadied the hand of the attacker when he was shooting the first four people?

You would have thought I had danced a jig with the devil. "A bigoted old man," one letter-writer called me, promising never to read my column again. Others were overflowing with theological explanations:

> *Mr. Strock failed to grasp what Jesus meant concerning "turning the other cheek."*
> *This passage in the Sermon on the Mount has to do with responding to personal insult. The use of force by the security guard in the Colorado church*

shooting had nothing to do with personal affront. Force was used to preserve life.

Justice is not a heathen idea that is incongruent with the ethics of Christianity. To assert such a viewpoint is to misunderstand men and women of faith who serve in the military, in law enforcement and on the bench in the judicial system—who may be called upon to take a life to preserve life.

Justice and love are both integral to the Christian faith. It would have been selfish, and not loving, for the guard to turn a deaf ear or stand idly by when it was in her power to stop the bloodshed.

At the moment of the shooting, it was not a question of acting contrary to one's faith (as Strock suggested), but rather a question of being courageous or cowardly. Thankfully, for the sake of others, she was brave. (Wayne Brandow, pastor, Bible Baptist Church, Galway)

This teaching [turn the other cheek] *is given in the context of seeking revenge. We are not to retaliate against another when they seek to hurt us. The difference is motivation. The security guard did not aim her gun for purpose of "payback" but to protect others from harm.* (Mary Beth Knapp, Princetown)

The same writer also had an explanation for why God didn't stop the madman in the first place:

God gives us the freedom to choose how we will behave. The gunman did not want God to stop him, he chose to act the way he did. The security guard did ask God to help her. Ultimately, God did intervene, and stopped the gunman through the actions of the guard who sought his help. God gives us the freedom to choose to follow him—or not.

Another writer, apparently a scholar, submitted:

> *A little investigation will show that in ancient Near Eastern societies, a slap on the cheek with the back of the hand expressed a severe form of public dishonor. Thus, by "turning the other cheek" Jesus tells his disciples to forgo retaliation and forfeit payback in deference to showing restraint toward the accuser. Strock's literal interpretation takes none of this into account.*
>
> *Hence, his complaint against Christians who see no inconsistency between "turning the other cheek," which discourages personal vengeance, and "protecting the innocent," which encourages public justice, strikes me as pure bluster. No inconsistency exists, and to say so merely invites another joust with the straw man.*
> (Jeff Kimble, Scotia)

It was like intelligent design all over again—they made up whatever suited their purpose. There was nothing in the Sermon on the Mount or anywhere else in the New Testament about distinguishing between personal affront and preserving life. Nothing about it being OK to kill someone in order to save innocent life. No exception made for the military or law enforcement. Jesus's instruction was clear and unequivocal:

Ye have heard that it hath been said, An eye for an eye, and a tooth for a tooth. But I say unto you, That ye resist not evil; but whosoever shall smite thee on thy right cheek, turn to him the other also... Ye have heard that it hath been said, Thou shalt love thy neighbor, and hate thine enemy. But I say unto you, Love your enemies, bless them that curse you, do good to them that hate you, and pray for them that despitefully use you, and persecute you...(Matthew 5:38–44)

An extremely inconvenient and, one might argue, impractical instruction, possibly even immoral—don't resist evil!—and clearly these Christians didn't buy it. But rather than just say no, that won't serve, they bent themselves into all kinds of pretzel shapes to explain it away with made-up interpretations that had nothing to do with the Bible itself. Pure rationalizations that would allow them to go on shooting their enemies just as heathens do, the Bible be damned, so to speak.

It got so far out that the New Bethel Church in Louisville, Kentucky, actually invited its parishioners to bring their guns to an "open-carry celebration," the pastor declaring, "God and guns were part of the foundation of this country." They trumpeted Biblical passages that suited their convenience, like the famous bit about homosexuality being an abomination, and either ignored or explained away other passages, like "love your enemies," which might have suited them when they were advertising the beauties of Christianity but emphatically did not suit them when they were being shot at. They picked arguments off the wall, like "the gunman did not want God to stop him," when the question is not what the gunman wanted but what God wanted. I had fine sport with this, to the point of indelicacy, almost, mocking their hypocrisy,

So when a discussion got going in the newspaper about gay marriage, and one believer wrote in to say, "If people would dust off their Bibles and look up Leviticus 18:22 they would discover how God feels about homosexuality and punishes sin" (Gerolene Snavely, Malta), I couldn't resist coming back with more rules from Leviticus besides the one that says if a man lies with another man as with a woman it's an abomination, which is what Chapter 18, Verse 22 says. Chapter 20, Verse 13 says not only that it's an abomination but that both men should be put to death. Why didn't anyone cite that? Why so selective? Did they take the Bible as the word of God or not? Chapter 24, Verse 16 says someone who blasphemes the name of the Lord should also be put to death. Chapter 19, Verse 28 forbids tattoos. Deuteronomy 22:20–21 says if a bride is found on her wedding night not to be a virgin, the men of town should take her the next morning to her father's door and stone her to death. And so on. Everyone knows this stuff, but believers have a remarkable ability to just turn their knowledge on and off as the occasion requires and to pick and choose the quotes that suit them.

Then there was Dr. Laura Schlesinger, a radio gabber specializing in personal advice, an Orthodox Jew, at least for a time, guided by Holy Scripture, who condemned homosexuality on the familiar grounds of Leviticus 18:22 and who thereby prompted some unheralded wit to write her the following letter, which circulated widely on the Internet:

Dear Dr. Laura:

Thank you for doing so much to educate people regarding God's Law. I have learned a great deal from your show, and try to share that knowledge with as many people as I can. When someone tries to defend the homosexual lifestyle, for example, I simply remind them that Leviticus 18:22 clearly states it to be an abomination. End of debate. I do need some advice from you, however, regarding some of the other specific laws and how to follow them:

When I burn a bull on the altar as a sacrifice, I know it creates a pleasing odor for the Lord—-Leviticus 1:9. The problem is my neighbors. They claim the odor is not pleasing to them. Should I smite them?

I would like to sell my daughter into slavery, as sanctioned in Exodus 21:7. In this day and age, what do you think would be a fair price for her?

I know that I am allowed no contact with a woman while she is in her period of menstrual uncleanliness—Leviticus 15:19–24. The problem is, how do I tell? I have tried asking, but most women take offense.

Leviticus 25:44 states that I may indeed possess slaves, both male and female, provided they are purchased from neighboring nations. A friend of mine claims that this applies to Mexicans, but not Canadians. Can you clarify? Why can't I own Canadians?

I have a neighbor who insists on working on the Sabbath. Exodus 35:2 clearly states he should be put to death. Am I morally obligated to kill him myself?

A friend of mine feels that even though eating shellfish is an abomination—Leviticus 11:10—it is a lesser abomination than homosexuality. I don't agree. Can you settle this?

Leviticus 21:20 states that I may not approach the altar of God if I have a defect in my sight. I have to admit that I wear reading glasses. Does my vision have to be 20/20, or is there some wiggle room here?

Most of my male friends get their hair trimmed, including the hair around their temples, even though this is expressly forbidden by Leviticus 19:27. How should they die?

I know from Leviticus 11:6–8 that touching the skin of a dead pig makes me unclean, but may I still play football if I wear gloves?

My uncle has a farm. He violates Leviticus 19:19 by planting two different crops in the same field, as does his wife by wearing garments made of two different kinds of thread (cotton/polyester blend). He also tends to curse and blaspheme a lot. Is it really necessary that we go to all the trouble of getting the whole town together to stone them?— Leviticus 24:10–16. Couldn't we just burn them to death at a private family affair like we do with people who sleep with their in-laws? (Leviticus 20:14)

I know you have studied these things extensively, so I am confident you can help. Thank you again for reminding us that God's word is eternal and unchanging.

Your devoted fan,

Many names have been attached to this masterpiece as it has moved around, but the author has never been firmly identified, as far as I know, which is a great shame, since whoever it is certainly deserves a prize of some sort, and I for one would be happy to bestow it personally. Maybe a Bible bound in pigskin?

Every year I enjoyed the National Day of Prayer, an event founded by Christian evangelicals that shares national headquarters with Focus on the Family and is chaired by Shirley Dobson, wife of James Dobson, both stalwarts of the conservative Christian movement. I would attend the festivities either on the steps of Schenectady City Hall or on the lawn of the Capitol building in Albany, and took pleasure, in my column, in quoting the Bible to them, as follows:

And when thou prayest, thou shalt not be as the hypocrites are: for they love to pray standing in the synagogues and in the corners of the streets, that they may be seen of men. Verily I say unto you, They have their reward. But thou, when thou prayest, enter into thy closet, and when thou hast shut thy door, pray to thy Father which is in secret; and thy Father which seeth in secret shall reward thee openly. (Matthew 6:5–6)

Like water off a duck's back. Didn't bother them a bit. They pretended to ecumenism too, the leaders of the national organizing task force, declaring, "People with other theological and philosophical views are, of course, free to organize and participate in activities that are consistent with their own beliefs," meaning they could get up their own day of prayer if they wanted to, but to be a volunteer on the national task force you had to sign a statement declaring, "I believe the Holy Bible is the inerrant Word of the Living God," which was the part I loved. You had to believe the Bible was the perfect word of God, but you had to ignore the exhortation in Matthew 6:5–6. You had to actually *organize* people to pray in public, like the hypocrites of old, so others could see you, which was the whole point of the National Day of Prayer.

The event in Schenectady was always small, but in Albany, in the park behind the Capitol, it was a big deal, with politicians falling over each other to get to the microphone and declare their enthusiasm for supernatural communication—"I pray every morning when I get up," promised Mayor Jerry Jennings. Catholic and Protestant clergymen led prayers for them, for the state legislature, for the military and even for the media (which made me duck for cover), as a limousine circled the park with a billboard mounted on its roof saying JESUS in 1920s show-biz lettering.

It was wonderful for anyone who had the least sense of irony. As wonderful as the Prosperity Gospel preached by such luminaries of the Bible circuit as Joel Osteen, Joyce Meyer and President George W. Bush's own spiritual advisor, Kirbyjon Caldwell, with their millions of followers. Their message: "God wants you to be rich," as summed up by one of the early Prosperity preachers, Jim Bakker, before he went to prison for fraud. And they lived it, too. Joel Osteen, who held services in an 18,000-seat arena in Houston, lived in a home valued at $1.3 million. Joyce Meyer of Missouri, who traveled in a private jet, said, "There's no need for us to apologize for being blessed." Kirbyjon Caldwell, an investment banker and bond trader before turning to the Christian ministry, wrote a bestseller, *The Gospel of Good Success: A Road Map to Spiritual, Emotional and Financial Wholeness*. The exquisitely named Creflo Dollar of Atlanta, founder of Christian World Changers Ministries, was proud owner of two Rolls Royces.

How did they do this in light of the celebrated instruction from Jesus, "Lay not up for yourselves treasure upon earth but lay up for yourselves treasures in heaven," and his statement that "It's easier for a camel to go through the eye of a needle than for a rich man to enter into the kingdom of God," and his further instruction, "If thou wilt be perfect, go and sell that thou hast and give to the poor"? Easy, as I discovered. They leafed through the Bible until they found a line that suited them—in this case, the greeting at the beginning of a letter from someone named John to someone named Gaius, neither further identified: "Beloved, I wish above all things that thou mayest prosper and be in health, even as thy soul prospereth." (3 John 2) In other words, Dear Gaius, I hope you're doing well. That was the basis for their saying God wants you to be rich, that was the

Biblical foundation for the "prosperity" label. It was enough to give an ordinary mortal a headache, and I had a merry time with it, further advancing my reputation as a basher of Christianity.

The leading embodiment of the Prosperity Gospel in the suburbs around Albany and Schenectady was Buddy Cremeans, known as Pastor Buddy, an immigrant from North Carolina who set up shop in a mall on Route 9 north of Albany and called it Northway Fellowship, for the highway that ran parallel to Route 9 with which many residents identified, thinking of themselves as living near a certain number exit. Pastor Buddy eschewed the tailored elegance of Joel Osteen but preached pretty much the same message, which was basically self-improvement; he just did it with his shirttail out. He was funky. He'd show up at a grand event, like his Easter service at the biggest civic center in the area, called at the time the Pepsi Arena, and you would think he was one of the janitors—shabby jeans, sneakers, spiky gelled hair, shirttail out—but it was him, Pastor Buddy, and 3,000 or 4,000 people would be there to hear him: "Jesus said, I can change your relationships, I can change your financial situation, I can even change your health." Any old thing he could make up on the fly, laid at the doorstep of the Lord and Savior. He would pace back and forth, or around in circles, very intent on explaining how "Jesus wants you to rise above mediocrity, Jesus wants you to rise to a new level." Old-fashioned Methodist or Presbyterian churches would have killed for the kind of following he had, all those middle-aged shopping-mall crawlers, clerks and data-entry specialists from the halls of state government filing into "the Pepsi" on Easter morning.

Pastor Buddy's teenage son got into the game also, with the same down-home enthusiasm. I was in a dressing room once, before a boxing match in Albany, when he led a prayer for a local fighter who was about to get in the ring. "God is in your corner," he promised with head bowed and eyes closed. "So let's go out there and kick ass!" Success of all kinds, that was the message. Jesus could do it, you can do it too.

I used to wonder that this new fervent brand of Christianity was so richly populated with scoundrels, people who rolled their eyes over Jesus while fleecing the flock, or inveighed against homosexuality while practicing it, or went into ecstasies over family values but slunk around sleazy motels on the side. People like Rev. Ted Haggard, who was finally ousted by his church's board of overseers for "sexually immoral conduct." The very head of the National Association of Evangelicals.

Or Claude Allen, President George W. Bush's domestic policy advisor, a born-again believer and prominent member of the Covenant Life Church in Gaithersburg, Maryland, who was arrested for switching goods and receipts at Target stores so as to get refunds for things he didn't actually return, which he explained by saying he had suffered a "loss of perspective."

Or Ralph Reed, boyish-looking executive director of the Christian Coalition, exposed as taking more than $1 million in fees to lobby against the expansion of casinos in Louisiana and marshaling anti-gambling Christians for that purpose without disclosing that he was working for other casinos, which were simply trying to beat back the competition.

Or Tom DeLay, born-again Republican ex-leader of the House of Representatives, who boasted that God "is using me all the time, everywhere, to stand up for a Biblical worldview in everything that I do and everywhere I am," and was convicted of money laundering.

Or good old Jim Bakker—if you remember him from his glory days with Tammy Faye on their "Praise the Lord" television show—who made millions from a theme park and resort until he was sent to prison for fraud.

Or Jimmy Swaggart, who called the Bakker scandal "a cancer on the body of Christ" until he was photographed skulking in and out of a motel room used by a prostitute and was defrocked by the Assemblies of God.

Or George Rekers, co-founder with James Dobson of the Family Research Council and author of *Growing Up Straight: What Families Should Know About Homosexuality*, who was photographed returning from a European vacation with a young fellow from rentboy.com.

But then I began to think, is all of this possible because evangelical Christianity is actually *founded* on dishonesty, gushing over the Bible while at the same time trampling on the greater part of it? A delicious thought. Judge Jones in the intelligent design case in Pennsylvania said it was ironic that school board members who touted their religious beliefs would time and again lie, and now I was beginning to think it wasn't ironic at all. It was perfectly consistent, the religious beliefs themselves being a hodgepodge of lies, contradictions and self-deception.

"We assume that by virtue of being bad we are at least safe from being hypocrites," wrote Robert Frost. These Christians demolished the assumption. There was, for example, the little disparity between Christian love and the vision of the future offered up by Rapture enthusiasts, a vision captured in the wildly popular "Left Behind" series of books by Tim LaHaye, a Christian conspiracy theorist, and Jerry Jenkins, a novelist. Never mind love. The whole point of these books was a gloating over the victory of believers, who would soon get whooshed up to heaven to be with Jesus, and the defeat of non-believers, who would get left behind on the awful final day and be consigned to hell. This was not some marginal and obscure vision among snake handlers at a gospel fellowship in Tennessee. By the time I got around to the books, they had already sold an astounding 63 million copies and had spawned three movies and a video game. Seven of the titles had been No. 1 bestsellers on *The New York Times* list. It was popular American Christianity, even if it was denounced by so-called mainstream churches like the Lutheran, whose Commission on Theology and Church Relations declared the Rapture vision "contrary to the teaching of Holy Scripture," and even if secular people had little awareness of it. I gave a talk about the books to the Friends of the Albany Public Library, a group of people largely liberal and of course well read, and found that not only had none of them read the books, none of them had even heard of them.

The vision was comical, based on a couple of snatches of scripture written when early Christians believed the end of the world was at hand, but the essential self-satisfaction—we're going to heaven, you're going to hell—was really nothing out of the ordinary. The "statement of faith" of any evangelical church says something like the one published by the aforementioned New Life Church in Colorado Springs:

> *Heaven is the eternal dwelling place for all believers in the gospel of Jesus Christ...After living one life on earth, the unbelievers will be judged by God and sent to hell where they will be eternally tormented with the devil and the fallen angels.*

It's straight Christianity, going back to the third-century doctrine of no salvation outside the church (*extra Ecclesiam nula salus*). In its heart it's about the farthest remove from love you can imagine, and I was happy to explain it in my modest little corner of the *Gazoot*. Not just explain it but hammer and bang on it with devilish gusto. I thought I was performing a service, even if I was venturing somewhat beyond the normal territory of a local columnist.

> *How many times does Strock have to attempt to pick apart Christianity and make all Christians out to be idiots? We get the point—he thinks Christians are stupid, ignorant and blind to the truth. Guess what? I think the same about him, so please, stop it! I have never heard Strock slander any other religion in his column, so it's not as if he is fairly beating up anyone who believes in a higher power—he purposely picks out only Christians.* (Jeremy Kergel, Ballston Lake)

Had some of his conclusions about Christians... been directed inclusively to another major faith— Orthodox Jews, Muslims, or to a minority subculture, there would be an outcry. (Reverend David H. Brown, former president, Capital District Association of Evangelicals)

He likes to attack Christians, or at least the televised Christian evangelists. I was surprised he took the time to use the term "assorted Christian gasbags" in his March 13 column on Eliot Spitzer. Shouldn't he give equal time to attacking other religions? Shouldn't he be more balanced in his attacks? He could have attacked Jews over the Spitzer scandal. After all, Eliot Spitzer is Jewish...I think the Gazette should request that Strock balance his hatreds. (Richard Vale, Schenectady)

He would not be able to redirect his inflammatory comments about Christians toward Jews without being labeled anti-Semitic, calling their beliefs "hokum" and so forth...I suspect that he would never single out moralistic, Hasidic Jews as closed-minded, exclusive hatemongers, or insensitive, or infer that their beliefs were "hokum." He would be called anti-Semitic. People would be asking to have his column removed from the paper, or at least be asking, if not demanding, for an apology. (Dave Hart, Cohoes)

Good points, I had to admit, though I thought I had an answer: "This great country of ours is awash in revivalist, evangelical, fundamentalist Christianity as it is not awash in any other religion. You can hardly drive a road in this country without seeing a billboard advertising Jesus." As for New York Governor Eliot Spitzer being Jewish, I replied that that was merely "incidental" to his patronizing high-priced call girls.

Furthermore:

> *Orthodox Jews, whatever the quaintness of their beliefs, don't browbeat the rest of us into accepting those beliefs. Nobody is lobbying Congress to outlaw the mixing of meat and milk...so why should I make fun of Jews? It's not comparable at all...I do grant: It would be in poor taste for me, as a Gentile, simply because of the long and gruesome history of Jewish persecution, whereas, having been raised more or less as a Christian, I feel freer to rag on those of that persuasion.*

So I wrote, and I thought it was a good defense. I did not appreciate the prescience of the letter writers. How could I, innocent that I was?

14

THE TEA PARTY

*"I'll keep my guns, freedom and money.
You can keep the change."*

When President Obama visited Hudson Valley Community College in Troy, next door to Schenectady, I judged I would do better to hang out in the street with the expected demonstrators than to go inside and listen to a teleprompted speech, and I was right. It was my first face-to-face encounter with the Angry Ones, as I had been calling them in print—all those righteous Americans who were fairly seething at big government—and I treasure it to this day.

"Sick of your lies, sick of your taxes, sick of your stealing, sick of your cheating, sick of your double-dealing, sick of your big government, sick of your B.S.," read the most detailed sign that I made note of. It was held by a sixty-four-year-old citizen from Pittsfield, Massachusetts, who told me, when I asked him, that the first time he had come out to protest all these outrages was just a few months previously. Meaning, he had lived through the Vietnam War, Watergate, the Iran-Contra scandal, the weapons-of-mass-destruction hoax, and just now, shortly after Barack Obama took office, he had finally hit the streets.

"What took you so long?" I asked him.

"I just got fed up," he said.

Yeah, right, I thought. You had no problem with big pernicious government until a black, or more accurately, a mixed-race Democrat became president and proposed a larger government role in health care, and then you had a fit. You didn't object to the squandering of hundreds of thousands of lives and hundreds of billions of dollars in futile wars based on lies, but you are so enraged by a health care plan that now, at the advanced age of sixty-four, you take Magic Marker to posterboard, drive forty miles to Troy, and plant yourself by the side of Vandenburg Avenue to display your indignation.

I was to find this over and over, but right now it was still new to me, this understanding that there was something more to the Angry Ones' anger than they owned up to. It was so wild, it was so irrational. When the local congressman, Paul Tonko, a Democrat, held a town hall meeting to answer questions about Obama's health care plan, the first question from the heckling audience was, "If the plan fails, will congressmen be willing to be executed?" You knew there was more to it than a healthy mistrust of government.

I went through the same thing with a former supervisor of Duanesburg and his business partner, who graciously invited me to a demonstration in Washington for which they had chartered a bus. (I thought I was finished with Duanesburg, but I couldn't shake it.) More than a march, a big "Liberty XPO Symposium," billed as "the largest conservative event in history." I asked them what their beef was that led them to this protest event, and the former supervisor said the usual: "Government is out of control, it's large, and it doesn't really listen to the people." He gave as an example "159 new government agencies" to administer Obamacare, which was one of the urban myths circulating on the Internet at the time. His business partner said, "Out-of-control spending, borrowing, printing money by the government." But I found with them, just as I found with the Troy demonstrators, that the first time they had publicly expressed their anger was when President Obama took office, even though they were both of advanced years. So I didn't believe them any more than I believed the others.

None of them in what was being called the Tea Party truly disliked big government. In fact, they liked big government very much when it was bombing other countries, torturing prisoners, or rounding up suspicious-looking immigrants. It was only when government was being benevolent—providing health care to poor people—that they had a fit. And when it was doing that under the leadership of a smooth-talking, dark-skinned, smart guy with an African-Muslim name they hated it so bad they wanted to burst. Little by little I could see that, and I wrote many an entertaining column accordingly—at least I thought they were entertaining. The Angry Ones themselves demurred.

I talked to a member of the National Rifle Association contingent at the Troy demonstration while Obama was inside speechifying about economic development, and he told me, as the others did also, that he was against socialism and for freedom. But it turned out he worked for the state Department of Transportation, which, as you might guess, takes tax money obtained disproportionately from rich people and builds roads and bridges for everyone equally. A socialist operation if ever there was one. I asked him his name, so I could report him to Fox News to see if they would "out" him, but he wouldn't tell me. Maybe he had skipped work for the day so he could protest socialism, and he didn't want his supervisors to know.

"I'll keep my guns, freedom and money. You can keep the change" was one of the bumper stickers in evidence, and I thought it was telling. The Angry Ones were very big on freedom, but when you pressed them, that's always what it boiled down to, keeping their money—meaning not paying taxes—and keeping their guns. There was never anything noble about it.

"Forced charity is thievery," one of them explained to me when I asked about paying taxes for the general good, reciting a *bon mot* of the movement. I shouldn't have been surprised that at the same time he lectured me about the saving power of Jesus.

"Their ideal," I wrote, "seems to be the lone ignoramus standing in the door of his cabin with a shotgun in the crook of his arm, scowling out at the world." I should have added a Bible to the picture, but I didn't think of it at the moment. The Angry Ones themselves didn't like to make too much of their religious motivation. They liked to talk about the Constitution and let on to purely secular concerns—excessive spending and that sort of thing—but a survey done by a couple of academics, David E. Campbell and Robert D. Putnam, found that the second-strongest indicator of Tea Party support, after being a Republican, was a desire to "see religion play a prominent role in politics."

"The Tea Party's generals may say their overriding concern is a smaller government, but not their rank and file, who are more concerned about putting God in government," they concluded. Which was no surprise if you were on the ground with these people. I remember the fellow at another demonstration, this one at the Corning Preserve in Albany on the banks of the Hudson River, who was holding a poster bearing the Ten Commandments, with the note at the bottom, "America's Moral Foundation." I always got a kick out of people being devoted to the Ten Commandments as guideposts to moral behavior, and I couldn't help calling this fellow's attention to Commandment No. 2, which said, on his poster, "Thou Shalt Not Make Unto Thee Any Graven Image."

"That's a very important one," I said. "Where would America be without that as part of our moral foundation?" But like so many Angry Ones, he suffered from Irony Deficit Disorder, and my attempt at humor went for naught.

The game was called, I thought, when the Angry Ones went berserk over empathy, if anyone still remembers that. President Obama had a Supreme Court seat to fill, and he declared, "I will seek someone who understands that justice isn't about some abstract legal theory or footnote in a casebook; it is also about how our laws affect the daily realities of people's lives, whether they can make a living and care for their families, whether they feel safe in their homes and welcome in their own nation. I view that quality of empathy, of understanding and identifying with people's hopes and struggles, as an essential ingredient for arriving at just decisions and outcomes."

An utterly innocuous statement, one might think, not to say a complete snoozer, but how the Angry Ones exploded:

"Crazy nonsense, empathetic!" roared Michael Steele, national chairman of the Republican Party, on his radio show. "I'll give you empathy. Empathize right on your behind!"

"We cannot sit by and allow this to happen," harrumphed the American Conservative Union.

"Empathy leads you to very bad decisions, many times," declared Glenn Beck on his Fox News program, as he cited Hitler's supposedly empathetic decision to kill a sick child as the first step toward the murder of six million people.

You might think in a civilized country a public figure would be embarrassed to belittle so fine a sentiment as empathy, almost like belittling bravery or generosity, especially if the public figure is a self-advertised Christian, but that turned out not to be so. Public figures representing the Angry Ones evinced nothing but contempt for Obama's proposed criterion for a Supreme Court justice.

Nor did they forget what he had said in a speech to Planned Parenthood two years earlier: "We need somebody who's got the heart, the empathy to recognize what it's like to be a young teenaged mom; the empathy to understand what it's like to be poor or African American or gay or disabled or old. And that's the criteria [sic] by which I'm going to be selecting my judges." Which was even worse. Not just empathy in general but empathy specifically for the poor and downtrodden, the very people that the Angry Ones scorn, as I was gradually learning. (If you wanted non-stop putdowns of gays, illegal immigrants and especially welfare recipients, you had only to tune in to Rush Limbaugh or the pundits of Fox News.)

When it emerged that Yassin Aref and Mohammed Hossain in Albany had been duped by the FBI and had not, on their own, done anything remotely connected with terrorism, I naively expected that the people who professed hatred of big intrusive government would rally to their defense, but no such thing happened. The people who rallied were your old-line civil libertarians, suburban mothers for peace, and liberals in general. Not a conservative among them. Not a single one who claimed to have put up with big bad government all his life until suddenly being awakened to its dangers by Barack Obama. And the same with Family Court. At one Tea Party demonstration I suggested to a genuine libertarian—Kevin McCashion of the New York Libertarian Council, as opposed to merely a right-wing Republican—that I would put more stock in the Tea Party's professed animus to big government if they would picket outside Family Court to protest the governmental snatching of children. That's the level at which government really intrudes in people's lives, I said, and he agreed with me, but nothing ever came of it. When it came to governmental bullying of poor or marginal people, whether by a sheriff in Arizona, the FBI in Albany, or Family Court and Child Protective Services in Schenectady, I found that the Angry Ones were indifferent. When I asked them at various events what they were angry about, not one of them ever mentioned those genuine governmental intrusions. What they cared about was taxes. Taxes and guns. They were a selfish, belligerent bunch, and I had a swell time pillorying them. That many of them were self-righteously Christian, forever insisting that the United States was a Christian country, added to the pleasure. Their dishonesty as Tea Pots formed a continuum with their dishonesty as followers of Jesus, I figured.

As for empathy, I couldn't help but note that its absence appears to be one of the constants of psychopathy. Our friend, the *Diagnostic and Statistical Manual of Mental Disorders*, so characterizes it and puts the condition under anti-social personality disorders. A psychiatrist who worked in the 1930s, Hervey Cleckley, described psychopaths as "charming and intelligent, unreliable, dishonest, irresponsible, self-centered, emotionally shallow, and lacking in empathy and insight." The current leading authority on the subject, Robert Hare of the University of British Columbia, scores his psychopathic test subjects on a range of qualities that include "parasitic lifestyle, pathological lying, conning, proneness to boredom, shallow emotions, lack of empathy, poor impulse control, promiscuity and irresponsibility," the constant being lack of empathy. Some of the qualities that go along with the lack of empathy are interesting too, when you think about entertainers like Beck and Limbaugh. The DSM-4 says psychopaths typically demonstrate "inflated self-appraisal and superficial charm," and Cleckley noted that they "talk entertainingly."

I don't want to suggest that talking entertainingly is necessarily an indication of mental disorderedness, as I have made my own efforts in that direction at any number of Rotary lunches, but isn't it curious that people who are numb to the feelings of others can also gab agreeably and be superficially charming?

When Glenn Beck made a stop at the ornate old Palace Theater in Albany as part of his national "Glenn Beck Live" tour, naturally I went, since he was a Tea Party hero, and whenever I asked at demonstrations who people watched or listened to for the news, his name was always mentioned, along with Limbaugh's. His television show was probably the gaudiest offering on Fox, hewing not at all strictly to the conservative Republican line hewed to by other Fox programs but veering off into the most fanciful conspiracy directions that any student of the Illuminati ever imagined, connecting John D. Rockefeller with Vladimir Lenin with Diego Rivera with George Soros, most of them tied one or way or another to Hitler, the whole crazy mental universe illustrated with blackboard diagrams of balloons and arrows and question marks that looked like the work of a demented eighth-grader. Beck, crew-cut and pudgy-faced, would stand in front of this blackboard with his piece of chalk and raise eye-rolling questions about what exactly Rockefeller had in mind when he commissioned socialist worker statuary for Rockefeller Center, and he would arch his eyebrows mischievously and make Limbaugh-like HHHHHMMMmmmmmmmmmm sounds, leaving you to conclude for yourself that there was a vast plot in place to take down Christian America and only Glenn himself was on to it.

The first thing I noticed was something I should have known all along, namely that television magnifies people and "live" brings them down to size. Glenn Beck on stage, seen from thirty rows back, was not a larger-than-life nutcase or an outsized conspiracy theorist as I had thought. He was just a radio gabber who had hit upon a shtick that for the moment made him a celebrity. He was the same drive-time motor-mouth that he had been since he was a teenager, the same guy who had bounced from radio station to radio station across the country—a year here, two years there—trying whatever juvenile gags worked, until he got fired and moved along. From Texas to Utah to Kentucky to Maryland to Arizona to Florida, wherever a station would have him. It was easy enough to see that his current self-presentation as a save-America conservative alert to socialistic dangers and devoted to Israel was merely another shtick, though there was no evidence that the rest of the audience perceived this. On the contrary, they laughed happily at his stand-up jokes, many of the bathroom variety, booed or hollered "noooooo" at his artfully timed mentions of

France or the United Nations, and applauded lustily at his patriotic platitudes ("It's not only the flag, it's the values...America will come roaring back to life...it's in our DNA to be free.")

And when, at the end of the show, addressing what he was going to do now that his Fox gig was coming to an end, he told them he was going to "pick up the hammer and start building what we need for global freedom...and you're going to be first...It's not for everyone, it's just for those with eyes and ears...the world needs leaders, you will be the first"—well, they rose to their feet and gave him a standing ovation that General Douglas MacArthur would have been proud of when he histrionically said goodbye before Congress. Them, right there, munching their popcorn and guzzling their intermission beer in the restored glory of the Palace Theater in downtown Albany, they were going to be the world's new leaders. And if you wanted to know what specifically old Glenn was going to do, well, he was going to manufacture shirts, for one thing, with significant if cryptic messages on them, like the Number 7 polo shirt he was actually wearing, and all the profits would go to charity, though "not to a U.N. charity," he promised, eliciting more cheers from the crowd. And he would manufacture the shirts right here in the United States, but without using any federal aid, eliciting still more cheers.

It was an interesting crowd. During intermission I walked up and down the aisles and toured the lobby and did not see a single black, brown, or yellow face, which was pretty remarkable when you thought about it, since the city of Albany, per the most recent census, was thirty-one percent black, nine percent Hispanic and five percent Asian. I doubt if you could have found 2,000 exclusively white people gathered together at any other place in town on this particular evening, or any other evening.

The homogeneity was actually a sore point with the Angry Ones, and they would often defend themselves by saying "We're not racist" even when no one had said they were. At the Corning Preserve gathering the most popular demonstrator was a black man in the kind of tri-corner hat favored by Tea Pots as an indicator of their affinity with the original American Revolution Tea Partiers. White demonstrators practically lined up to have their picture taken with him, arm in arm, I suppose so they would have something tangible to demonstrate their non-racism. They would drape their arm around this guy's shoulders and beam for the camera, and he would beam too, apparently relishing the attention, and there you would have a snapshot of a little moment in American history.

The Tea Party business, with its anger and mean-spiritedness, as well as its Glenn Beck sappiness, made a very nice fit with hallelujah Christianity, and I was beginning to feel I was onto something, finding a way to report on the local at the same time as the divine. Pretty soon the Catholic Church—holy, Roman and apostolic—would help me with that endeavor, which was not something I could ever have anticipated. The fact that many of the *Gazoot*'s readers were Catholic— descendants of Italian, Polish and Irish immigrants— would be a complication, but surely I could handle it.

15

ST. KATERI

"The Vatican scrupulously investigates miracle claims for proof that recovery was not a result of medical or surgical intervention."

It was quite the story for the little Mohawk Valley towns just west of Schenectady: They were going to have their own saint. A real saint, recognized, glorified and canonized by the Vatican itself. She would be a feather in the cap for Auriesville and Fonda, for sure, and for Montgomery County as a whole. Kateri was her name—a corruption of Catherine, bestowed on her when she converted to Christianity—Kateri Tekakwitha, in full, the last name supposedly indicating "bumps into things," as a result of partial blindness caused by smallpox. She was the daughter of an Algonquin Christian mother and a Mohawk chief father who had lived her short life more than 300 years ago, from 1656 to 1680 to be precise, and who already had two shrines to her memory, the large National Shrine of Our Lady of Martyrs in Auriesville and the more modest National Kateri Tekakwitha Shrine outside the village of Fonda. She had been declared "venerable" in 1943 by Pope Pius XII and had been "beatified," as the church calls it, in 1980 by Pope John Paul II, who turned the Vatican pretty much into a saint factory. She was thus officially denominated as "Blessed Kateri," awaiting only Vatican certification of a miracle to qualify for sainthood. And then it came, approved by Pope Benedict XVI, and of course that was quite the story for the *Daily Gazoot*, too, which was the principal newspaper for those small towns.

We reported it just as any newspaper in America would have reported it, that is, with full solemnity. We quoted the museum coordinator at the National Shrine of Our Lady of Martyrs (also known as the Shrine of North American Martyrs) as saying, "I hear almost every week someone say how their prayers were answered through the intercession of Blessed Kateri," and we quoted the bishop of the Albany Roman Catholic Diocese, Howard Hubbard, as saying, "I am thrilled to learn about the authentication of the miracle attributed to Kateri's intercession." The next day we caught up with the miracle itself, which we noted had occurred in the state of Washington:

> *The Native American boy named Jake was playing baseball in 2006 when he suffered a facial injury.*
> *That injury led to a fever, and doctors discovered he was suffering from flesh-eating disease.*

"Nothing seemed to work until his parents began to pray to Blessed Kateri," Steed said. [Friar Mark Steed, of the national shrine.]

The disease is almost always fatal, he said.

"The illness began to abate and he was completely healed. Doctors authenticated that's never happened before," Steed said.

That is pretty much how our competitor newspapers reported it also, and it's pretty much how *The New York Times* wrote about it a year and a half later when it ran a feature story on the subject. Full solemnity, full credulity. Taking a Catholic friar's word for medical claims and not inquiring at all into the details of this alleged miracle, not inquiring into the metaphysics behind it, and not even inquiring into what sort of medical treatment the boy Jake might have received and whether that might have had something to do with his alleged complete healing. It was as sorry a job of journalism as I had ever seen. Like receiving a report of a haunted house and just earnestly passing along a few of the claimed details—whooshes in the attic, moans in the closet—and a few quotes from people already convinced of the report's veracity. (*The New York Times* did say, "Some doubt the truthfulness of her story as told by the church," but that was in reference only to Kateri's personal history, not to the supposed miracle, and the "some" who doubted were Native Americans who preferred their own supernaturalism to that of Christians.)

A quick Google search turned up more details. A six-year-old boy in the state of Washington by the name of Jake Finkbonner had cut his lip playing basketball (not baseball), the cut quickly became infected, and the infection spread into his face. He was taken to Seattle Children's Hospital, one of the top pediatric hospitals in the country, where it was determined he was under assault by what's known as flesh-eating bacteria and was put into the Intensive Care Unit. His family was Catholic, and his father was a member of the Lummi Indian tribe, besides which there was the disfigurement connection— Kateri Tekakwitha had been scarred by smallpox, and now Jake was having the flesh of his face eaten away. So the parish priest asked his flock to pray to Blessed Kateri on the boy's behalf. Pretty soon a representative of the Society of the Blessed Kateri visited Jake in the hospital and left a medallion with an image of Kateri on it. Jake's mother put the medallion on the boy's pillow, and lo and behold, the next day the infection had stopped, according to the story widely circulated in the media.

Interesting, no? Fascinating, no? Absolutely mind-blowing, no?

The metaphysics behind the story, as near as I could make out, was this: There is an invisible man up in the sky who is all-powerful and who loves us but is too preoccupied to see to the details, so he relies on intermediaries to bring matters to his attention. The invisible man is a forbidding figure, with a vast white beard and frowning visage, so ordinary folks like the Finkbonners might be intimidated by the thought of approaching him directly. They would rather go to someone a little more human, someone who might be more understanding, like a pockmarked Indian girl, even if the pockmarked Indian girl has been dead for three centuries. That girl (or her spirit) "intercedes," as the church says, with the invisible man, meaning she goes and has a private word with him. She tells him about little Jake Finkbonner lying in a hospital bed in Seattle, his face being consumed by some dreadful bacteria that came from God knows where, and the invisible man, moved by the story, waves an omnipotent finger, and little Jake is saved. That is the idea, stripped of its ecclesiastical trimmings and reduced to plain English. That is what the Catholic Church teaches, that is what the faithful believe, and that is what newspapers judiciously avoided spelling out.

The Vatican spent three years investigating the story before concluding, in the words of the priest who led the investigation, "We have received assurances that [Kateri] now stands in heaven before the throne of God."

USA Today reported, lest anyone doubt, "The Vatican scrupulously investigates miracle claims for proof that recovery was not a result of medical or surgical intervention."

I am a humble soul and do not wish to boast, but I believe I was the only journalist in the world who actually called Seattle Children's Hospital to inquire into the treatment the boy received there. At least my Google searches have not turned up any other. Can you believe such a thing? Can you believe that a rusty old religious institution can make such a fantastic claim as the Catholic Church was making in this case without any journalist making the obvious phone call? Without anyone even ascertaining that in addition to prayer, the boy had also received antibiotics? Without anyone even checking with a medical person for a second opinion, so to speak, but just swallowing that miracle story like a wide-eyed child in a Sunday school class? But that is exactly what happened, and if any other journalist did make such a call, I am ready to be corrected.

First I checked with the Centers for Disease Control and learned that the mortality rate for the kind of infection Jake Finkbonner had is ten to fifteen percent, meaning that eighty-five to ninety percent of patients survive it, contrary to what the friar told the *Gazoot* and what the *Gazoot* printed. There could have been no doctors who "authenticated that's never happened before." Further, a quick search of online images revealed that the boy was not "completely healed," as we had reported, but remained severely disfigured, requiring massive plastic surgery. The infection had been arrested; its effects had not been reversed.

Finally I spoke with Dr. Craig Rubens, a pediatric infectious disease specialist who was one of the team leaders who treated the boy at Seattle Children's Hospital. He told me it was the worst case of such an infection he had ever seen and that the boy was several times close to death during the approximately three weeks he was in intensive care. He said the medical team administered antibiotics to fight the infection, known as necrotizing fasciitis, which was moving so fast they could actually see it spreading, and gave other medication to control the boy's blood pressure. They performed surgery every day, sometimes more than once a day, to remove dying tissue from under the skin of his face, put the boy in what I took to be sort of a decompression chamber to provide him with a high level of oxygen, and took other drastic steps to keep him alive. All of this around the clock, twenty-four hours a day for three weeks. He also informed me that when the infection finally abated it did so gradually, not all of a sudden, as some of the more breathless news stories had it.

Naturally I asked if he considered the boy's survival to have been beyond the laws of nature, which is how Thomas Aquinas defined miraculous, but there he demurred. "I will leave it to those who are theologists to decide if this is miraculous," he said. "That's not my domain." He did say the boy's recovery was "truly remarkable for as close to death as he was." He would not answer my question as to whether he was Catholic.

It is not to aggrandize myself that I say I'm the only journalist who gathered this elementary information, but rather to expose the slavishness of the rest of the news media when it comes to religion. It was becoming clearer to me all the time that under the unwritten rules of the press I was getting away with murder when I ragged first on evangelical hypocrites and now on the Catholic Church, not just for their behavioral shortcomings, like patronizing prostitutes and sexually assaulting altar boys, but for their fantastical worldview.

And it wasn't just the expressed worldview—the magical, the supernatural, the miraculous. It was the corollary, often left unexpressed, which was the disdain for real knowledge. Readers wrote in, angry at my disrespectful treatment of Catholic beliefs. I responded:

But I'll tell you something no one was angry about. No one was angry that the mighty Roman Catholic Church, with its billion-plus followers, failed to acknowledge the power of hard science and the dedication of teams of doctors in the saving of that six-year-old boy in Seattle.

I recounted the details of the boy's medical treatment, which I characterized as "applying knowledge gained by the application of reason over three centuries or so beginning with what historians call the Enlightenment," and added:

The Catholic Church explained it by means of a fairy tale, a fairy tale on the same level as Jack and the Beanstalk, and used it to promote itself. The pope signed off on the fairy tale, and the bishop of the Albany Diocese declared himself thrilled. Isn't that something to be at least moderately disgusted with? I think so. They broadcast their medieval nonsense just if the last few hundred years of human progress had never happened, and the press, I'm sorry to say, reports it with a straight face.

Can you imagine uttering such blasphemy in a minor-league newspaper in a minor-league city in upstate New York, a city with almost as many Catholic churches as traffic lights? Can you imagine uttering it in any mainstream newspaper at all, large or small?

A lot of other people couldn't either.

In his recent columns...Carl Strock trumpets his bigotry. He ridicules the Catholic Church for promulgating a "fairy tale" and "medieval nonsense." God is "an invisible man up in the sky" as well as "a forbidding figure, what with his vast white beard and frowning visage." Clearly, it is Mr. Strock who is the "forbidding" one: He denies Catholics the respect that characterizes civility and that betokens the virtue of tolerance. (Marcus Plieninger, policy analyst for the Catholic League for Religious and Civil Rights, New York City)

A few billion people on Earth believe in God and/or in Christianity. Billions have believed over the centuries. Strock obviously thinks himself brighter and more enlightened than all of them. What an ego, what hubris! (Reverend Thomas Morrette, pastor of Holy Trinity Catholic Church, Johnstown)

A reader in Rotterdam informed me that she had sent my columns to a cousin in Florida, and the cousin had seen to it that a Mass was said for me and a novena started. (I didn't even know what a novena was, and I believe the Mass was a first.)

Now, I will divulge that I did get a phone call from a parish priest, whose identity I will take with me to the grave, telling me I was "absolutely right," and that the Vatican creates saints and peddles miracles just as a way to keep the masses happy, which gave me heart. And a Catholic friend assured me that not even the bishop believed the medieval nonsense of Blessed Kateri but went along with it out of political necessity. Of course, those were exceptions.

I raised a few more injudicious questions: if there is an invisible man up in the sky who loves us and who is capable of healing one sick child, why doesn't he heal all sick children?

If he is all-powerful in addition to brimming with love, why did he let little Jake Finkbonner get infected in the first place?

And seeing as how he is the creator of all things, why did he create the flesh-eating bacteria, *Streptococcus pyogenes*, in the first place?

I proposed that if a doctor had done what this supernatural being had done—create a dangerous organism, allow it to attack a child, let it run rampant in the boy's face for three weeks before finally stopping it, and then fail to repair the damage, leaving the boy gravely disfigured—he would lose his license. He wouldn't be given hosannas.

I was not unaware that I was raising the basic nagging question of Christianity: If there's a loving God up in Heaven, how come my body is covered with boils and my camels have all been stolen? Nor was I surprised that more than one reader had the conventional answer: It's my own damn fault for being a sinner. Or if not my fault directly, then Adam and Eve's fault and mine by inheritance.

In the words of a letter-writer who identified himself as a part-time philosophy instructor:

> *Evil, in its primary sense, requires human intent, and in fact the Christian answer to the problem of evil is that evil entered the world through human free will. But, indeed, the Bible has*

an answer as to why things like disease and natural disasters were allowed into the world as well: as a punishment and result of the misuse of that free will. (Stephen Riker, Schenectady)

In the words of another:

The Bible teaches that all sickness, pain, sorrow, death, etc., are a direct result of the sin and disobedience of mankind. I'm not talking about the little boy's sin, but the whole world is in a "fallen state away from God." [1 John 5:19] Also, we have an enemy, Satan, who along with his fallen angels afflicts us and wars against us constantly...(Janet Mueller, Glenville)

A little boy was at death's door with a rare bacteria devouring his face, and that was how they explained it. The smugness of it! By God, I would have liked to give them a kick in the pants.

From time to time I would get an invitation to speak to one group or another, to provide a spot of entertainment after a lunch of chicken Milanese and green beans, and one of my favorite such groups was the retirees of Knolls Atomic Power Laboratory in Niskayuna, who naturally tended toward the scientific and the managerial and had more tolerance for my perverse sense of humor, perhaps, than the Rotterdam Kiwanis, though I by no means disparaged Kiwanians. (They bought the newspaper too.) The next time the retirees invited me to join them at the Woodlin Country Club on Glenridge Road, I impishly suggested "God" as a topic. I thought I could cook up an entertaining talk on the subject. I would point out that "God" was not alone in the universe of human beliefs, and to ask if someone believed in him was, in a way, to beg the question. It was to assume that there was such a being, the question being merely, do you acknowledge him? Whereas, in fact, there were all kinds of supernatural beings loose in the universe of the human imagination: Ganesh, Vajrapani, Allah, Quan Am, Huitzilopochtli, not to mention all the leprechauns, angels, devils, saints, djinns and trolls that have been posited by thinkers high and low over the centuries. If you say I'm an atheist—a word I object to—because I don't believe in your Christian or Jewish "God," can't I just as well say you're an atheist because you don't believe in Huitzilopochtli? Then I would get into the little problems of necrotizing fasciitis and why an omnipotent, omniscient God needs an intermediary to bring suffering to his attention—does he doze off, or what?—and maybe I would touch on evangelicals skulking around motel rooms while preaching family values, and I was sure I could fill a half-hour and get a few laughs in the process, especially considering that the audience would be weighted with scientific types.

My host said no, it would be too controversial, and urged me to find another topic, which really left me empty. He finally suggested something vague, like "Stirring the Pot," and that's what went into the printed program. But, alas, when the time came and the chicken and green beans had been disposed of, I couldn't help myself. I talked about why it wasn't a good idea to give a talk about God, which amounted to much the same thing as I had planned anyway, but with an ironic twist, I hoped.

"I don't have to listen to this bullshit," one man in the audience groused as he got up to leave early in the talk. "I don't have to listen to you insult my God."

"Then leave!" someone called out to him as a couple other people also got up and walked out.

I was nonplussed for a minute, just as I had been in the great evolution-creation debate. But a few other people hollered to me, "Keep going," which gave me heart, and I did keep going, and I think I pulled it off, and after the talk we had a lively and intelligent Q-and-A session. But it was sort of a turning point. It was the first time I had ever polarized an audience. Even when I had spoken about the Albany Muslim trial or the excesses of Family Court or Jack Carroll, an accused child molester, I had kept the audience with me, without any walkouts.

Similarly at the *Gazoot*, I had always, or almost always, been supported, or at least ignored. Now there were getting to be raised eyebrows. "What's the point?" the general manager asked me regarding my jibes at the Catholic Church. "Do you think you're going to change the minds of the little old Italian ladies on Goose Hill?" There was no question of silencing me— "I'm not going to censor Carl Strock," the editor assured me—but the fact that the thought crossed her mind was something new.

I couldn't really blame them. The *Gazoot* of course depended on the support of its readers and its advertisers, and many of those readers and advertisers were Catholics or evangelical Protestants—or Jews, about whom I'd had nothing yet to say—and did it make sense to offend them? The question was raised by the reporter who wrote the first lame-brained story about Blessed Kateri, the one that quoted the friar saying little Jake Finkbonner's survival was unprecedented and the boy had been completely healed. "Does it make sense to offend so many of our readers?" he e-mailed the editor. I hadn't thought of it like that.

16

O JERUSALEM

"Nowhere is it written that males need to work.
It's good enough if the wife works."

I wanted to see Jerusalem. Having a little extra money available, Pearl and I had been taking a major trip each year for the past few years—major for us—and had been fetched by the charms of such ancient human nests as Varanasi in India and Fez in Morocco, places that fairly groaned with antiquity, with their forbidding walls, their crooked streets, their cloaked and turbaned inhabitants, and after each such trip I would write a how-I-spent-my-vacation column. Jerusalem, or at least the old part of it, seemed a fair choice for our next destination, from what I had been able to learn, so we got ready to do it. We booked a flight, made reservations at a tiny "boutique" hotel, and set about studying maps and guidebooks.

Presently my office phone rang, and it was a doctor in neighboring Niskayuna who belonged to a group called J Street, which I had never heard of, and he was inviting me to a program the group was having in a few days at the Jewish community center in Albany, the Golub Center. J Street, he informed me, believed in what he called a "two-state solution" to the problem of Israel and Palestine, and the program would feature three former Israeli soldiers holding forth on their experiences, it being understood that their views would be in harmony with those of J Street and they would favor an independent Palestine, which is what the "two-state solution" amounted to, an Arab Palestine alongside a Jewish Israel, the two living in peace.

Amazing, I said. It just so happens I'm leaving for Israel in about a week, which he had no way of knowing. What a coincidence, and what a great opportunity. How had he happened to think of me? He said he remembered a column I had written about a peace conference in Albany, a national gathering of leftists, in which I had mocked the participants for their knee-jerk and unanimous denunciations of Israel and their refusal to say anything unkind about Islamic fanaticism. I had apparently impressed him with my fairness.

So of course I went, and it turned out the meeting was an eye-opener to me. The ex-soldiers—two men and a woman, now graduate students in the United States—had all served in the West Bank and one had participated in the evacuation of the Jewish settlements in Gaza in 2005, and they were all dismayed with the Israeli treatment of Palestinian Arabs. One of them described it as "a cancer eating at our society," and said Israel was "a democracy for seven and a half million people but ruled ten million." They were obviously bright people, they had been soldiers—one of them said his grandfather had fought in the 1948 war, known in Israel as the War of Independence, and his father had fought in the 1967 war—and now here they were, condemning Israel for its brutal treatment of Palestinians, in which they themselves had participated. One of them had been court-martialed for refusing to engage any further in the bullying of Arabs in the West Bank.

This was all new to me, and I'm embarrassed now at how ignorant I was. The Israel-Palestine matter was to me an intractable problem that had been going on all my life and to which I had nothing to contribute. I figured two tribes were laying claim to the same land, you probably had your fire-breathers on both sides, and there was nothing I could do about it and maybe nothing anyone could do about it. I wasn't going to worry my head over it as I had once worried my head nearly to destruction over Vietnam. Let others fret and analyze and tear their hair. There seemed to be no shortage of people willing to do so.

Now I was set to pondering, and a few days before our departure, following the advice of one of these ex-soldiers, I took to reading not only the *Jerusalem Post* online, as I had been doing for a few weeks, but also *Haaretz*, a wider-ranging and more liberal newspaper, and *+972 Magazine*, which was militantly critical of the Israeli occupation of the West Bank.

When the phone rang the next time it was the head of the Jewish Federation of Northeastern New York, Rodney Margolis, whom I likewise did not know. He had heard from a Schenectady rabbi, Matt Cutler, that I was going to Israel, and he wanted to help. Indeed, Rabbi Cutler had sent an e-mail to both him and the director of community relations for the Jewish Federation, Shelly Shapiro, saying he wanted me to "experience Israel through the eyes of Israelis" and asking if they could set me up with people who would show me "various political and social ideas within Israel, especially those who are attached to the Likud Party and/or the ruling government."

Shelly Shapiro had responded, "He is an important voice," referring to me, and promised to "meet and work on this," which is how Mr. Margolis came to be on the phone with me, telling me he had a friend from upstate New York, David Baker, who worked in the press office of Prime Minister Benjamin Netanyahu. He had taken the liberty of contacting this friend, proposing that he get me in for a chat with the press secretary.

This did not necessarily please me. I was going on vacation with a lady who does not like to be left alone even briefly in foreign lands, and though I hoped to educate myself on matters previously obscure to me, the main activity I envisioned was the two of us walking hand in hand through picturesque lanes and plazas, maybe getting pelted with stones by religious zealots for the holding of hands, in which case we would let go, but that was the general idea. It did not include an interview with a government official who presumably would inflict on me statements of government policy. Nevertheless, accommodating as I am and eager to please, I agreed, and the appointment was made. I suggested that the end of my trip would be a better time than the beginning, since by then I might have something intelligent to ask, but the press secretary, Mark Regev, was fully booked then, so it had to be the beginning. In the event, this proved awkward, at least for me, since on my second or third day in Jerusalem I still knew next to nothing and could only ask such penetrating questions as, "So, what about the settlements?" Mr. Regev, to his credit, was gracious and indulgent, though he did feed me some explanations that later I was able to recognize as cotton candy, when I had ventured out of Jerusalem into the West Bank and had learned a little on my own.

And then another call—I was beginning to feel loved—this one from Rabbi Cutler himself, of the Schenectady reform synagogue, Congregation Gates of Heaven, who had studied in Jerusalem, sometimes led tours there, and knew the place in detail, it appeared. He gave me travel pointers, offered to lend me a couple of guidebooks, which I accepted, including one that oddly enough was written for religious Jews and included prayers to be said at various Holy Land sites. What was I supposed to do with that? After all my mockery of Tea Party Protestantism and saint-saturated Catholicism, all my ragging on the Invisible Man in the Sky, it was no secret in Schenectady or its environs where I stood on religion. I did make note of a little hole-in-the-wall shop he recommended to me, the shop of the Kippa Man, in the Ben Yehuda pedestrian shopping area of Jerusalem, which was actually where Pearl and I were going to stay. The Kippa Man sold kippas, better known to Americans by the Yiddish name *yarmulke*, which are the skullcaps worn by observant Jews in obedience to the Talmudic prescription, "Cover your head in order that the fear of heaven may be upon you."

The Kippa Man in Ben Yehuda, I eventually saw with my own eyes, had skullcaps in every conceivable design—from the embroidered skyline of the old city of Jerusalem to the logo of the New York Yankees, in velvet, satin, or crocheted cotton, whatever you could imagine and more. Floor to ceiling, in a shop barely big enough for two people to squeeze into. As it was described to me, it sounded like a good place to pick up souvenirs for Jewish friends, and I made note of it. Matt, I thought, you are a capital fellow and I will keep you in my prayers. I did scratch my head later when a congregant of his reported back to me that he was concerned upon learning I had arranged to visit the West Bank on my second-to-last day in Israel. He said he wished I could make that visit earlier "so we could have another crack at him." The remark puzzled me, but I put it aside.

The visit to the West Bank had been arranged through the good offices of my new J Street friends, two of the most gracious people I have had the pleasure to meet, and it pained me that what I eventually wrote for the *Gazoot*, after all their efforts on my behalf, to some extent aggrieved them. They had an Arab friend in the West Bank city of Ramallah who was a like-minded soul, good-hearted and eager for peace and reconciliation, and they would contact him, and if all worked out he would see Pearl and me through a checkpoint and drive us around the area I had always heard of but had not the slightest idea what it was. West Bank? It could have been a muddy riverbank for all I knew, or it could have been a depopulated desert or almost anything else. It was a troublesome area, was all I carried in my brain. Israel occupied it in the 1967 war—I knew that; Jews built "settlements" there; Palestinians threw rocks at them; the United Nations passed resolutions about it; and so forth into an endless murk of tribal hatred and international politicking that passed me by as I fretted instead over the drowning of kittens and the snatching of children. I admit I was now excited at the prospect of seeing it. I was happy to be a tourist in Jerusalem, but I was happier still to have the chance to see something beyond the predictable tourist sights and to fill in a blank in my mental landscape. By God, I'm going to see the West Bank, is what I thought. Maybe I'll meet some terrorists! Maybe I'll meet some "settlers" and they'll invite me into their covered wagons or their log cabins or whatever they have and we'll talk about making the desert bloom, which I had also heard about.

I will not claim that I went to Jerusalem with a pure heart. I had studied up on the religious attractions there and was fully prepared to work them for a laugh, particularly the Christian religious attractions, which seemed especially suited for the treatment. The chief Islamic attraction, the great Dome of the Rock, might be workable in its claim to be the launching place of the Prophet Mohammed to paradise on his horse, Buraq, but it was a splendid edifice from the outside and was closed to infidels on the inside, as I knew from my researches, so I didn't expect I would be able to do much with it by way of satire. The principal Jewish attraction, the remains of a retaining wall of the so-called Second Temple, known as the Western Wall or sometimes the Wailing Wall, I wasn't sure about. As a Gentile, I had misgivings about making light of things Jewish. It seemed in poor taste, given the horrors of history, but I did look forward to photographing the bearded, black-hatted worshippers there. Pictures aplenty were available on the Internet, so I had an idea what it looked like, and I was ready with my Nikon D700 to have a go.

Things began to sour right away on the flight over, or even earlier, in the Newark airport, when luxuriantly bearded Orthodox dudes among the passengers took to their prayers, cloaking themselves in fringed shawls, tying little black boxes to the top of their heads and wrapping long black leather thongs around their bare right arms so tightly that the flesh bulged between the wraps. To my innocent eye, it looked like some kind of S&M getup, which I eventually noted in my column. And then they prayed, bobbing their heads like dippy birds as they muttered over their prayer books, all of this not in any retiring way, the better to commune with the Great Spirit, but ostentatiously in front of everyone, even in the airport, where it would have been easy enough to repair to an inconspicuous corner. In the airplane they would form a bunch of four or five near the restrooms, blocking the passage and making a sanctimonious show so that in my irreverence I couldn't help praying myself for a bout of turbulence. I watched them from a distance of a yard, in my aisle seat, and mischievously imagined what they would look like if the airplane took a plunge of about a hundred feet and then bounced back up. I meant no harm, but I had the same reaction to them as I had to Christians praying on the steps of City Hall.

I say they were Orthodox, but I'm not sure about that, as I had a hard time telling the mere Orthodox from the more elevated ultra-Orthodox, who in turn are divided into so many sects and cults, distinguishable sometimes only by the color of their stockings or the cut of their coat, that only an anthropologist specializing in the subject can tell them apart. On our first full day in Jerusalem, which was a Saturday and therefore the all-important "Shabbat," we attended services at the Great Synagogue on King George Street, an Orthodox establishment that had been recommended to me by Rabbi Cutler, and the men there dressed and looked much the same as the men in the airplane, though I do not offer that as conclusive evidence, since the distinctions can be so fine. I had taken the precaution of buying a skullcap the day before in the Mehane Yehuda market, believing it might be necessary for entrance to this house of worship, but it turned out that my L.L. Bean rain hat was perfectly acceptable, so that's what I wore, just as I later wore it at the Western Wall. Yahweh apparently insists only that the head be covered; he doesn't insist on a wafer-like little cap that must be held in place with bobby pins. That is a human convention, or at least such was my understanding. I do not pretend to Talmudic expertise.

In the Great Synagogue, while I sat downstairs with the men my wife had to sequester herself out of sight up in the balcony with the women. Orthodox Jews do not trust themselves to control their sexual urges any more than Muslims do, apparently. Similarly, the Western Wall, access to which is controlled by the ultra-Orthodox, is divided into a male section and a female section, separated by a partition, and you won't be surprised to learn that the male section is much bigger. My experience with Islamic mosques is that at prayer time the main part of the floor is for men only, and women are relegated to the rear, sometimes to a rear corner, where they are concealed by a screen. Sexual tension, I suspect, is an essential element in every major religion, with the possible exception of Hinduism. In the holy and filthy city of Varanasi, Pearl and I watched Hindu men and women alike immerse themselves in the Ganges River, we watched them pray together in the few temples that admitted us, and I was aware of the erotic sculpture for which Hinduism is known, even though I did not see any of it with my own eyes but knew it only from books.

We visited the grubby-gray Mea Shearim neighborhood of Jerusalem, plastered with Hebrew posters. It supposedly resembles a nineteenth-century European *shtetl*, and it well may, for all I know. It was built before the modern state of Israel was a glimmer in Theodor Herzl's eye, and reports say many of its black-clad residents to this day reject the nation-state as an unholy presumption, the messiah not yet having arrived to authorize it. This is where the open letter had been posted demanding that a certain rabbi-scientist "burn all his writings," which I read about when I was immersed in the creation-evolution controversy. Here also we got a further taste of sexual uptightness. Signs warned, in English, "To Women & Girls...Please Do Not Pass Through Our Neighborhood in Immodest Clothes." We thought we were in compliance, but lo, when I emerged from a little shop where I had negotiated the purchase of a silver pointer for reading the Torah, poor Pearl, who had waited for me outside, was in distress. She had been accosted by a pregnant young woman with two little children in tow who had yelled at her in either Hebrew or Yiddish, aggressively gestured at her clothing, and more aggressively gestured for her to go away. Was it because her wrists showed? Because her hair was loose? Because her pants were too tight? We didn't know, but Pearl insisted we leave, and we left. It was no loss. They were an unfriendly bunch anyway, these Haredim, as they're known in Israel. I tried to strike up a conversation with a few of them who were selling religious goods—pictures of bearded holy men and the like—after ascertaining they spoke English, and got only rude rebuffs. The hell with them, I said, let's get out of here. You see them in the United States sometimes, especially in New York, and they seem a quaint and picturesque people, like the Amish, but you see them in their own territory and they are less quaint and less charming.

I wrote in the *Gazoot*:

> They're a curious people, the men devoting themselves entirely to study of the Torah, while the women bear children and work outside the home as well, to support their worthless men.

One of these men, extravagantly bearded and curled, had earlier accosted me in the crowded Mehane

Yehuda market, where people mix freely, thrust a plastic-covered sheet of paper in front of me, and demanded, "Please, money," not politely but peremptorily. The paper was written entirely in Hebrew except for a small heading that he stabbed his finger at, which said, "Torah Study Institute." The bugger wanted me to give him money so he and his fellows could more conveniently spend their days memorizing the primitive taboos and archaic prescriptions handed down from their supposed ancestors 2,500 years ago.

It was a shame I didn't have a few choice words of Hebrew for him.

Did I say "worthless men"? Well, yes, I did. It was just a bit of hyperbole, like saying the prayer getup looked like S&M gear, and I soon felt bad about it, since surely no human being is worthless. But I had learned from a leader of a reform group, the Israel Religious Action Center, that these Haredi men were not only still exempt from military service at that time—military service that was required of other Israeli Jews—but they were also exempt from the requirement to demonstrate need in order to get welfare payments, called income supplements. They qualified automatically, by dint of being full-time, lifelong students of the Torah. Their wives bore an average of 8.6 children, causing the Haredi population to expand faster than any other, but still sometimes the women had to work outside the home to supplement their welfare payments while their husbands studied holy writ. At the time I hadn't seen it, but I later read a remark by the Deputy Health Minister, Yaakov Litzman, on this subject, which I could have used if I'd had it at the time: "Nowhere is it written that males need to work. It's good enough if the wife works." I could have incorporated that quote into my column, and then I wouldn't have felt half so bad.

I e-mailed Rabbi Cutler:

> *Just to let you know we are up to our ears in Jerusalem... from the old city, to Mea Shearim, to the splendid Israel Museum...utterly engrossing, all of it...and I'm getting good use out of the guidebooks you loaned me...thanks again for your guidance.*

The "good use" of the guidebooks was of course a courtesy. I actually had only scant use for the prayers.

I e-mailed Rodney Margolis:

> *Just to let you know, I met David today and more at length his boss, Mark Regev, and am grateful to you for making that happen...I am still fairly overwhelmed with the experience of being in a new and such multi-layered place, behind on sleep and trying to do too much each day, but look forward to talking to you when we return next week.*

The "multi-layered" sounded like a blurb for a bad movie, like "richly textured" or something, but again, I was trying to be polite.

On my way back from the interview with the prime minister's press secretary I ran into a parade of American evangelicals led by the Reverend John Hagee, the Texas megachurch pastor who gained national fame when John McCain had to renounce his endorsement on account of Hagee's anti-Catholic pronouncements. He was in town with his Christians United for Israel, and just the night before, as I learned from the news, Prime Minister Netanyahu had addressed their convention, and this subject had actually come up in my conversation with the press secretary, who assured me Israel was very grateful for the support of right-wing Christian wackos, though of course he didn't say it that way.

They were parading down Ben Yehuda, carrying Israeli and American flags and placards proclaiming "Israel You Are Not Alone," and in their evangelical enthusiasm some of them would break off and hug random passersby and spectators and snap pictures of each other. The reader may not believe it, and I hardly believed it myself, but one of them leaped at me and wrapped his arm around me, apparently taking me for an Israeli in need of Christian bolstering, and as he did so who should appear but the beautiful Pearl, who had been sitting on a bench waiting for me, and she snapped a picture of the two of us, me and the Christian, both of us smiling and him with his arm around my shoulders, and I said, that is one for the album. It was definitely one for the album, especially in light of what was yet to come. I could have used it as an exhibit in my defense.

17

BELIEVERS

"He Is Not Here, For He Is Risen."

The guidebook told us there was only one door to the large and labyrinthine Church of the Holy Sepulchre, and this was a cause of woe many years ago when there was a fire, but Pearl and I, wandering lost one day, found another. It was around back on a lower level, and it gave into the dingy little Ethiopian precinct, tended by a monk as ragged and forlorn-looking as if he had just endured forty days in the desert, or forty years. Without expression or comment he pointed us up a narrow flight of stone stairs to the main part of the church. It made me feel like a discoverer myself, and I resolved that I would write to the publisher of that guidebook when I got back and tell him about our find.

It was a joy and delight to see the genuine tomb of our Lord and Savior being guarded by Israeli police. They were present because the Christians in this holy place cannot get along sufficiently to provide order

themselves and need armed Jews to keep order for them.
I had to cover my mouth to keep from laughing. Tourists
like us line up in the gloom for a chance to squeeze into
the cramped little space resembling a Hopi bread oven
where the body of Jesus was supposedly entombed,
and it is these police officers, pistols on their hips,
who keep us from trampling each other and keep the
various monks and priests from tearing each others'
eyes out. Not just that, but the church is occupied by
six different species of Christians— Roman Catholic,
Eastern Orthodox, Armenian, Coptic, Ethiopian and
Syriac, if I remember correctly—and they cannot even
agree on when to open and close the establishment,
so, as an English Franciscan monk confirmed for me,
the keys are entrusted to a family of *Muslims*, who
carry out opening and closing duties and have carried
them out for some six centuries! You go to Jerusalem
from Schenectady and you have to recalibrate your
sense of historical time. Schenectady is proud of its
Stockade neighborhood, which was mostly built in the
nineteenth century and is on the site of the original
Dutch stockade, which was torched by French and
Indian marauders in the seemingly antediluvian year
of 1690. When that great event happened, the keys to
the Church of the Holy Sepulchre had already passed
from generation to generation over and over within
that same family! I could hardly grasp it. And the idea
of Muslims controlling access to this dubious Christian
site and Jews policing it because Christians cannot get
along sufficiently to perform those offices themselves—
well, you could have written that column yourself.

I say dubious, because persons of sober disposition do not take the tomb any more seriously than persons of sober disposition take Plymouth Rock seriously, but of course there are many persons *not* of sober disposition who are drawn to Jerusalem. So many, in fact, there is something called Jerusalem Syndrome, a temporary mental disorder brought on by proximity to so much holiness. Symptoms include dressing in white robes, excessive cleanliness and nail-clipping, speaking in tongues, and generally carrying on like a lunatic. There is actually a mental health center, Kfar Shaul, which specializes in treating sufferers of this affliction, most of whom are said to be Christian evangelicals. I wanted to go have a look, but with Reverend Hagee's crowd in town I thought it might have its hands full and I didn't want to impose.

The tomb was discovered—or invented—only in the fourth century, when Helena, mother of Emperor Constantine, a newly minted Christian, journeyed to Jerusalem for the express purpose of identifying holy sites and relics. Her success was astounding. She found not only the tomb but also the cross on which Jesus had been crucified, the nails that had held him to it, the rope by which he had been led, and the tunic that he had worn—more than 300 years after the fact!—and she distributed these goods around the Christian world to be appropriately adored and cherished. She also found the place where Jesus was born, in Bethlehem, and the place whence he rose to heaven, on the Mount of Olives. It was amazing work for someone not trained in archeology.

We spent a day exploring the Mount of Olives and got so hopelessly lost and disoriented that I can't tell you if we saw that sacred launching pad or not. The famous hill, actually a ridge, is mostly covered by Jewish cemeteries of pale beige stone, where I was told Jews who could afford it have long bought burial plots so as to be first in line for their own resurrection, since that's where *their* messiah is expected to land. From this large and mostly barren high ground you get a nice view down to the glittering Dome of the Rock, and some of the faithful, according to various guidebooks, believe that, come the day, a rope will stretch from the top of the hill down to the dome, people will walk that rope like Nik Wallenda walking his rope over Niagara Falls, and the righteous will arrive but the unrighteous will fall off and go to perdition. I was not eager to make the experiment and was relieved the end didn't come while we were there.

I observed a group of African-Americans from an AME Zion church, wearing white caps for identification, climb off their tour bus. When a stoop-shouldered Arab man hurried across the road and held out a plastic cup to them, begging for alms, they looked determinedly straight ahead and kept walking. It was a curious-enough sight, a member of one downtrodden group begging from members of another and getting the cold shoulder, right there in the Holy Land.

Pearl and I never take guided tours, but we relented on our first day in Jerusalem and, just to get our bearings in the crooked Old City, we tagged along on a free one-hour walking tour led by a Hebrew

University student, a personable young man originally from Pennsylvania. He recommended to us a paid tour of the Mount of Olives—the free one in the Old City was apparently a way to gin up business—and told us if we preferred to go there on our own we should be careful of pickpockets, since they were thick as flies and would swarm over us and distract us while brazenly thrusting their hands into our pockets. (The inhabitants of the Mount of Olives are Arabs.) But when we did go on our own, we found no such thing. The one or two Arabs we stopped to ask directions of were perfectly hospitable. The Arab taxi drivers at the summit ignored us. And the closest we saw to a hustle was that one shambling man begging from the black American tourists, which wasn't very close. And one other man in headscarf, holding a donkey and offering to pose for pictures for a tip.

One of the expressions I fall back on when I wish to avoid blasphemy is "Jumping Jehoshaphat," which I must have gotten from an old comic strip, so when I saw on my map that the tomb of the actual Jehoshaphat was near the Mount of Olives, along with the tombs of Absalom and Zacharaiah, I was naturally in a lather to see it, and so was Pearl, who was determined to take my picture there. "I want to see Jumping Jehoshaphat," she kept saying. But we couldn't find it, and we couldn't find the tomb of the Virgin Mary for a while, either. (I didn't know the Virgin Mary even *had* a tomb.) In our search we did stumble upon a little church or chapel that a sign identified as Dominus Flevit, and there we met a congenial monk who turned out to be from California. He explained to us that Dominus Flevit means "the Lord wept," and he said the little chapel was built on the spot where Jesus wept as he approached Jerusalem and looked out over the city (Luke 19:41), just as we looked out over it now. He graciously directed us to the tomb of the Virgin Mary, but as for the tomb of Jumping Jehoshaphat, the modest pile of rocks and an iron gate that we thought might be it—"That's not confirmed," he said. I couldn't help asking him if Dominus Flevit had been confirmed. "Well, it's tradition," he said humbly.

There is a lot of tradition in Jerusalem. There is not only the tomb of Jesus preferred by the six denominations above-mentioned, there is another tomb, the Garden Tomb, preferred by Protestants. We had a look, for which we waited in line behind a congregation of Koreans. A sign inside it said in English, "He Is Not Here, For He Is Risen." It was closed on Sunday, when we first tried, which I thought was the very day it should be open, so we came back another day, after making our way through the Muslim Quarter of the Old City, where we drank icy-sweet lime juice and admired the embroidered robes of bulky Palestinian women, and then trudged uphill from the Damascus Gate. We were not to be denied.

There is the Stone of Unction, just inside the Church of the Holy Sepulchre. This is a slab of rock maybe eight feet long by three feet wide on which the body of Jesus was supposedly laid when he was taken down from the cross. The Bible doesn't mention any such detail, but believers crowd around that slab, stroke it and kiss it and lay their crosses and amulets on it to soak up the holiness anyway. I snapped a picture of a boy about ten years old bending over and kissing it as he laid his toy assault rifle across it.

There is the Via Dolorosa, the sorrowful route that Jesus is supposed to have walked on his way to his crucifixion—a marked way through the narrow cobblestone lanes leading from St. Stephen's Gate to the Church of the Holy Sepulchre. The first such route was laid out in the fifth century, I learned, but this most recent one only in the eighteenth century, so you can safely put it in the same category as the tombs as far as historical reliability goes. Flocks of pilgrims wearing color-coded ball caps so as to stick with their tour groups clog these lanes to such a degree that if any messiah stumbled along here nowadays, or any Roman soldiers, they would get swept up and carried away and find themselves at last on an air-conditioned tour bus headed back to a hotel rather than to Golgotha, and history would be different.

I had the impish idea to try to find out where I could obtain a cross. I had figured in advance I might write a column or two from Jerusalem, and this seemed a swell hook, as we call it in the news game. I had seen pictures of the more enthusiastic type of male pilgrims, half-naked and daubed with red paint to simulate blood, carrying crosses along this trail, and I figured they could hardly have brought the crosses with them from Texas or Poland or wherever they hailed from. They must have acquired them locally.

"Wait, let me ask," I said to Pearl, who suddenly decided to pretend she didn't know me. I stopped a monk or two and a pilgrim or two, and I inquired in a souvenir shop or two, and finally I got an answer. You could rent a cross at the Sanctuaries of the Flagellation and the Condemnation, just down the lane, near the beginning of the trail, and sure enough, a monk there who identified himself as Firos, nationality undetermined, told me the tariff would be fifty U.S. dollars. Pretty steep, I thought, but what the hey. I asked him how many he had—I was in reporter mode now—and he asked back, "How many do you need?" evidently taking me for a tour leader. I didn't want to disabuse him of his impression but only said I'd like to see them, as if I were an especially discerning customer. He didn't have the key to the storeroom where they were kept, but one cross was out in the courtyard where I could see it and heft it, and it seemed to me entirely suitable for a symbolic walk, if not quite large enough for serious business. So I was satisfied and said I would be back—and maybe some day I will.

It's only a short walk from this most holy place in Christendom to the Western Wall, the most holy place in Judaism, and it was a special pleasure to visit one after the other and, what's more, when at the Wall to look up and see Al-Aqsa mosque, the third-holiest place in Islam, for those who rank such things. So much madness condensed into so small a space! And as a bonus, the glittering Dome of the Rock, too, both it and the mosque sitting on the vast stone platform, the size of several football fields, known as the Temple Mount, of which the Western Wall forms a partial support. Such a massing and shaping of stones! It gave me the same feeling as I get at the ruins of Teotihuacan in Mexico: How the blazes did they do it?

At the wall I watched a group of black-suited, side-curled men lacing up for prayers as other men had laced up on the airplane, winding black leather thongs tightly around their arms till it looked like the circulation must have stopped and fastening tiny black boxes to the top of their heads. They had set up a table with some books on it, a distance back from where the actual praying is done, and I took the liberty of approaching them and asking if they spoke English. They did. I presented myself as the curious tourist I was and asked what sect they belonged to, and one said, not very helpfully or encouragingly, "We are Jews of the Holy Land." I asked why they wore the little noggin boxes, and he said, "We do what God told Moses to do." And that was as far as I got, though he did advise me that if I could prove my grandmother was a Jew I could join them.

I later wrote in my column, for the edification of the *Gazoot's* readers:

> *I found out about the little black boxes tied to the noggins of faithful men at the Western Wall, and the black leather straps on their arms. They're called "t'fillin," and they are based on the rather cryptic words of Deuteronomy 11:18: "You shall put these words of mine on your heart and on your soul; and you shall tie them for a sign upon your arm, and they shall be as totafot between your eyes," the meaning of "totafot" being unclear.*
>
> *With that for a guide, they get themselves up like S&M cultists.*

It's a good thing Deuteronomy didn't tell them to swan-dive off the Western Wall, which is sixty feet high, or there would be an awful mess to clean up at the bottom.

These words, playful and harmless to my innocent mind, would be found offensive by some and cause me great grief.

I will say for Christians that they never harass me about whether I am one of them before showing hospitality. I stroll in and out of their churches and engage them in conversation, as I engaged the monk at Dominus Flevit, and they seem perfectly happy and sometimes even eager to tell me what they are up to. I once even engaged a worshipper of Santa Muerte in Mexico City, and he was happy to explain to me that he had tried praying to both the Virgin of Guadalupe and San Judas Tadeo but that he got better results from Santa Muerte, or Saint Death, who is not recognized by the church but is popular nonetheless. He was a student of orthodontia and said he prayed for good exam scores and for money.

Jews I engaged in Jerusalem often wanted to know right off the bat if I was Jewish. It struck me as impertinent. I wouldn't dream of asking someone if he was an atheist and turning away from him if he said no. Walking the streets one day among the skullcapped strollers I had the thought that the national slogan should be "Whoopee, I'm Jewish." Muslims wanted to know if I was Muslim only when I approached a mosque, which was bad enough, if not as broad as the

Jewish interest. Wandering the Muslim quarter of the old city one night, we ventured down a dark lane and a couple of kids emerged from a doorway, pointed at us and asked, "Muslim? Muslim?" and when we shook our heads no they waved us away.

People talk about the moral benefits of religion, and I feel those benefits myself when church groups help people rebuild their homes after a flood in Schenectady and Schoharie counties, but I didn't feel them in Jerusalem. I felt exclusivity and sanctimony, especially from Jews. For friendliness away from holy sites, like in markets, I recommend Muslims. This is a large generalization to derive from so brief an experience as mine, and the reader may take it for what it's worth. I considered wearing my Mehane Yehuda skullcap for a day to see what different experiences I might have, but I dropped the idea.

A wall is a curious thing to go into religious ecstasy about, if you can take a step back and view the matter objectively. The Western Wall supposedly supported one flank of a temple that was the center of Jewish worship until it was destroyed by the Romans in the year 70 CE, but that's all it is, just a portion of a retaining wall, as I described it in one of my irreverent reports in the Gazoot. And the temple of which it was a small part, the so-called Second Temple, we know little about, a fanciful model of it at the Israel Museum notwithstanding. We know details of the animal sacrifices and other rituals that were performed there, Judaism being preoccupied with such matters, but we don't know much else. We don't even know if there was a First Temple, there being no archeological evidence for one, but only Bible stories, as I learned at the Israel Museum.

Watching worshippers at this wall groaning, moaning and indeed wailing it occurred to me that a large part of Judaism is worship of their own history, even though much of that history is imaginary, like the covenant with Yahweh, the captivity in Egypt, the Exodus back to the Promised Land under the leadership of Moses, the hardships endured en route, and the kingdom of David and Solomon. It would be a curious thing to worship even if it were genuine, but to go into convulsions about a *mythological* history—how odd it seemed to me. I hadn't thought about it until I stood at the wall and watched. And watched and watched. I didn't yet know about Yeshayu Leibowitz, Hebrew University professor and editor of the *Encyclopedia Hebraica*, deriding the exhibitionism at the Wall as "religious disco," or I would have worked that into a column. I liked the phrase very much.

I did take note on a visit to the Israel Museum, which is not otherwise shy about glorifying Jewish history, that the scholars there could not quite swallow the foundation mythology themselves. A wall plaque said, "While the Biblical story of the Exodus relates that the Israelites came from Egypt, many archeologists believe that they actually originated in the Land," meaning the land of Canaan, now Israel. They didn't conquer Canaan, as per Joshua. It was their native digs. The triumphant coming into "the Land" was a campfire story. All of this I wrote up in my column, for the entertainment and possibly enlightenment of the readers back in Schenectady.

I further confirmed my understanding of these historical, or unhistorical, matters later at home when I read, for just one example, *The Bible Unearthed* by the archeologists Israel Finkelstein and Neil Asher Silberman, who go into all sorts of swoons about the alleged brilliance of the Bible stories, but when it comes down to hard facts sober up. Forty years of wandering in the Sinai desert?

> *Even if the number of fleeing Israelites (given in the text as 600,000) is wildly exaggerated or can be interpreted as representing smaller units of people, the text describes the survival of a great number of people under the most challenging conditions. Some archeological traces of their generation-long wandering in the Sinai should be apparent. However, except for the Egyptian forts along the northern coast, not a single campsite or sign of occupation from the time of Rameses II and his immediate predecessors and successors has ever been identified in Sinai. And it has not been for lack of trying. Repeated archeological surveys in all regions of the peninsula, including the mountainous area around the traditional site of Mount Sinai, near St. Catherine's Monastery, have yielded only negative evidence: not a single sherd, no structure, not a single house, no trace of an ancient encampment. One may argue that a relatively small band of wandering Israelites cannot be expected to leave material remains behind. But modern archeological techniques are quite capable of tracing even the very meager remains of hunter-*

*gatherers and pastoral nomads all over the world.
Indeed, the archeological record from the Sinai
Peninsula discloses evidence for pastoral activity
in such eras as the third millennium BCE and the
Hellenistic and Byzantine periods. There is simply
no such evidence at the supposed time of the Exodus
in the thirteenth century BCE.*

As for campsites identified in the Book of Numbers,
one is Kadesh, on the border between Israel and Egypt,
where "repeated excavations and surveys throughout the
entire area have not provided even the slightest evidence
of activity in the Late Bronze Age, not even a single sherd
left by a tiny fleeing band of frightened refugees."

Another is Ezion-geber: "No trace of wandering
Israelites."

Another is Tel Arad: "No remains whatsoever from
the Late Bronze Age," when the Biblical events were
supposed to have occurred.

Similarly on the east side of the Jordan River, where
the Israelites supposedly battled at the city of Heshbon:
"No Late Bronze city, not even a small village there."

How about the battle with the Kingdom of Edom?
"Archeology has shown us that there were no kings of
Edom there for the Israelites to meet."

All these stories were written centuries later. As
any level-headed reader can discern simply by reading
them, and without any knowledge of archeology, they
are tales, part of a continuum with the tales of the
Garden of Eden and Noah's Ark. Moses and Abraham,
like Agamemnon and Aeneas, are literary figures,

meaning that Judaism to a large extent is "literature misconstrued as history," as I wrote in my farther-and-farther-reaching column.

I had all these stimulating thoughts and experiences, and I didn't even know anything about the West Bank yet. We were going there tomorrow.

18

THE WEST BANK

"They understand nothing but force."

I discovered that the West Bank is neither a muddy riverbank nor a depopulated desert but rather a rocky country, thickly populated, about eighty miles long by thirty miles wide, with Jerusalem an indentation in the side of it. Houses built of stone or cement. The Arab cities of Ramallah and Nablus more congested and chaotic than Jewish West Jerusalem, more suggestive of Mexican cities like Tlaxcala, to my eye. But Jews here, Arabs there, and no question about who's in charge, even in Ramallah, the capital of the Palestinian Authority, where we visited the white marble mausoleum of Yassir Arafat. We rode with a helpful and congenial Palestinian Arab, Raed, by arrangement with our J Street friends in Schenectady who had helped set this up. On the ride we saw for the first time the famous wall that Israel has been building, apparently to carve the territory into non-contiguous sections that will make an independent Palestinian state impractical, for all the lip-service given to the "two-state solution." A horribly ugly and depressing thing, politics aside. We visited the native village of Raed's mother—all ancient stone walls, where local leaders showed us the kindergarten quarters they had been building in an old unused mosque and displayed the musical instruments they had just acquired, reminding me again of Mexico, since that is the sort of thing Mexican villagers would do, show visitors their civic achievements.

I wrote for the *Gazoot*:

> *You've heard about Israeli settlements in the occupied West Bank, but if you haven't seen them, you haven't seen them.*
>
> *They are clusters of houses set apart from their Palestinian surroundings by chain-link fences topped by coils of concertina wire. At the entrance is a barrier, and overlooking the houses, or overlooking the rocky approaches, is a guard tower of the kind you see at a military base, and indeed a military base is often nearby.*
>
> *If you tell your driver you'd like to stop and have a closer look, he says, "You want to get shot?"*
>
> *Nearby there is inevitably a Palestinian town or village, and you learn that the settlement was built on land belonging to that town or village—not by purchase or negotiation but simply by force.*
>
> *Israeli Jews moved in with the encouragement of the government, or occasionally without the encouragement of the government, and started building, and the Israeli Defense Forces protected*

them, regardless of government encouragement or lack thereof.

You see Israeli soldiers lollygagging around Ben Yehuda in downtown Jerusalem, and they look for all the world like college students on break, but once you cross over into the West Bank, it's a different story. In the West Bank, part of the once-was and now-aspiring nation of Palestine, they are armed guards for the pioneering land-robbers known delicately as settlers. These settlers occupy the land of people who have lived on it and cultivated it for centuries. They come from Russia and Europe and America, carrying guns, and they say it's ours. We are the children of Israel. We're coming home, and tough luck for you Arabs.

...Keep in mind that the Jewish settlers are armed, the Palestinian villagers for the most part are not, and one of the jobs of Israeli soldiers is to make sure things stay that way, which they accomplish by breaking down doors and ransacking houses, without warrants, without charges, without any legal formalities. Just by main force and as the prerogative of conquerors.

I dimly understood this before I came here, but I never gave it a great deal of thought. I figured you had your religious-tribal fanatics on one side and your religious-tribal fanatics on the other side, and it wasn't my fight. There was nothing I could do about it, and I wasn't going to worry my head.

Now I see things in a new light, having seen with my own eyes.

In one day of driving around Ramallah and Nablus and surrounding hills, I saw dozens of these land-occupation settlements. Some of them looked like tidy housing developments, some looked like junky trailer camps but all of them were fortresses, with their barbed wire and their guard towers— not established with the slightest effort to be good neighbors or to get to know the people they had displaced, if such a thing were possible—but just flat-out Jewish-only enclaves protected by Jewish soldiers, and the hell with you Arabs. Get too close, and we'll shoot you.

...Strolling through the congested market of Nablus, I fell into conversation with a cheese vendor who told me he lives in a village not far away, that after a Jewish settlement was built nearby he and his fellow villagers were restricted in the hours they could cultivate their own olive trees: from 7 a.m. to 2 p.m. only, and for just one week. As a result olives are often left on the trees to rot.

What is the reason for such a restriction? They don't know.

By what earthly right does one tribe invade the land of another tribe and dictate when people may work their land? That's a question that it's not politic to raise. But if you don't obey, you're likely to get shot.

This was all new to me. In my meeting with Mark Regev, the prime minister's international press secretary—who, by the way, was from Australia—I knew just enough to ask how it would be possible for Israel to give up the West Bank in peace negotiations if 300,000 Jewish settlers were living there, and he asked me in return, "Why should it be presumed that no Jews would live in a Palestinian state if 1.5 million Arabs live in Israel?" I didn't have an answer, but now I could see there was a little difference between Jews living in Palestine as armed occupiers of other people's land and Arabs living in Israel as a remnant left behind after being conquered. To equate the two was a bit of sophistry that I didn't know enough at the time to challenge, and I thought, hmm, you've got a point there.

I had the vague sense that Jewish "settlers" were somehow neighbors of the Palestinian Arabs they lived among, and now I was embarrassed at my ignorance. They are neighbors only in the sense that the white settlers of the American West were neighbors of the Indians they lived among. More accurately, they are conquerors, and just as the Indians were conveniently perceived as savages, Palestinian Arabs are conveniently perceived as terrorists. The only thing to do: round them up and put them in reservations, which is basically what Israel was doing with its walls and fences.

"They understand nothing but force," quoth Benzion Netanyahu, the father of Benjamin Netanyahu, in an interview he gave in 1999. The only solution is "strong military rule." And it applies not only to the occupied West Bank but also to those Arabs who make up twenty percent of Israel's citizens: "I think we should speak to the Israeli Arabs in the language they understand and admire—the language of force," declared this elder statesman.

Arabs who fire homemade rockets at Israel from Gaza are terrorists, of course, but Jews who set fire to mosques, who chop down olive trees, who shoot Arab villagers when they get too close to Jewish fortified villages, who assassinate Palestinian leaders, who throw stones at Palestinian children on their way to school, who lock people up without charges, are settlers, or better yet, "defense forces."

I wrote when I got back:

> It came as a shock to me that the modern, prosperous, supposedly democratic country I was in operates a police state in its backyard. And I don't mean a metaphorical police state, or a hyperbolic police state, but a real, literal one...

The self-image of Israel as a small beleaguered nation, beset on all sides by irrational Arabs who hate them just because they are Jews, was beginning to look a little different. So I wrote about it, piling trouble on top of trouble for myself. Ragging on Israel was not like ragging on the Schenectady police or the Stillwater school board, I would soon learn.

Actually, liberal Jews both in Israel and in America speak more harshly of the country than I did. They call the rule of the West Bank an "ethnocracy," and they call Jewish supremacy "racist," referring to such incidents as Jewish soccer fans in Jerusalem spilling over into a shopping mall and attacking Arab maintenance workers, shouting "Death to the Arabs"; or Jews in South Tel Aviv mobbing Sudanese refugees, beating them and smashing windows, denouncing them as a "cancer on our body"; or the Ministry of the Interior deporting the Israeli-born children of Philippine health workers because those children are a "demographic threat."

I preferred "tribal" to "racist." I thought it was more accurate, since physical differences between Jews and Palestinian Arabs can be minimal or even non-existent. If someone's mother or grandmother was a certified member of the Jewish tribe, then that person is a member, regardless of religion or race, neither of which enters into the equation. That person, whether from Russia or Brooklyn or Ethiopia, enjoys what is called with a straight face the "right of return," whereas Arabs, even if born in the land, enjoy no such right, and if they don't watch their step are subject to deportation. In the occupied West Bank, two million Arabs live basically as illegal aliens in the land of their birth, while recent immigrants officially certified as Jews can and do take their land, fence them off from their orchards, and shoot at them if they get too close, all of which was new and fascinating to me and made me glad we had journeyed to Israel rather than to Myrtle Beach for our vacation. It was so novel.

The prayers in the religious guidebook that Rabbi Cutler had loaned me, *Israel: A Spiritual Guide—A Companion for the Modern Pilgrim,* by Rabbi Lawrence A. Hoffman, made the matter clear. One was, "Blessed is God who guards our people Israel forever." Not all people, but our people. Another, quoting the Book of Genesis, was, "God said to Abram: 'Raise your eyes and look out from where you are...To the north and south, to the east and west, for I give all the land that you see to you and your ancestors forever.'" Actually, misquoting Genesis, since God obviously didn't give the land to Abraham's ancestors but rather to his descendants, or his seed. A little screw-up by the author there, but I knew what he meant.

An essential part of the tribal lore is that the Romans drove the Jews out of the Holy Land after putting down a revolt in 70 CE, and Jews thereupon dispersed throughout the world to live in the Diaspora, from which they are latterly returning. Alas, there is no evidence to support such an exile. The best defense that can be mustered for it was offered by one Zachary Esterson, in a blog dedicated to such matters:

> *The tradition may not be history by strictest standards. But it has been believed to be historical for so much of the intervening history, including, if not especially, by Palestinian Christians and Muslims, as itself to constitute a kind of history.*

Which is to say, it may be baloney, like the captivity in Egypt and the Exodus, but a lot of people believe it, so it's as good as true.

I wrote in the *Gazoot*:

> *Israel in the Bible had shifting meanings and uncertain boundaries, but that doesn't matter. It's real. Palestine, however, also of shifting meaning and uncertain boundaries, is not real. It does not figure in the archeology of the otherwise magnificent Israel Museum, and it doesn't figure in the national myth.*

*"There were no such thing as Palestinians,"
quoth the former prime minister, Golda Meir. "They
did not exist."*

*"They're an invented people," agrees Israel
booster Newt Gingrich today.*

*Which of course makes it easier to cut down
their trees, demolish their houses and put them
in prison without charges. You can go a long
way toward understanding Israel's predation of
Palestine by understanding the tribal outlook.*

*Did I say tribal? Tel Aviv has a government-
sponsored counseling program to discourage Jewish
girls from dating Arab boys. A survey in 2007 found
that a majority of Israelis considered marriage
to non-Jews to be "national treason." Not that
"marrying out" is even possible under the rules of
the Chief Rabbinate, which leaves even Reform Jews
out in the cold.*

I sat on a bench in pleasant Ben Yehuda, with its
clean walks, its outdoor cafes, its cheerful strollers, and I
asked myself what we would say about any other country
in the world that did not permit "intermarriage"—
the very word redolent of Jim Crow America and
apartheid South Africa. What would we say about a
nation that regards children born to foreign workers as
a "demographic threat" and deports them? Or about a
prime minister (Benjamin Netanyahu) who talks about
part of the population, the Arab part, as a "demographic
bomb"? Imagine living somewhere where you and your
children are viewed in such a light, especially if it's the

very land where you were born. "Tribal" was the most neutral term I could think of to convey the attitude. I meant no harm by it.

Only later did I learn about the national identification card, which every Israeli sixteen years or older must carry and which used to identify the carrier according to his or her *le'om*, a word that usually gets translated as "nation" or "ethnicity" but I believe could fairly be rendered as "tribe." It definitely does not mean "nationality" in the usual sense, since there was never an Israeli *le'om*. One's *le'om* was either Jewish or Arab, or some minority designation like Druse. The line was eliminated in 2005 not because of the awkward associations with old South Africa, with its racial ID papers, but because the Orthodox rabbis with state power objected to people being identified as Jewish who had been converted by liberal Reform rabbis. Those people were not real Jews, in their eyes, so in a compromise the line was left blank for everyone. Something to think about when you hear Jews proudly describe Israel as the Jewish state. That's what it is, even if Jewish with an Orthodox asterisk after it. It is certainly not the state of Arabs who were born there and who make up a fifth of the population, nor of the small communities of Christians or Druse who have lived there forever. It's certainly not the state of the Filipinos, Thais and Indians who are there to do the dirty work, nor of their children who happen to get born there.

Israel is forever beating its national breast about how the Palestinians refuse to recognize its right to exist, which seemed to me a good point before I went there. How can you negotiate with someone who refuses to recognize your right to exist? I had to go there to learn that what Palestinians object to is the existence of Israel as an officially Jewish state— tribal supremacy guaranteed—to which anyone with a Jewish mother can immigrate and automatically become a citizen but to which native-born people who are not Jewish have no right to return once they have left, and in some cases are subject to deportation. And if they live in the West Bank, have almost no rights at all.

As for the Arabs who lived in what is now Israel before the war of 1948, they left voluntarily, I was told by any number of even liberal Jews, evidence to the contrary having been suppressed until recently. It's the party line, or the tribal line: when in the wake of the Holocaust Jewish immigration to Palestine vastly increased, the United Nations responded with a partition plan, dividing Palestine into a Jewish state and an Arab state. The Arabs resisted, the Jews declared independence, and Arab armies invaded. The Zionists heroically fought back, and in the course of the fighting some 700,000 Palestinian Arabs out of a total of possibly a million packed up their pots and pans and skedaddled—because they desired to skedaddle.

Israel has seen to it that contradictory facts remained hidden.

The New York Times, Jerusalem, October 23, 1979:

A censorship board composed of five Cabinet members prohibited former Prime Minister Yitzhak Rabin from including in his memoirs a first-person account of the expulsion of 50,000 Palestinian civilians from their homes near Tel Aviv during the 1948 Arab-Israeli war.

Mr. Rabin says that some Israeli soldiers refused to participate in driving out the Arabs and that afterward, propaganda sessions were required to soothe the consciences of embittered troops.

Many [Palestinians] *left in panic after the Israeli massacre at the village of Deir Yassin outside Jerusalem, which remains a name of infamy in the Arab world. There, contingents of the extremist Stern gang and Irgun attacked the village and lined men, women and children up against walls and shot them, according to Red Cross and British documentation.*

All this is well enough known by now, as a new wave of Israeli scholars has gained access to more and more Israeli archives. There have been books like *Righteous Victims* by Benny Morris, and *The Ethnic Cleansing of Palestine* by Ilan Pappe, disclosing "Plan Dalet" to drive Arabs out of the land the Zionists desired, which included not only the land apportioned them by the United Nations, which was already fifty-five percent of Palestine, but half again as much, which is what they conquered by force of arms. Still the party line, or the tribal line, remains unchanged, and I have been lectured on it by liberal Reform Jews as well as by overt zealots. The land is ours by legal right, and the Arabs who left during the war of 1948 did so freely and voluntarily, and of course *they* have no right of return.

In the Nablus market I picked through a display rack of trinkets, looking for a souvenir, and came upon an enamel pendant with the Palestinian flag on one side and a key on the other. I asked the vendor what it signified, and he told me that when the Arabs fled their homes in 1948 before the advancing Zionist forces, many of them took their house keys with them, expecting they would shortly return, and the key represents that now-forlorn desire. No doubt many alert citizens in the world are aware of this situation, but I was not aware of it. It was news to me, the scenario of aggressive well-armed Jews from Europe driving out the native population of Palestine and continuing to bully them in the more recently conquered West Bank. I read an interview with Benny Morris, the aforementioned historian and defender of Israel:

> *A Jewish state would not have come into being without the uprooting of 700,000 Palestinians. Therefore it was necessary to uproot them. There was no choice but to expel that population.*

I had absorbed by osmosis the notion of Palestinians as terrorists and Israelis as creators of an admirable democracy. Now I thought, well, I'm getting an education.

At one point driving through the hardscrabble hills near Ramallah, Raed told us his family used to go to a certain park for picnics, but now a Jewish settlement had been built nearby and his mother wouldn't go for fear of being shot. I wanted to see, so we went, dragging poor Pearl along, though she would have been much happier back in Ben Yehuda in an outdoor cafe. It wasn't much of a park, just another rocky mound of a hill with some low scrubby trees and here and there a few picnic tables. A cluster of tile-roofed houses surrounded by chain-link fencing and barbed wire was visible on another rocky mound, maybe 100 yards away. It didn't look particularly threatening, but Raed said the danger was that the Jewish settlers who lived there could come out and chase us away. How would they do that? They would throw rocks or even shoot guns.

We started slowly up the hill, and then Raed suddenly grabbed my arm and said, "Wait." Up ahead, through the trees, we could see three or four young men perched on a picnic table. We moved slowly and cautiously, not to draw attention to ourselves, and then stopped to listen when we could hear their voices. "It's OK," Raed said after a tense minute. "They're Palestinians."

For me it was a new way of looking at the world.

Of course, when I thought about Judaism I still relished the primitive taboos and ritual instructions of the first five books of the Old Testament, the Jewish holy of holies, just as I relished them when I was ragging on Protestants who claim "inerrancy" for the whole caboodle of the Bible:

> *If a woman gives birth to a boy, she shall be considered unclean for a week. If she gives birth to a girl, she shall be considered unclean for two weeks. Then, after a period of purification,*

she shall bring a lamb to the tabernacle to be sacrificed. (Leviticus 12:1–7)

If a man commits adultery with another man's wife, both the man and the woman shall be put to death. (Leviticus 20:10)

Don't boil a kid in its mother's milk [interpreted to mean, don't mix meat and dairy products in any manner, to the extent of keeping separate sets of dishes]. (Exodus 23:19, 34:23, and Deuteronomy 14:21)

Keep only foreigners, not fellow Israelites, as slaves. (Leviticus 25:44)

If you lend money, it's OK to charge interest to outsiders but not to fellow Israelites. (Deuteronomy 23:19–20)

Don't eat the meat of a pig, a rabbit or a camel. A pig because it has split hooves but does not chew the cud, a rabbit because it chews the cud [allegedly] but has no hooves, and a camel likewise. (Leviticus 11:4–8, Deuteronomy 14:7)

Don't wear clothing made of two different kinds of material, like linen and wool. (Leviticus 19:19)

If a friend or family member tries to convert you to a different religion, kill him. (Deuteronomy 13:6–10)

You can eat winged creatures that go on all fours if they have jointed legs, like locusts, crickets and grasshoppers, but not otherwise. (Leviticus. 11:20–24)

If an Israelite offends God, he should bring to the priest an unblemished bull for a sacrifice.

The priest shall kill the bull, then dip his finger in the blood and sprinkle it seven times before God. And the priest shall put some of the blood on the horns of the altar of aromatic incense ...and all the blood of the bull he shall pour out at the base of the burnt-offering altar...and all the fat of the bull of offense offering, he shall set aside from it the fat covering the innards...the two kidneys and the fat that is on them, which is on the sinews, and the lobe on the liver, together with the kidney, he shall take away...[and so on and so on]. (Leviticus 4:1–10)

If a man has an unseemly discharge from his male member, he shall be deemed unclean. A week after being free of the discharge he shall take two young pigeons to the priest and the priest shall sacrifice them to atone for the man before God. (Leviticus 15:13–16)

Such bizarre prescriptions and proscriptions make up three of the five books of the mighty Torah: Leviticus, Numbers and Deuteronomy. Mythological history makes up the other two: Genesis and Exodus.

A liberal Jewish friend, anxious that I perceive the goodness of his religion, quoted to me the old saw about Rabbi Hillel, who lived and died at about the time of Jesus, being asked if he could recite Jewish Law while standing on one foot, and replying, "That which is hateful to you, do not to your fellow." Essentially what Christians know as the Golden Rule. But the perspicacious reader of the Torah will see that the laws laid down therein are the queer and merciless laws of a primitive desert tribe, nothing more, and anyone endeavoring to live by them today would quickly be confined to an insane asylum, if not first arrested for murder. They have nothing to do with treating one's neighbor as one would wish to be treated oneself, and in any case, one's "fellow" in the Torah clearly meant one's fellow Jew, not one's fellow human being.

But I was now fired up over the exclusivist aspect of the Jewish state more than over the comical laws, which I had already spoofed anyway, and I considered it my unique contribution, at least as far as Schenectady went, to make the connection between the religion and the nation––"Israel, Like Judaism, Is for the Tribe," I headlined a column––indicting religion as the motivating force behind the malevolent occupation of other people's land:

> One thing that struck me about Judaism on my brief visit to Jerusalem is that it's a tribal religion. The god that it posits—the ineffable YHWH—is the god of a particular people, his Chosen People, in opposition to other gods of other peoples.
>
> That's the way it originated in Biblical times, when YHWH had to compete with Ba'al and other disreputable types, and that's the way it still seems today.
>
> Christianity, for all its warts, is at least intended for everyone.
>
> Islam claims to be for everyone, but its god speaks only Arabic and you have to be able to pray in Arabic if you want to have any show with him.

Judaism makes no pretensions to universality.

This matters because Judaism is the heart of the state of Israel. The state is not for everyone either. It's for members of the tribe, as made clear in its declaration of independence and its national anthem. Its central conceit is that modern-day Jews, whether from Poland or Ethiopia, and regardless of physical type, are all lineal descendants of the Israelites of the Bible.

After 2,000 years they have come home. You hear this all the time in Israel. I heard it most memorably from an aggressive guy in downtown Jerusalem who buttonholed me and tried to get me to sign a petition against the division of Jerusalem, not that any such division is in the works. "We waited 2,000 years!" he shouted at me, though I was not offering any resistance.

It turned out he was from New York, though he could as well have been from Kiev or Marrakech.

True, Zionism began as a secular, socialist movement, not as the religious-chauvinist cult it has become, but the tribal folklore that motivated it was never separable from the religious folklore.

"This country exists as the fulfillment of a promise made by God himself," insisted the nominally secular Golda Meir. "It would be ridiculous to ask it to account for its legitimacy."

I was pleased with myself for figuring all this out as a mere tourist on a pleasure trip. I'll probably get a prize for writing it up, I thought. Maybe Schenectady will give me a ticker-tape parade when I get back.

Leaving the West Bank to re-enter Jerusalem, we had a choice between the main checkpoint, Qalandia, used by Palestinians going to work in Israel, which I was warned might be time-consuming and irksome, and another one farther away, used by everyone else, most notably by commuting Jewish settlers. We opted for Qalandia. Whatever inconvenience Palestinians put up with to enter Jerusalem (which of course used to be half theirs) we would put up with too, to see what it was like. But in the end I couldn't do it. To make ourselves available for searching and questioning we had to herd ourselves into a long, narrow cage, in the nighttime darkness of a concrete holding area more dispiriting than a prison. A couple dozen downcast Palestinian men were already ahead of us in this tunnel-shaped cage, wide enough for just one human body, and more were coming behind us, so in another minute or two we would be packed in, unable to move, our shoulders wedged against the bars, bodies jammed in front of us and behind, wire above us so we couldn't even climb out in an emergency. We were told the wait would be at least an hour and a half. My breathing had become a desperate panting, and I felt like my brain was going to explode. I frantically backed my way out, pulling Pearl with me.

This was how Palestinians from the occupied West Bank who held work permits lined up every day to go their menial jobs in Jerusalem. It was not for security. Anyone could have strolled up and thrown a grenade without entering the cage. There weren't even any guards around. The guards were on the other side, waiting to frisk us after we had gone through the cage. It could only have been to "sear the consciousness," as I later learned the Israeli military calls its more perverse exercises.

Through the good offices of a friend, arrangements were made with a taxi bearing a yellow Israeli license plate rather than a green Palestinian one, and that taxi drove us twenty minutes to the other crossing point, where settlers go through. At Qalandia we had been coached that we would have to show our passports, we would be searched, and any bags would be examined, which is what we were crowded into the cage waiting for. At the second crossing we got waved through without having to show any identification and without even getting out of the taxi. How come? We were the same people, coming from the same West Bank, entering the same Jerusalem as before. "They thought you were Jewish," the taxi driver said.

Now, I was not so naïve as *not* to realize I might be giving offense with my observations on Israel and Judaism. I figured I had established my *bona fides* with my ridicule of Protestant fundamentalism and Roman Catholicism, so no one could single me out as being specifically anti-Jewish, but at this point I thought it might be prudent to take a whack at Islam too, just to further demonstrate my ecumenism.

I had already written a couple of years earlier about both the Qur'an and the Hadith in my self-assigned capacity as the Gazoot's theologian-in-residence, the Qur'an being of course the holy book of Islam, supposedly dictated by God himself, and the Hadith being a rambling and repetitious collection of anecdotes related by the Prophet's followers over the next couple of centuries, supposedly capturing and illustrating the Prophet's teachings.

I did it with what I thought was an appropriate level of awe, that level being rather low. Of the Qur'an:

> It's almost all browbeating: God is great! He has no partners! Unbelievers will burn in hell!
> ...Like the God of the Bible, the God of the Qur'an is an egomaniac, the most important matter in the world to him being that we believe in him. The main difference is that Christians are enjoined to love God, Muslims to fear him. Hardly a Qur'anic page goes by without the injunction, "Fear God!"

Of the Hadith:

> ...the Prophet himself, that old billy-goat, "used to go around (meaning, have sex with) all his wives in one night, and he had nine wives."
> ...Nor was he particular that these wives be of mature years. His favorite was Aisha. "The Prophet (in his fifties) married her when she was six years old and he consummated his marriage when she was nine years old"...
> Nothing further is said about the matter; it's presented entirely matter-of-factly, as if it were the most normal thing in the world. Today, of course, it would get him up to twenty-five years in prison.
> Islam was born in war—don't let anyone kid you about its being a religion of peace—and the Prophet Muhammed was a military leader as much as a religious leader.

Now, trying to burnish my non-discriminatory credentials, I was moved to recall some of Islam's recent barbarities: the stoning to death of a thirteen-year-old Somali girl for having been raped; the extradition of a Saudi writer from Malaysia back to his homeland on charges of insulting the Prophet in tweets; a Dutch moviemaker and shot and stabbed to death for slandering the holy faith.

I thought I had also made myself clear a couple of years earlier when I attended an event in Albany called the United National Peace Conference, featuring a lineup of left-wing outfits ranging from the Women's International League for Peace and Freedom to Voices for Creative Non-Violence. It was my report on this conference that led the J Street people to reach out to me as someone obviously not biased against Israel. The flavor of the conference, I reported, was:

> ...that the United States along with its partner Israel is the Great Satan of the world. Nobody used those exact words, but that's the idea. As for Islamic jihadism, the less said the better.

I mocked a participant for claiming "the greatest threat to global security is the United States and Israel," and I took sarcastic note of Noam Chomsky, famous linguist as well as relentless critic of U.S. foreign policy, saying by video hookup with regard to terrorism by Hamas and Hezbollah, "Those acts pale in comparison to U.S. and Israeli acts."

I sneered at a gentle soft-spoken woman, an alleged voice for creative non-violence, who tried to explain away the internecine bombings and murders in Afghanistan and Pakistan by sectarian fanatics as an example of "strategizing" by poor oppressed people. "If you've never got a teeny fraction of the military power of the United States, what are you going to do? How do you fight back?" she asked. Which made me very nearly throw up.

> *And as for the medieval fanaticism that leads to the shrouding of women, the burning down of girls' schools, the beheading of adulterers, the imprisonment of mentally retarded people for insulting the Qur'an, nothing was said. Not by Chomsky, not by anyone. Not even by the women's groups that were represented.*

I didn't think I could be any more fair and balanced than that. But it didn't do any good. Not any good at all.

19

THE MAD RABBI

*"…sometimes for the sake of peace,
truth needs to be buried."*

It began right away, before I'd been back in Schenectady more than a day or two. I was about to pop over to Congregation Gates of Heaven to deliver to Rabbi Cutler the skullcap I had bought for him at the Kippa Man shop, a nice one, with the skyline of the Old City embroidered on it—cost me fifteen bucks—when a Gazoot secretary showed me a letter to the editor she had just received from him. It was a scorcher:

> *I write to share my outrage over Carl Strock's columns on his recent trip to Jerusalem. I spoke with him prior to his trip…He made it clear that what he wanted were extremists, not rational or mainstream voices.*
>
> *He painted a distorted view of Jerusalem—offensive to many people of faith: Jews, Christians*

and Muslims. I have read his columns over the years and found them at times interesting and thought-provoking—but these articles went too far. They were not only infuriating, full of inaccuracies and sloppy reporting, they were inflammatory, containing distortions and bordering on anti-Semitic.

As a Jew who were wears t'fillin (the leather phylacteries referred to by Strock as "S&M cultists' toys"), I have prayed for the return of Jews to the land of Israel...To imply that Jews are occupiers of a land that has been the spiritual center of their faith is repugnant! To imply that the death of Jews at Masada is "historical fiction" is the type of historical revisionism that spurs hatred. History is clear, but Mr. Strock's research fell short of discovering it.

Just prior to Strock's visit, southern Israel was under attack. Rockets from Gaza rained down, forcing 2 million Israelis to seek shelter. Schools were canceled. In one day alone, 107 rockets crashed throughout the region. If you and I had to live under this type of threat, wouldn't checkpoints and additional security measures be seen as essential?

In our synagogue, there is a poster of Gilad Shalit (the Israeli solider who was kidnapped by Hamas terrorists and held for several years); next to that is a poster of the hundreds of Israeli citizens who were murdered by homicide bombers. One congregant noted that in order to obtain the freedom for one Israeli soldier, those responsible for the deaths of hundreds had to be permitted to go free. This is why these rules were enacted.

I am a Jew who firmly believes in the existence of the state of Israel. I am also one who is empathetic to the plight of Palestinians. Yet even I was surprised by the one-sided and blatantly biased approach to covering the situation.

Mr. Strock's reporting left readers with questions unanswered because he did not follow through by speaking with Israeli authorities. The result was inaccurate perceptions.

Good sport that I am, I delivered the skullcap to the synagogue anyway, with a note saying I had seen the letter but appreciated his help nonetheless. A couple of days later I got the cap back in the mail with a note from him saying he could not accept it.

His letter was published with all its calumny, and I was not happy. I responded in my column:

I was especially pained by the letter in yesterday's paper from the rabbi of Congregation Gates of Heaven in Schenectady, who had graciously counseled me before I embarked on my journey.

Now he says my reports are "bordering on anti-Semitic," which is a charge so shabby that I will not embarrass either of us by responding to it... He says my research "fell short of discovering" the truth about Masada ... though in fact I didn't do any research at all on that subject but just passed along what the Israel Museum says ... He also says I "did not follow through" on my personal adventures "by speaking with Israeli authorities," who presumably would have set me straight, though in fact I had a half-hour meeting with Prime Minister Netanyahu's international press secretary [at his instigation, I should have noted.]

... *He tells us that in his synagogue there hangs a poster of an Israeli soldier who was "kidnapped by Hamas terrorists" and another of "hundreds of Israeli citizens murdered by homicide bombers," wherein we see again the tribal perspective. No posters of any of the 1,463 Palestinian children killed by Israelis since 2000 (according to the website ifamericansknew.org), as opposed to 124 Israeli children killed in Palestinian attacks.* [This was before the Gaza battle of November 2012, which yielded similarly lopsided results.]

No posters of Hana Shalabi, the Palestinian woman who fasted forty days to protest her detention—I saw those posters in Ramallah, land of the other tribe.

Nor posters of any of the other 300 Palestinians that Israel acknowledges holding in what it calls "administrative detention," without charges, without sentences.

His synagogue honors victims from its own tribe, including a soldier, but ignores the more numerous victims from the other tribe. Then he tells us, eyes heavenward, that he is "one who is empathetic to the plight of Palestinians."

Let him get squeezed into the holding cage at the Qalandia checkpoint with a few dozen Palestinian men trying to get to work and then come back and talk to us about empathy.

I waited to see if there would be an outcry about a house of worship being used as a platform for nationalist propaganda, but there was not. But that bit about the Israeli soldier being "kidnapped" really got me. Not captured, but kidnapped, an event that I'm told precipitated a five-year orgy of sentimentality in Israel, an orgy in which this rabbi evidently participated. A poster in his synagogue! What kind of house of worship was this? Wasn't I exactly right that Judaism was strictly for the tribe? Damn right I was.

There were other letters too, as my education continued to expand:

> I refuse to give credence to Carl Strock's anti-Semitic series with a point-by-point response to his skewed statistics and xenophobic comments. (Rabbi Rose Durbin, Knesseth Israel, Gloversville)

> On the subject of religion, Strock has a lot to learn...It is suggested that Mr. Strock take a class in comparative religion to understand that the God of Abraham is the one God common to the Jewish, various Christian and Islamic faithers. (Michael Fischer, Saratoga Springs)

> I am dismayed at your printing the prejudiced and hateful rantings of Carl Strock...His making fun of the religious articles and manner of dress of the Orthodox he saw in Jerusalem shows his intolerance and ignorance...Strock seemed to be comparing the Israeli army's treatment of Palestinians to Nazis. That's more than outrageous, it is anti-Semitic. (Debbie Gatoff, Schenectady)

...three weeks of incessant bashing and ridiculing of Israel, Jews and Judaism...Strock's words are not harmless. They are biased, distorted and dangerous... Six million innocent Jews, including my grandparents' families, were systematically murdered by the Nazis...When Jews are unjustly characterized as running an "undisguised police state" or [as] "land robbers," and when Judaism is called "tribal," it has the real potential of inciting prejudice, discrimination and violence against Jews. Historically, anti-Semitic violence, including the Holocaust, has begun with accusatory anti-Jewish rhetoric. (Rabbi Moshe Mirsky, Congregation Beth Israel, Schenectady)

The Gazette has joined the ugly chorus of hate that is drowning out thoughtful, respectful public discourse by publishing columns ridiculing all religion, their prayers and rituals...Mr. Strock reveals a stunning ignorance of Judaism and the Jewish people. (Megan Levine, Niskayuna)

Shame on you, Mr. Strock. Your lack of knowledge of the history of the Middle East since 1948 and your blatant intolerance and lack of respect for other cultures repels us. (Judy and Asa Kaplan, Charlton)

I think he might be biased, lacking in any historical background or the area of simply shooting from the hip due to pure ignorance. (Jonas Kover, Amsterdam)

There was even a letter from the Anti-Defamation League in New York City, where the *Gazoot* was not widely circulated, to put it mildly, meaning that someone in Schenectady must have helpfully supplied it:

> *Carl Strock's preconceived biases toward Israel and Jews are evident in the offensive and defaming notions permeating his recent columns to describe Israel, Jews and Jewish religious practices...Strock is not an objective commentator...his trip seems to have reinforced his premeditated animosity toward the Jewish state...Had Strock spent time in Tel Aviv, he would have experienced a diverse city with a strong secular and intellectual culture, and an internationally recognized gay-friendly community that is unique to the Middle East.* [I later learned that Tel Aviv's gay-friendliness is a government talking point; Israeli dissenters refer to it as "pink-washing."] *Yes, Israel, a land which Jews have called their religious, spiritual and cultural home for over 3,000 years, is not a perfect country... It's a shame that Strock failed to see beyond his own preconceived anti-Israel and anti-Jewish biases..."* (Ron Meier, director, New York Regional Anti-Defamation League)

The original of this letter, as it arrived at the newspaper, was more colorful, accusing me, among other things, of comparing Jews to Nazis, which I had not done. The editors removed the bald misstatements before publishing it.

There was also a letter that the *Gazoot* did not publish at all, from the deputy chairman of the Schenectady County Legislature, Brian Gordon, who not so subtly pointed out that the *Gazoot* was the official newspaper of the county, meaning it was where legal notices were placed, to the financial benefit of the newspaper. "In the future, I hope that the *Daily Gazette* utilizes better judgment in selecting which articles to publish and understands its role as the official newspaper of Schenectady County," he wrote.

And there was a letter in the *Jewish World* newspaper from students at Maimonides Hebrew Middle School, saying, "Mr. Strock's inciting hateful writing recalls the 1930s Nazi 'Der Sturmmer' propaganda, awful caricatures that led to the Holocaust horrors!"

Part of my alleged incitement, of course, was my use of the world "tribe," so I was especially pleased that in that same issue of *Jewish World* there was a report on a national Jewish youth conference called TribeFest, with the word "TribeFest" displayed in a banner across the front page.

Of course there were friendly letters, and quite a lot of them, mostly to me personally but a few for publication, and they provided balm for the sting. The one that most struck me was from the mother of a young woman who had lived in the West Bank for the past six years:

> *My husband and I wanted you to know that your accurate description of the area is noted every day by our daughter. She, herself, while volunteering for the NGO in Beit Sahour, was attacked by settlers. The NGO she was with had built a playground for the children of Beit Sahour. The settlers would repeatedly vandalize the playground at night and harass the children during*

the day. One day, Elizabeth and a group of volunteers happened to be on the site when the settlers showed up. The settlers began shouting and throwing things, and an object struck our daughter in the head. She finally said something to them in Hebrew which stopped them in their tracks as they are not used to someone responding to them in their own language. The Israeli soldiers appeared then, and everyone dispersed. Sadly, the playground was eventually dismantled and removed to a less suitable location in Beit Sahour. (Eva and Chuck Vandrei, Schenectady)

I was fairly reeling by now despite such encouragement. Cutler and two other rabbis even wrote an op-ed piece for *Jewish World*, a regional newspaper based in Albany supported by the Jewish Federation, in which they directed readers to a "Boycott the Gazette" Facebook page, urging people "to voice their disapproval by canceling their subscriptions," which the Jewish Community Center promptly did.

The three rabbis wrote:

Mr. Strock openly admits that when he went to Jerusalem, he went to meet with fringe elements in society [upping the rhetorical ante; now I openly admitted it]...*He defines the modern state of Israel as a "police state"* [I had said it "operates a police state in its backyard."]...*He regards Jewish claims to the land based on Torah as "mythology" as if "Greece hanging its national hat on the Iliad and Odyssey."* [I thought it was a good analogy, even if the rabbis did garble the grammar.]

More ominously, they wrote:

> *Recently, Shelly Shapiro, director of community relations of the Jewish Federation of Northeast New York, convened a meeting of the three pulpit rabbis in Schenectady, the executive director of the Schenectady Jewish Community Center and representatives of the leadership of the local Federation. Their plan is to meet with the editorial staff to voice their disapproval of Mr. Strock's words. While appreciating the importance of free speech and a free press, this group is concerned that such a tone is prompting a rise in hatred and racism in our community. They are also concerned that much of what was written is inaccurate and misleading. The primary goals for the Jewish community are to defend against the attack on all religions and to hold the Gazette accountable for the words used by one of its columnists. It also seeks to advocate for the legitimacy of the state of Israel. The Federation's executive director, Rodney Margolis, said that these columns should be taken seriously and addressed by a clear, definitive and united voice.*

We had gotten angry reaction when I mocked the Catholic story of St. Kateri and also when I ridiculed Protestant creationists, but "this feels different," the general manager of the *Gazoot* told me, and indeed it did.

I suspected part of the problem was that the Jewish Federation was irked that their effort to spin me had misfired. Considering me an "important voice," they had directed me to the right-wing "Likud Party and/or the ruling government," per Rabbi Cutler's request, which turned out to mean Netanyahu's press secretary, no doubt hoping I would adopt the official perspective as my own and come back and write accordingly, maybe clucking my tongue about poor Israel surrounded by a sea of crazy Arabs—the party line—with perhaps a sentimental word for an Israeli soldier "kidnapped by terrorists," and it didn't work. Rabbi Cutler was even concerned that his fellows wouldn't get "another crack" at me after I saw the West Bank with my own eyes, I now remembered. When my columns started appearing in the *Gazoot*, it must have been awful for them. A real kick in the pants.

I imagined Rod Margolis and Shelly Shapiro giving the rabbi a chewing out: "What the hell were you thinking when you sent this guy to us? Didn't you ever read what he wrote about religion? Bibi will never trust us again [Bibi is Netanyahu's nickname.] The next time we ask for a favor he'll throw Strock up to us and tell us we're self-hating Jews," which is the equivalent of anti-Semite for members of the tribe.

It would be all over for them. No more red carpet when they made their pilgrimages to Eretz Israel, as tribal mystics call the country. They might even get detained at Ben-Gurion airport and shipped back home, for God's sake, like some pitiful left-wing demonstrators from Europe.

Pretty soon Rabbi Cutler took to the pulpit of the First Reformed Church in Schenectady's Stockade neighborhood, when the pastor happened to be traveling in Europe—his synagogue had an exchange agreement with the church—and there he devoted his sermon to me and my poor columns, saying he had been "consumed" by them and that they were "in our hearts and souls highly inflammatory and bordering on anti-Semitism."

All I could be grateful for at this point was that I was still just "bordering" and had not yet been fully inducted into the company of Josef Goebbels. I wasn't present for this unusual sermon, which I regret, since I'm sure I would have enjoyed it, but it was tape-recorded and posted on the church's website, so I was able to enjoy it later in the comfort of my home:

> *As a Jew I have been exposed to anti-Semitism throughout my life. Anti-Semitism left unchecked causes hatred to grow by exponential power that brings about a Holocaust whether you like it or not...When someone attacks Jews because their religious garb is like a sado-masochistic cult, that hurts, and when I look at my t'fillin, which is an S&M cultist's toy, this is what my grandfather brought over from Europe ...it's not a sexual fetish, this is something that was sacred, important to him, and to demean it in any other way is just hurtful... Anti-Semitism is when you attack Jews for being Jews, like calling an Orthodox Jew who wants to spend his life studying, worthless.*
>
> *A thirteen-year-old gets in the mail last week that she is responsible for the death of Jesus because of blood libel. That is anti-Semitism...It's anti-Semitism to say Jews learned from the Nazis...I have a strong connection to Israel. Israel is my*

spiritual homeland…For sixty-four years there has been a state of Israel, it's not a European conquest thing, per the president of Iran…The inhabitants of Israel have never had a day of peace…There are things the Israel government does that I'm not proud of…Certain things are pretty awful…Carl Strock was held in a containment area in the West Bank in a demeaning way…but my nephew didn't go to school [because] *107 missiles fell on southern Israel.*

Who's telling the truth? I will tell you it doesn't matter. Rabbi Israel Salanter, a medieval sage, said that sometimes for the sake of peace, truth needs to be buried.

It was weird: first using someone else's pulpit to fire rhetorical rockets at a lowly newspaper columnist, which made some parishioners squirm, as I soon learned, and then taking a cavalier attitude toward the truth, which is hardly what you expect from a clergyman. You expect a clergyman to argue that truth is absolute, emanating from God. But:

Truth, I will tell you, is a relative term in my eyes. You have your truth, and I have my truth… that doesn't mean you're right and I'm wrong, or I'm right and you're wrong …it means truth has different places in different settings.

Weird. And to quote some nineteenth-century sage (not medieval) as saying that for the sake of peace, truth sometimes needs to be buried—what the devil did that mean, that I should have kept quiet about what I saw in the West Bank? That the truth about Israel ought to be hushed up?

I was beginning to think of him as The Mad Rabbi, without realizing he was just getting rolling.

He e-mailed me directly:

> *I write to make a personal plea for you to stop degrading Jews, Judaism and Israel...You may not see yourself as anti-Semite nor your words hurtful, but both conclusions can be made...Since these articles have appeared, there has been an increase of unrest directed at the Jewish community. Since you made your observations, many of us have been consumed with responding to the increased fear and anger that is emerging among many in the community. In addition to that, I have received 3 visits from various law enforcement agencies because of threats to the community and to me personally. A man has come to the synagogue saying that he is prepared to defend the Jews and he has the weapons to do it. Several 7th and 8th grade students have received hand-addressed envelopes, containing anti-Jewish material—some of them have come to my daughter. The titles are called the "Passover Plot" and the "Blood Libel," which reference that the Jews are responsible for the death of Jesus and the "only way to avoid punishment for this sin is to embrace Jesus." I have received phone calls in the middle of night. While we cannot prove that your columns are the spark of many of the incidents, let me say that in 17 years in the community I have never*

encountered these all at once...I beg you to stop your tirades before someone gets more than their feelings hurt. Unlike any other of your talks on religion, this one has created a threat of violence—knowing that, it is irresponsible for you to continue!

(A man with weapons? A year later we learned, partially, what was going on, when the FBI arrested two men connected with the Schenectady GE plant of trying to build a sci-fi machine to zap Muslims with deadly radiation at long distance. One was a GE mechanic, member of a local Tea Party group and self-described Ku Klux Klanner; the other was a GE contractor with a background in computer software. The mechanic, we learned, had gone to Rabbi Cutler's synagogue to offer "a type of technology that could be used by Israel to defeat its enemies," according to the FBI complaint. The synagogue's secretaries who spoke to him referred him to the Jewish Federation of Northeastern New York, which I thought was revealing, and then, after he left, called the police. This is the zaniness that the rabbi implied I was responsible for.)

But it was hard to believe: me, blamed for Jesus-freak propaganda in junior high school! Blood libel! A man with weapons ready to defend the Jews! I've got to shut up or there will be violence!

I wrote back:

Matt: This has got to stop, you accusing me of anti-Semitism and bad-mouthing me around town, even laying responsibility for hate incidents at my doorstep. Someone has weapons and is prepared to defend Jews? It goes beyond criticism and fair commentary and borders on hysteria.

I understand that as a man of the cloth you would like religion to be exempt from ridicule, but I'm sorry, I think the world would be a better place if religion were demystified and subjected to the same treatment as any other human endeavor, and I will continue to write accordingly.

Disagree all you like, but I implore you to stay within the bounds of rationality, and for God's sake, lay off the anti-Semite stuff. It does you no credit.

To which he responded tersely:

And this is why I want to see you fired.

The guy has gone off his rocker, I thought. Whatever he has is worse than Jerusalem Syndrome, and it's only a shame the Kfar Shaul mental health center is too far away to get him there in a timely manner.

When he finally calmed down enough to put his thoughts in order, it wasn't any better. He had figured out the criteria for anti-Semitism, and he measured me by them. His criteria were:

> *a. Hatred of Jews for being Jews*
> *b. Death or physical harm to Jews*
> *c. Mocking Jewish beliefs*
> *d. Denouncing the Torah and religious texts*
> *e. Denouncing Israel's right to exist*
> *f. Degrading Jews*

He decided to upgrade (or downgrade) me from his previous "bordering." He allowed that I didn't call for "death or physical harm to Jews," but he wrote:

> *5 out of 6 is a passing grade—you fit the term: anti-Semite.*

Me, for Chrissake. In the same sub-type of the species as those who think Jews are in cahoots with the devil.

> *This is hardly over, Carl. It is not my call nor yours to end it...I wish you well, not malice. But I do want to see you removed as a columnist for spewing anti-Semitism.*

Now, the reader is no doubt aware that anti-Semitism is a very real pathology with a long and ugly history, entailing such beliefs as that Jews are collectively responsible for the death of Jesus ("Christ-killers"), that they drink the blood of Christian children (the "blood libel"), that they are in conspiracy to take over the world (per the fraudulent *Protocols of the Elders of Zion*), and so forth, and that this pathology has manifested itself over the centuries in periodic murderous rampages in Europe and Russia, culminating most grotesquely in the gas chambers of Auschwitz. It has been promoted not only by ignorant peasants and megalomaniacal tyrants but also by such notables of Western civilization as Martin Luther and Henry Ford. In its milder, less murderous form it was an off-note of American society well into the first half of the twentieth century, when proper country clubs would deny membership to Jews and Ivy League universities would discreetly limit their acceptance. But the reader who has not lived in a cave for the past half-century is probably also aware that there has been a vast change in this department and that anti-Semitism is now the property of a small and impotent lunatic fringe, while persons of the Jewish persuasion, despite their modest numbers, have become fully accepted as Supreme Court justices, members of Congress, and leaders in every field imaginable, from academia to business to the arts to journalism, so that if anyone today were to arch an eyebrow and slyly insinuate that a certain candidate might not be suited for office because he is, ahem, you know what I mean, that insinuator would be laughed to scorn and would never again enjoy a public platform. If you want to find a red-blooded anti-Semite today you have to hunt up a survivalist militia in the canyons of Idaho, and even that wouldn't be easy. So it's extremely curious that at the same time this most salutary development has occurred, there has arisen among many prominent Jewish citizens and organizations the conviction that anti-Semitism is everywhere, bubbling barely beneath the surface, and that a second Holocaust is imminent if we're not careful. Organizations like the Anti-Defamation League, the Simon Wiesenthal Center and the American-Israel Public Affairs Committee, to pick just the most prominent examples, positively make their living promoting this anachronistic fear. Rabbi Cutler in Schenectady is just a small example of it. Scholars say the counter-experiential shift in Jewish consciousness followed upon the spectacular success of Israel in the

1967 war, but still cannot explain it. It seems to make no sense except as a weapon for compelling deference to the newly empowered state of Israel. I was just learning about it, and it took me very much by surprise.

20

THE END

"You know what? You were absolutely right."

One prominent member of the local Jewish community not yet heard from was Neil Golub, president and CEO of the Golub Corporation headquartered in Schenectady, owner of the Price Chopper supermarket chain with some 125 stores in New York and neighboring states, which was No. 116 on the Forbes list of the nation's largest private companies with $3.4 billion in revenue in 2011. He was the area's highest-profile philanthropist, and he had helped form the Metroplex Authority to rebuild downtown Schenectady. The headquarters of the Jewish Federation of Northeastern New York was named for him, and the *Jewish World* newspaper operated out of offices that he donated.

Rabbi Cutler told someone who told me that Golub was furious about my columns, but I dismissed it. "Neil Golub has never been shy about expressing his opinions," I said, "and we haven't heard from him."

Indeed, he had occasionally called me in the past, sometimes with a minor complaint about some comment or other I had made about the Metroplex Authority, sometimes with a suggestion for a column against the labor unions that were trying to organize his employees, and he occasionally wrote a letter to the editor too. But after a couple of weeks of Jewish furor over my reports from Israel, there had been nothing.

Then the phone rang, and there he was. "What about the Holocaust?" he demanded, and he proceeded to give me a lecture about Jewish history and my ignorance thereof. "We are not a tribe," he insisted. (I didn't ask him about TribeFest.) He told me I hadn't read anything about Jewish history, which he of course would have had no way of knowing, and I meekly replied that if he would recommend books for me to read, I would be sure to read them. He promised to send me a list, but alas I never got one. Maybe it got lost in the mail. He also told me about a program that he sponsored in local schools called "A World of Difference," promoting tolerance and diversity, and expressed disgust that I didn't know about it. (Only later did I discover that this was a program of the Anti-Defamation League, principal purveyor of the anti-Semitism panic, and he was just the underwriter.) Finally he demanded that I apologize for my unflattering words about Israel and Judaism, and I said I would not.

But I was shaken. Neil Golub was not a rabbi having a convulsion because his grandfather's leather thongs had been made light of. He was Schenectady's first citizen, practically, and not incidentally one of the *Gazoot's* biggest advertisers.

It didn't get better. Rabbi Cutler and his Jewish Federation friends did demand a meeting with the *Gazoot* editor to air their complaints and press their demands, as promised in the *Jewish World* op-ed piece, and this meeting would be held at Golub's corporate headquarters, a new green-glass monument a few blocks from the *Gazoot's* own headquarters. I thought it was not just a poor plan but an outrageous one. It amounted to the *Gazoot* being called on the carpet and acquiescing in it. Anyone else who had a gripe with us—even the FBI and the U.S. Attorney —came to our turf, and the discussion was on the record, with a reporter taking notes and a photographer recording the occasion, all for publication. That was standard procedure, and in my years at the newspaper it had never been different. In the case of the FBI and the U.S. Attorney, I had written about the meeting myself and had mocked them for their presumption. The idea of us shuffling over to someone else's turf for a private dressing down I thought was a craven abrogation of journalistic principle, but I was overruled. "I think it's just what we ought to do," our general manager said, "go out into the community."

Out into the community! For a tongue-lashing by a hysterical rabbi who thought I was precipitating a second Holocaust and by a major advertiser whose tribal sensibilities had been offended, all of it off the record, our readers not to know about it.

I wasn't going. I wasn't invited and probably wouldn't have gone if I had been. The purpose in any case was not to dress *me* down but to dress down the management of the newspaper for publishing my columns. The editor of the editorial page, my friend and colleague Art Clayman, was going, and that was heartening, since not only did he support my work, and not only was he Jewish, he was also a member of Rabbi Cutler's congregation. With him defending me, it would be hard to make a case against me of Hitlerism. But as luck would have it, he took a spill in a bicycle event two days before and at the time of the meeting was in a hospital bed in New York City.

So the meeting took place—nine or so outraged citizens led by Rabbi Cutler and Neil Golub berating me to *Gazoot* management. I was never told the details, but after that everything went downhill. I was forbidden to respond any further to the campaign against me and was advised that henceforth my column would be closely edited, as it never had been before. "Everyone needs an editor," was the word. I was told that my writing on religion, including Judaism, had been "mean-spirited" and "obsessive" and I was doing it "just for the sport of it," none of which, however, had been said before the rabbi's campaign against me or before the fateful meeting, all of my columns having been published without demur. A group of supporters, many of them Jewish, who came from Albany to argue in my behalf were dishonestly told by the editor that nothing had changed and I was free to write as usual. Very soon a tagline was attached to my column specifying that "opinions expressed in his column are his own and not necessarily the newspaper's."

I did not know at the time that the people who had really been gotten to were a couple of cousins of Jack the Musician who had lately decided to involve themselves in the affairs of the newspaper and were pressuring management to silence me, but it hardly mattered. Whether originating with management or with family members who had previously been remote, the effect was the same. The *Gazoot* was caving.

I will not burden the reader, or myself, with all the intermediate details. Suffice it that I spent many hours over the ensuing months trying to reconcile myself to these new limitations on me. At first I reduced my output to one column a week, simply not having the heart to work full-time any longer. But producing one column turned out to be not essentially different from producing three if I wasn't at liberty to write as I saw fit and if I had to submit to nitpicking editing. I told myself not to be resentful, that I'd had a good run and should be grateful for it. I was old enough to retire, and in fact was already technically retired, working as a contract employee, to my financial benefit, though that was little known. *Gazoot* management wanted the arrangement kept secret so other aging employees wouldn't ask for the same thing. That is, they wanted it kept secret until the campaign against me, and then they added that confidential information to the tagline at the end of my column, advising readers that I was a "freelance columnist," along with the information that my opinions were my own, not necessarily those of the newspaper, thus further distancing themselves from me. It was as if they said, we want nothing to do with this guy.

I could mutter to myself all I wanted that I'd had a good run and should be grateful, but I was not grateful.

I was bitter and disappointed. I wanted my privileged position to go on forever, and it had come to an end. Not the position itself, but the privilege. I would now be treated like any other employee, I was told, that is, subject to supervision and second-guessing. I couldn't swallow it. I tried, but it didn't work. Still I hung on, writing nothing that would ruffle anyone's feathers so as not to be subject to the further humiliation of being rewritten, reluctant to recognize what every day became more obvious, that I was done. One more week, I told myself. One more column, one more paycheck, one more armload of accumulated papers and memorabilia discretely lugged home, until there was no more putting it off and I finally, formally, officially had to quit.

I thought back to the day, almost exactly thirty-one years earlier, when I walked into the office of Jack the then-editor and tried to impress him with my international experience, and with one eye he gazed straight at me and with the other stared over my shoulder and told me he was a musician. As a descendant of the family that founded the newspaper in 1894, he held various titles at various times—publisher, editor, managing editor—but the one constant was his discomfort at having anything to do with the actual running of the paper, which he didn't so much delegate as abandon to others. I remembered when he moved his office to a far corner of the sports department, shielded by a wall, and whispered to me with satisfaction, "Nobody will know I'm here."

Now he retained only the title of publisher and was rarely seen on the premises, having lately saved a friend from bankruptcy by buying her failing restaurant, where he could be seen from time to time planting flowers in a strip of earth alongside the building. His *Gazoot* office, with its model trains and stacks of unread mail, was locked.

When I reached him on his cellphone I could hear the silence at the other end and could picture the aggrieved look on his face. He was thinking, Oh, shit, Strock wants to drag me into some problem of his and get me to make a decision. We met at the Stewart's shop on Van Vranken Avenue, over hot chocolate. "What's up?" he asked, trying to sound casual.

"I'm leaving," I said. "I'm finished," at which point a disinterested observer might have expected him to respond, "I'm sorry to hear it," or, "Why?" or, "I wish you luck." But Jack the Musician just looked at me, dreamy, as if lately back from the marijuana patch, the same as he had thirty-one years earlier, out from behind his full beard, now gray, and it fell to me to continue the conversation, to recall our first meeting in his office and his hiring of me, which was why, I said, I felt it right and proper to advise him of my departure before I told the people who actually ran the paper.

Yes, he said, he had heard about the flap over my Israel reporting. In fact, Neil Golub had called him and asked him to attend the meeting at which I was to be denounced, and he had declined. "I have an engagement," he said he told Golub.

Golub had insisted, but Jack the Musician was not to be dragged into practical matters of the newspaper that he had inherited and of which he was the accidental owner. He told Golub that the editor would attend and that was sufficient. So he didn't go, as anyone who knew him could have guaranteed he would not. Indeed he would not have been sitting there with me now if he could have thought of a quick way to avoid it, I well knew.

It was all predictable, but when a few minutes later, chatting, I mentioned something about Israel again, he said in the slow spacey way he had, "I was in Israel—in 1974—and you know what? You were absolutely right."

As casual as can be! Over the sticky Formica table and the paper cups of hot chocolate! I was absolutely right! From the very owner and publisher of the newspaper! I didn't give any weight to his views on Israel, but the point is, that was his view, and it did not occur to him to express it to a prominent advertiser who was on the phone trying to crush me for what I had written on the subject, much less to the editor or the general manager of the newspaper who were sawing my legs off. And it certainly wouldn't have crossed his mind to go to that shameless private meeting and say, "I was in Israel, and you know what, Neil? You know what, Matt? Carl was absolutely right—so go shove it."

You have to know him to appreciate that. It wasn't that he was afraid to stand up to powerful people in the community, and it wasn't that he was afraid of losing advertisers and subscribers—his editor and his business manager could worry about such mundane matters. It just wouldn't occur to him. It would be the farthest thing from his mind, just as it was far from my mind to ask him why he hadn't done it. This was the same Jack, after all, who had built a wall so no one would know he was there. I had been happy with the wall for most of thirty-one years, left free to write and report according to my own flickering lights, from Duanesburg to Jerusalem. Just this once it worked against me, and now I was done.

So we shook hands and said goodbye. I had paid for the trip to Israel; he paid for the hot chocolate.

Afterword

At least I was not alone in my final dismal experience as a columnist, I had that for comfort. Within a short time of my misadventure, either before or after, the following occurred:

M.J. Rosenberg, a disaffected former staff member of the American-Israel Public Affairs Committee (AIPAC) who had joined the liberal group Media Matters as a commentator on Israeli matters, felt obliged to resign from that group after arousing anger with his repeated use of the term "Israel firsters" to describe Jewish advocates who seem to put Israel's interests before those of the United States. One such advocate, Alan Dershowitz, professor of law at Harvard University, led the national charge against him, promising, "I am beginning a serious campaign on this issue, and I will not let it drop until and unless Rosenberg is fired from Media Matters." The problem with Rosenberg, he said, was that he "didn't engage in careful, nuanced critiques of Israel, which is fine. He engaged in hyperbole, name-calling." The label Israel-firster is of course derived from the "America-firsters" who tried to keep the United States out of World War II. American Jews of Zionist persuasion object to it as suggesting "dual loyalty," which they take as a slur, and even worse than that, since it alleges the two halves of the duality are not equal. It seems a funny thing for people to get huffy about when they are perfectly open about championing Israel at every turn and even declaring it to be their "spiritual homeland," as the rabbi did in his sermon denouncing me. In any event, Dershowitz and like-minded persons from a knocked-together Emergency Committee for Israel went so far as to take out a full-page ad in *The New York Times* denouncing Rosenberg, and poor Rosenberg finally had to settle for a blog.

The Washington Post ran a photograph on its front page of a Palestinian man, his face contorted with grief, holding a white-wrapped bundle that a caption informed us was his eleven-month-old son, who had been killed by an Israeli air strike on the family's home in Gaza during the Israeli attack of November 2012. The man was not a Hamas fighter but a journalist, employed by the BBC. It was a touching scene, the man surrounded by other men, reaching out to him. The baby itself was not visible, only its wrapping, so there was no question of poor taste, which sometimes arises when newspapers run gruesome photos of dead or injured people. It was a picture of human grief. Reaction was such that a week later the newspaper had to run a defense by its ombudsman, Patrick B. Pexton. "Jewish groups and American Jews in large numbers wrote to the ombudsman and to *Post* editors, protesting the photo as biased," Pexton explained. Biased, because it wasn't offset by a comparable photo of a grieving Israeli or a dead Israeli child. The *Post* did not apologize but did explain: "The *Post* cannot publish photographs that don't exist. No Israeli civilian had been killed by Gaza rocket fire since Oct. 29, 2011, more than a year earlier," which I'm willing to bet not many readers would have known, given the level of publicity about rocket fire from Gaza. The *Post* also pointed out that on the same day it ran the front-page photo in question, it did run a photo on an inside page of "an Israeli mother taking refuge in a bomb shelter with her young children," but obviously that wasn't enough. The problem was the prominent and sympathetic portrayal of Palestinians, any Palestinians, as victims of Israel rather than as deranged terrorists. Such a thing was clearly not acceptable. It later emerged that the baby boy was probably the victim of a misdirected Hamas rocket, not of an Israeli airstrike, but no one knew that at the time so that was not a factor.

The same problem, inducing sympathy for Palestinians, appeared to be at the root of the protest against an exhibit scheduled earlier at the Museum of Children's Art in Oakland, California, titled *The Child's View from Gaza*. It consisted of pencil and crayon drawings by Palestinian children following the Israeli bombardment of Gaza in 2008–2009, which killed hundreds of civilians, children among them. The drawings were produced in therapy sessions supported by the Middle East Children's Alliance. I didn't see them, but if they were anything like the drawings I used to see in Saigon, made by children who fled from American bombing in the countryside, they would have shown flames belching from aircraft and stick-figure people down below running and dying. The exhibit was canceled after a meeting of Jewish leaders with the museum's directors, whereupon the Jewish Federation of the East Bay tweeted: "Great news. 'The Child's View From Gaza' exhibit has been canceled thanks to some great East Bay Jewish community organizing."

In early 2012 the CBS news program "60 Minutes" broadcast a report about the punitive effects on Arab Christians of the Israeli occupation of East Jerusalem and the West Bank, which to my eye was moderate and understated, not even mentioning the Jewish "price tag" practice of spray-painting "Jesus is a monkey" on Christian churches, but still it made Israel look bad. The occupation was oppressive not only to Muslims, which anyone might expect, but also to minority Christians, many of whom were packing up and leaving. The story was reported by longtime correspondent Bob Simon, whose credentials ran to having been captured in Iraq during the Gulf War and tormented over the course of forty days for his own Jewishness. It did him no good. The reaction started as soon as it became known that the program was in the works. Israel's ambassador to the United States, Michael Oren, called CBS chairman Jeff Fager to try to stop production, claiming the report would be a "hatchet job." After the show aired, Matt Brooks, executive director of the Republican Jewish Coalition, called it "absolutely outrageous." Gerald Steinberg of NGO Monitor, an Israeli group that rides herd on human-rights organizations critical of Israel, claimed the show "uncritically adopted the standard Palestinian narrative." The Anti-Defamation League charged that it "failed to pursue the issue of anti-

Christian persecution by the Muslim population of the West Bank." Lela Gilbert of the Hudson Institute said, "The hypocrisy of the '60 Minutes' attack on Israel is astonishing." Clifford May of the Foundation for Defense of Democracies, an Israel-aligned group, asked, "Is this the result of ignorance or bias of some cocktail of the two?" The Israeli newspaper *Haaretz* reported that no less a power than Prime Minister Benjamin Netanyahu had been "fully informed on the affair almost since its start." Indeed, officials in the prime minister's office later boasted that their efforts had made the final version of the "60 Minutes" report "softer."

Peter Beinart, prominent American journalist, former editor of the *New Republic*, and practicing Orthodox Jew, wrote a book, *The Crisis of Zionism*, deploring Israel's increasingly hard-line anti-Arabism, religious fanaticism and disdain for democracy. A *cri de coeur*, you might call it, or whatever the Hebrew equivalent would be—a member of the family lamenting the family's waywardness and not incidentally supporting a boycott of goods made in the occupied and undemocratic West Bank, though not the full "boycott, divestment, sanctions" program called for by left-wing groups. In fact, he asked for "an equally vigorous embrace of the people and products of democratic Israel."

"Why does Beinart hate Israel so?" asked *The Jerusalem Post* in its review of the book. He "employed several formulations favored by anti-Semites," said *The New York Times Book Review*, dusting off the favorite canard of the Jewish establishment. Pamela Geller, leader of the anti-"Ground Zero Mosque" movement, dubbed him a "vomit-inducing kapo," kapo being the slang term for a Jewish collaborator with Nazi guards in World War II concentration camps.

Beinart was to have been one of fifty-two authors at a book festival at the Marcus Jewish Community Center in Atlanta, Georgia, but after complaints from members, his invitation was canceled. "Our membership isn't closed to anyone or any one idea," said the president of the center, "but the negative reaction was significant."

A little farther back in time there was Helen Thomas, the seemingly immortal White House correspondent, formerly of UPI, latterly of Hearst Newspapers, who had covered every American president since Eisenhower. In an impromptu interview with a rabbi on the White House lawn during American Jewish Heritage Celebration Day she had said Jews should "get the hell out of Palestine," and when asked where they should go, replied, "They should go home... Poland, Germany...America, and everywhere else." The White House Correspondents Association promptly denounced her remarks as "indefensible," and she was dropped by both her speaking agency and the co-author (or ghost-writer) of her books. She put out a statement saying, "I deeply regret my comments I made last week regarding the Israelis and the Palestinians. They do not reflect my heartfelt belief that peace will come to the Middle East only when all parties recognize the need for mutual respect and tolerance." But it was too late, and a couple of days later she resigned from Hearst. ("I knew I would be fired," she later clarified.) Still the condemnation went on. President Obama called her comments "offensive" and "out of line." The Society of Professional Journalists dropped its Helen Thomas Award for Lifetime Achievement, because "no honoree should have to decide if the possible backlash is worth being recognized for his or her contribution to journalism."

M.J. Rosenberg said when he left Media Matters, "The bad guys didn't 'get' me,' but they did create the climate that made me decide to leave." I knew what he meant—I could have said the same thing—and I knew what Helen Thomas meant when she said, "You cannot criticize Israel in this country and survive," which if I had heard earlier I would have thought was ridiculous. I would have said this is a free country; we have free speech; we can criticize whatever we want.

I learned that not even synagogues are exempt from the stern attentions of what I sometimes think of, playfully, as the Jewish mafia. There was, for example, poor Congregation B'nai Jeshurun on the Upper West Side of Manhattan, a liberal redoubt if there ever was one, its musical services attracting several thousand worshippers, who often included politicians and entertainers. When the United Nations upgraded Palestine to "non-member observer state" in late 2012, the synagogue put out a statement welcoming the move as "a great moment for us as citizens of the world" and "an opportunity to celebrate the process that allows a nation to come forward and ask for recognition." *The New York Times* (once identified by the *Columbia Journalism Review* as "the hometown newspaper of

American Jewry") made this parochial little matter into a major news story, which in a way it was: a synagogue—any synagogue—welcoming heightened recognition of Palestine.

Reaction again was prompt, led by Professor Dershowitz, who sometimes seems to function as unofficial Minister of Enforcement for the Jewish establishment, or mafia, or whatever you want to call it. Writing in *The Jewish Daily Forward*, a century-old, New York-based newspaper, he denounced the "extraordinarily naïve rabbis and lay leaders" of the synagogue for supporting something that could give the Palestinian Authority standing to haul Israel before the International Criminal Court on charges of war crimes. A blast and a half, done in soap-box oratorical style. "Do the rabbis realize...? Do the rabbis understand...? Do the rabbis intend...?" The outrage was joined by some members of the synagogue itself, who professed to have been caught off-guard by the statement from their leaders. Within a few days, the leaders backed down, claiming that "through a series of unfortunate internal errors, an incomplete and unedited draft of the letter was sent out which resulted in a tone which did not reflect the complexities and uncertainties of this moment," and more in that mealy-mouthed vein, which followers of these matters will recognize without difficulty.

M.J. Rosenberg speculated on his blog that the synagogue was simply threatened with the loss of financial contributions: "Part of the deal, when you accede to pressure, is that you do not reveal what actually went down. But it is obvious what happened. Threats were made. They didn't have to be direct. No one has to tell those working for organizations (or synagogues) dependent on donations from the Jewish community what they can and cannot say. In most cases, they don't need to be warned. They impose prior restraint on themselves."

It was also Dershowitz who, a few years earlier, prevailed on DePaul University, a Catholic institution in Chicago, to deny tenure to Norman Finkelstein, an assistant professor of political science who had distinguished himself first by exposing, in his book *The Holocaust Industry*, the shameless hustle by Jewish organizations for bloated reparations from Switzerland and Germany; second, by unmasking the scholarly shabbiness of the book *From Time Immemorial* by Joan Peters, which claimed that the Arabs of Palestine were only recent arrivals in that land, and thus by implication could make no legitimate claim of ownership—a book that had been enthusiastically received by such eminent Jewish writers as Saul Bellow, Barbara Tuchman, and Martin Peretz but has since been discredited even in Israel; and third, and worst, by debunking a book by Dershowitz himself, *The Case for Israel*, which had amounted to a defense attorney's brief for the state. Finkelstein did this in *Beyond Chutzpah*, which methodically picked apart Dershowitz's arguments, ruthlessly examined the factual (or non-factual) claims behind them, and concluded that the work was "a threadbare hoax." According to *The Guardian* newspaper, cited by Wikipedia, Dershowitz tried to get the University of California Press to cancel publication of Finkelstein's book and went so far as to ask Governor Arnold Schwarzenegger to intervene, albeit without success.

After publication, with Finkelstein up for tenure, Dershowitz lobbied the president of DePaul University and the chairman of the Political Science Department, as well as other administrators and faculty members, to try to block the appointment. "At one point," according to *The New York Times*, "the 12-member Arts and Sciences' Faculty Governance Council, annoyed by Dershowitz's pressure, unanimously voted to send letters to the presidents of DePaul and Harvard complaining of Dershowitz's interference." Finkelstein was approved by a committee from the Political Science Department and by another from the college as a whole, but a dean overruled them, and he was ultimately denied tenure and was thus out of a job, even as the university acknowledged that he was "a prolific scholar and outstanding teacher."

Brooklyn College announced an event promoting BDS—the "boycott, divestment, sanctions" movement aimed at Israel, previously mentioned. The speakers would be Judith Butler, a Jewish feminist philosopher out of Berkeley, and Omar Barghouti, a Palestinian activist out of the University of Tel Aviv. A decidedly minor event, sponsored in part by the college's Political Science Department, which became major when Dershowitz got wind of it—Dershowitz again, invariably identified in news stories as a noted Harvard law professor without mention of his larger role. In a fevered op-ed in the New York *Daily News*, he denounced the coming event as a "propaganda hate orgy." The *Daily News*, owned by Mort Zuckerman, a leading financial backer of support services for the Israeli military (Friends of the IDF), helpfully followed with an editorial headlined "Brooklyn College is no place for an Israel-bashing lecture."

Jewish politicians like Lewis A. Fidler, assistant majority leader of the City Council, joined in, threatening to cut grants to the college if the program were to proceed. "We believe in the principle of academic freedom," he wrote to the president of the college. "However, we believe in the principle of not supporting schools whose programs we, and our constituents, find to be odious and wrong." (The *Daily News* also supported academic freedom: "The right of faculty members to foster expression and discussion is unquestioned," it wrote in its editorial demanding that the BDS program be canceled—just as the three rabbis of Schenectady, writing in *The Jewish World*, tipped their kippas to "the importance of free speech and a free press" as they tried to squelch both, and just as the Mad Rabbi declared in his church sermon that my own work "wasn't about a constitutional right, it wasn't freedom of speech or freedom of the press.")

This time it backfired. Mayor Michael Bloomberg, Jewish himself and obligatorily admiring of Israel, said, "If you want to go to a university where the government decides what kind of subjects are fit for discussion, I suggest you apply to a school in North Korea." (What might happen if more public figures were so bold?)

Still, the Anti-Defamation League took out an ad in *The New York Times* scorching the mayor and calling the BDS program "anti-Semitic at its very core" and a "hate-fest" that aims at "the destruction of the Jewish state through demography," an expression that earlier would have passed me by but that now had the ring of an old friend. "Constitutional freedoms," the Anti-Defamation League predictably echoed, "are not at issue here." The cost of the ad would have been at least $100,000, though realistically that is no huge expense for an organization with an annual budget in excess of $50 million.

Alas, the college president, Karen Gould, bless her heart, stuck to her guns, and the mighty if parochial *Times* came out on her side. "Such intimidation" as threatening funding cuts "chills debate and makes a mockery of the ideals of academic freedom," said the chin-scratchers of the editorial page. Well, good for them. I wish I'd had them on my side in Schenectady.

Not yet finished, the Consulate General of Israel protested the editorial, saying in a letter that the BDS demand for a "one-state solution" for Israel-Palestine was merely "a euphemism for the annihilation of Israel," but it was too late by then. The tide was turning, and the program went on as scheduled, though with several hundred Zionist protestors loudly dissenting outside in the street. Would you be willing to bet, though, that the next college to consider hosting a boycott-divestment-sanctions program will think very carefully, just as *The Washington Post* will think very carefully the next time it considers running a photo of Palestinian victims of Israeli bombing? I believe it would be a safe bet.

The *Times* also noted ruefully what I and many others have noted, that "there is more honest discussion about American-Israeli policy in Israel than in this country." Indeed, if I want straightforward reporting and intelligent analysis of matters Israeli, I turn to

Haaretz, not to the *Times* or any other American paper, and I consider the cost of an online subscription well worth the money. Thus has my education advanced since my own innocent journey to the Holy Land.

And more yet. Around this same time—that is, late 2012, early 2013—Senator Chuck Hagel was mentioned as a candidate for secretary of defense, and the establishment quickly recalled that a few years earlier he had said of Capitol Hill, "The Jewish lobby intimidates a lot of people up here," and further, "I'm a United States senator, not an Israeli senator," explaining why he didn't sign letters circulated by AIPAC. So of course his nomination was opposed by the American Jewish Committee, the Anti-Defamation League, the Israel Project, the Zionist Organization of America, and unofficially by AIPAC. It was wrong of him to say "Jewish lobby"—a whiff of anti-Semitism there, per *The Wall Street Journal*—and it was wrong to say "intimidates," because that "ascribes to the so-called Jewish lobby powers that are at once vast, invisible and malevolent," which was pretty funny, Israel calling itself the Jewish state but objecting to its lobby being called the Jewish lobby and feigning indignation that it should be considered effective. The nomination was rescued when Hagel assured everyone that he was actually a solid supporter of Israel and humbled himself before the Senate Armed Services Committee, whose members badgered him with demands for a show of loyalty, a performance that provoked an over-the-top satire by Jon Stewart's "The Daily Show," in which Senator John McCain demanded to know if Hagel would be willing to perform oral sex on a donkey if requested by Prime Minister Netanyahu. The Hagel character hesitated, but another senator-character piped in, "For Israel I'd do it in a second—but then, I grew up on a farm." The producers had the good sense not to put anything so scurrilous on the air, but the skit did appear on the Internet, and that was sufficient to ignite Abe Foxman, president of the Anti-Defamation League, who wrote in solemn protest that the skit "reinforces the pernicious notion of Jewish control over this government," along the lines of "anti-Semitic conspiracy theorists." He had earlier declared of Hagel that "the sentiments he's expressed about the Jewish lobby border on anti-Semitism." (The Anti-Defamation League, I was beginning to understand, would be nowhere without a steady and ever-burgeoning supply of anti-Semitism.)

To go a little farther back in time, there was poor Richard Goldstone and his famous, or infamous, *Goldstone Report*. Richard Goldstone: distinguished member of South Africa's equivalent of the United States Supreme Court and, not incidentally, Jewish. Not incidentally, because he was chosen by the United Nations Human Rights Council to head an investigation of possible war crimes by both sides in Israel's attack on Gaza at the end of 2008 and the beginning of 2009. His credentials ran to prosecuting war crimes in the former Yugoslavia and Rwanda on behalf of the U.N.'s International Criminal Tribunals. (One can only imagine the alarm if an Arab had been appointed.)

As all the world knew, in response to repeated rocket fire from Gaza, Israel attacked that densely populated strip of land with rockets of its own, with bombs, and with incendiary white phosphorous, incinerating not only hundreds of Hamas fighters but also some 762 civilians, including 382 children. (As opposed to three Israeli civilians killed by Gazan rocket fire, plus two Israeli dogs, which were given lavish sentimental coverage in the Hebrew-language press, according to *Haaretz*.) It was these attacks that were the subject of the children's drawings banned from the Oakland Children's Museum.

Israel refused to cooperate with the Goldstone-led investigation, notwithstanding the tribal affiliation of its chairman, as it refuses to cooperate with almost all international investigations of its conduct, but the commission proceeded anyway and eventually concluded, not surprisingly, that Israel had engaged in a "deliberately disproportionate attack designed to punish, humiliate and terrorize a civilian population." The establishment's reaction was fierce. Prime Minister Benjamin Netanyahu declared that Judge Goldstone ranked with Hamas rockets and the Iranian nuclear program as one of Israel's "three major strategic challenges." The Israeli interior minister wrote Goldstone a letter telling him the report "gives legitimacy to terror organizations," and challenging him, "Where was your voice?" when a Jewish settler family was murdered in their beds by a Palestinian villager.

Dershowitz called Goldstone "a traitor to the Jewish people," and, speaking on Israeli Army Radio, said the report was "a defamation written by an evil, evil man," adding, "I regarded him as a friend, but I now regard him as an absolute traitor." A synagogue in Johannesburg initially barred Goldstone from participating in his grandson's bar mitzvah, though it later relented. Goldstone declared himself a Zionist, just as Congregation B'nai Jeshurun in New York professed its love for Israel, but he said he "did not intend to visit Israel any time soon, for reasons of personal security," according to a report in *Haaretz*.

Finally he ate bitter crow, under what *New York Times* columnist Roger Cohen called "intense pressure from Israel, the U.S. Congress and world Jewish groups." He wrote an op-ed for *The Washington Post* explaining abjectly that he didn't have the full picture when he led the investigation: "If I had known then what I know now, the *Goldstone Report* would have been a different document." His three co-authors reasserted the validity of the report, but that was just so much the better for him, affirming his subservience to the establishment as opposed to the United Nations. It was a very close call for him. I look at him, and I give thanks that I got off so easily.

Going farther back, anger over tribal apostasy extended even unto a historian-philosopher as distinguished as Hannah Arendt, an early Zionist who fled Nazi Germany and established herself in America, where she became best known, at least in academic circles, for her classic *The Origins of Totalitarianism*. She got in trouble when she accepted an assignment from *The New Yorker* magazine to report on the trial of Adolf Eichmann, who had been kidnapped in Argentina and bundled off to Israel to answer for Nazi war crimes in which he was accused of having participated in his capacity as organizer of deportations.

It was her great insight that Eichmann was not the hate-filled monster pictured by the Israeli state prosecutor but rather a commonplace, self-serving bureaucrat, an example of what she memorably called "the banality of evil." Not a comic-book fiend but an ordinary, small-minded functionary, able to justify to himself the shipping of hundreds of thousands of Jews to their near-certain deaths as actually doing them a favor. More frightening perhaps than the deranged Hitler, if only because more everyday and less easily detectable. He could be your neighbor. Arendt wrote a brilliant series of articles explaining this wretch and supporting Israel's right to kidnap him, try him and hang him. It became a book, *Eichmann in Jerusalem: A Report on the Banality of Evil*, which I read for the first time only after returning from my own adventure in Jerusalem and was laboring to educate myself.

Her deviations from the party line, or the tribal line, were twofold: first, portraying Eichmann as something other than the virulent anti-Semite that Zionist orthodoxy demanded; and second, noting in passing that Jewish leaders in Europe's ghettos had actually cooperated with the Nazis, Jewish Councils providing the names of Jewish residents to be deported (meaning, murdered) and Jewish police often doing the actual rounding up, which they justified by saying it would have been worse if the Nazis had done it themselves. The historical accuracy of this observation, initially documented by Raul Hilberg in his groundbreaking *The Destruction of the European Jews*, published in 1961, is no longer in dispute, though it continues to be an embarrassment to the Jewish establishment, which prefers to celebrate the exceptional Warsaw Ghetto uprising and to present Nazi-era European Jews as heroic resisters rather than as pitiful "sheep going to the slaughter," or worse yet, collaborators.

The reaction upon publication of Arendt's work back in 1963 was merciless. The Anti-Defamation League denounced it as an "evil book," and one of the league's officials called it "a well of poisonous slander for all enemies of our people to draw from." The headline in the *Intermountain Jewish News*, published in Denver, was "Self-Hating Jewess Writes Pro-Eichmann Series for *New Yorker* Magazine." (Self-hating! Pro-Eichmann!) The president of the American Jewish Congress charged that Arendt had presented Eichmann as "a sweet misguided man," a complete inversion of the truth, which actually became common, and no less a personage than Barbara Tuchman, distinguished Jewish-American historian in her own right, accused Arendt of a "conscious desire to support Eichmann's defense." It was incredible. Today Hannah Arendt is recognized as a major thinker and writer, but within the tribal establishment she was "American Jewish Public Enemy Number One," in the words of historian Peter Novick.

For the Jewish establishment of Schenectady and Albany to rag on me for my impudent and disrespectful remarks published in a newspaper with no reach beyond

the confluence of the Hudson and Mohawk Rivers—
well, that will not even merit a footnote if the history of
this phenomenon is ever written.

Hannah Arendt, be it noted to her everlasting
credit, never apologized, never backed down, never did
a Goldstone.

The pressure of the non-existent Jewish lobby to
defend and glorify Israel is probably most intense in the
United States, but it is not unique to our fair land. In the
midst of the Israeli election campaign of early 2013, *The
Sunday Times* of London published a cartoon showing
Prime Minister Benjamin Netanyahu plastering up a
wall in which were trapped the contorted arms and
faces of Palestinians, the dripping plaster being blood-
red. The caption ran: "Israel elections. Will cementing
the peace continue?" The reference was presumably
to the much-condemned wall that Israel is building
around and through the West Bank, appropriating to
itself more territory.

The Board of Deputies of British Jews declared the
cartoon to be "shockingly reminiscent of the blood-libel
imagery more usually found in parts of the virulently
anti-Semitic Arab press," and *The Jewish Chronicle* of
Britain called it "the worst anti-Semitic blood libel"—
leading me to believe those parties attend the same
coffee klatches as the Mad Rabbi of Schenectady. The
European Jewish Congress denounced the cartoon as
"sickening" and "offensive" and demanded an apology.
An organization called Honest Reporting, whose stated
mission is "defending Israel from media bias," ran the
cartoon on its website with an overlay saying, "What

started as cartoons in the 1930s ultimately led to violence and tragedy. This is a lesson that *The Sunday Times* has clearly not absorbed," again mirroring the thinking of the Mad Rabbi: criticize or, heaven help us, ridicule Israel, and you're taking the first step toward another Holocaust. It seconded (or thirded) the familiar charge of "blood libel." The *Times* at first stood by the cartoon but soon backed off, and in most impressive fashion, its all-powerful owner, Rupert Murdoch, deploring the "grotesque, offensive cartoon," and the paper publishing a statement saying, "The publication of last week's cartoon was a serious mistake. We apologize unreservedly."

Even the cartoonist himself, after making the ritualistic disclaimer, "I am not, and never have been, anti-Semitic," like some poor movie producer answering to Senator McCarthy about possible Communist affiliations, conceded that publication of the cartoon on what happened to be Holocaust Remembrance Day amounted to "very unfortunate timing," though he did not explain why remembrance of World War II genocide should exempt the leaders of Israel for their oppression of others. And for just one day, apparently. Nothing, either, about *Nakba* remembrance, *Nakba* meaning catastrophe, which is what Palestinian Arabs call the conquest of their homeland by European and Russian Jews. To hell with that. Arab citizens of Israel who try to commemorate the *Nakba* are actually penalized by the Israeli government, of which the less said the better. Holocaust remembrance is the thing. "They call upon you to celebrate their victories over you, and if you refuse you will be punished," wrote the Palestinian poet Mahmoud Darwish.

Speaking of Great Britain, around the same time as the cartoon embarrassment there was David Ward, Member of Parliament, who wrote in a memorial book for the Holocaust: "Having visited Auschwitz twice—once with my family and once with local schools—I am saddened that the Jews, who suffered unbelievable levels of persecution during the Holocaust, could within a few years of liberation from the death camps be inflicting atrocities on Palestinians in the new State of Israel and continue to do so on a daily basis in the West Bank and Gaza." The reaction was the same, and so was the outcome. The Holocaust Educational Trust, which like many other organizations promotes endless Holocaust consciousness, charged Ward with "Holocaust equivocation and anti-Semitism." The Jewish Leadership Council and the Board of Deputies of British Jews condemned him in the customary terms, and Ward's own Liberal Democratic Party officially censured him, while ordering him to meet with its Friends of Israel chapter to "identify and agree on language that will be proportionate and precise," should he wish to say anything about Israel-Palestine again. I figured I got off easier than he did. At least I didn't have to meet with any Friends of Israel to agree on suitable language, and I'm glad I didn't.

Then soon enough there was the BBC canceling at the last minute a documentary by an Israeli filmmaker first titled *Exile: A Myth Unearthed* and then cautiously retitled *Jerusalem: An Archeological Mystery Story*, before being scrubbed altogether. The film reportedly presented the case that there was really no Roman exile of Jews from Palestine after the Jewish revolt of 70 CE, as moaned about in Jewish folklore, and that today's Palestinian Arabs are at least partly descended from those ancient Jews, or Israelites, which would be ruinous to Israel's ethnic case for itself. The filmmaker, Ilan Ziv, accused the BBC of "a mixture of incompetence, political naiveté, conscious or subconscious political pressure and ultimately, I believe, a lack of courage."

The film was shown in Canada and was scheduled to be shown in France and Switzerland. I have not seen it, but it is common knowledge that there is no contemporary evidence of any Roman expulsion of Jews from the Holy Land—"Nowhere in the abundant Roman documentation is there any mention of a deportation from Judea," wrote Shlomo Sand in *The Invention of the Jewish People* —nor any reason to believe that such a thing occurred, the Romans hardly having the means to deport hundreds of thousands of people. It is, however, essential for justifying the Zionist enterprise: "We waited 2,000 years!"

I, toiling in Schenectady, endeavoring to shine my poor flickering light on school boards and family courts, didn't know any of this background, or knew it only dimly, until I took to the library upon my return. I did not know that a bubble of immunity surrounded Israel and that Jewish organizations worked assiduously to maintain and strengthen it, so that if you spoke or wrote critically you would be labeled an anti-Semite and efforts would be made to block publication of your works, to shut down your lectures, to get you fired. I didn't know that the mass murders of World War II, later dubbed "the Holocaust" and treated as a singular event in human history, were used to reinforce the immunity. You couldn't deplore the Jewish dispossession of Arabs, photograph the victims of Jewish bombing, or poke fun at Jewish ritual practices, because, as the grocery king of Schenectady demanded of me, "What about the Holocaust?" (All I could think at the time was, Huh?)

Israel, not God, was at the center of this new Jewish universe, I discovered. You could disbelieve in God, that is, be a "secular Jew," and still be welcome at the tribal campfire, but you could not disbelieve in Israel. And if you were a non-Jew, or *goy*, like me, heaven help you if you spoke ill of the glorified nation. In the first case you were a self-hating Jew, in the second an anti-Semite, and in both cases a blasphemer. "An anti-Semite used to mean someone who hates Jews; now it means anyone Jews hate," I read in *The Folly of Fools: The Logic of Self-Deception in Human Life*, by Robert Trivers, as I pursued my researches, and that now sounded right.

If the traditional God of the Bible enters the picture at all, it is only to defend the nation: "**Heavenly Father, Israel's Rock and Redeemer, bless the State of Israel... strengthen the hands of the defenders of our Holy Land; grant them deliverance, our God, and crown them with the crown of victory," runs a prayer in the Koren Seder published by the Orthodox Union.** It is "a new form of idolatry," in the opinion of liberal Jewish thinker Michael Lerner, a *prima facie* apostate.

I had no idea what I was walking into when I fired my feeble little barbs at this new nationalistic religion, and no idea how I would come out of the storm that followed. When the inevitable imprecations rain down, members of Parliament crumble, nominees for defense secretary grovel, White House correspondents with prizes named after them slink away, art museums run up the white flag, liberal synagogues whimper—what could anyone expect from me? What could anyone expect from the *Daily Gazoot?*

Since my demeaning departure from that newspaper, which was my haven and my platform for so many years, I have thought long and hard about whether I would do things differently if I could do them over. Would I undo our visit to the West Bank? Would I go to Disney World instead of Jerusalem for vacation? Would I write more deferentially about Judaism and the Zionist enterprise? And I can honestly announce, after prayerful reflection, that I would not. I regret very much the consequences of my Israel columns, but I assure you, dear reader, I do not regret having written them, and I surely do not regret having learned what I learned. I can only hope that Helen Thomas and the others felt the same. May the lord bless us and keep us all. Amen.